The Church of Exemptions*
*A Farce with Footnotes

The Church of Exemptions*

*A Farce with Footnotes

by **Luis Granados**

Humanist
PRESS

© 2019 Humanist Press LLC
1821 Jefferson Place NW
Washington, DC 20036
www.humanistpress.com

Luis Granados
The Church of Exemptions: A Farce with Footnotes

Published by: Humanist Press LLC
Editor: Jennifer Bardi
Cover and interior design: Sharon McGill
Printed book: ISBN: 978-0-931779-80-0
Ebook ISBN: 978-0-931779-81-7

Contents

To all the lawyers I've known,
none of whom resemble any character herein.

June 7: Buzzard Point

"I should just shoot her."

"You can't do that," said Nick, turning around anxiously to check whether anyone else was close enough to hear. He knew his brother was only venting, but figured that playing along might help. "You'd get caught. Besides, you'd chicken out. You'd be there in the bushes, everything all planned. She'd walk up, everything's perfect. And you wouldn't pull the trigger. 'The mother of my children ...' or some shit like that. Luca, you need something that can actually work."

Luca stared blankly at the lush green field of Washington's new Buzzard Point soccer stadium. An hour into the game, neither side had seriously threatened to score. It was as pointless as trying to deal with his ex-wife Yvonne.

"I tell you, she's killing me. I fork over every nickel I make. Scratch that. I fork over more than every nickel I make. All she does is sit around and think up ways to claw more money out of me. You know the latest? Ballet lessons for Trina. Gotta have ballet lessons."

"Lots of little girls do ballet lessons."

"Yeah! In a class! For what, twenty, thirty bucks a week? Fine. But no—Trina needs private lessons, at a hundred a pop. She's five years old, for Chrissake."

Nick failed to suppress a smirk. "Is that in the divorce decree?"

"I don't know what's in there. All I know is, she had the toughest lawyer on this earth, and I had the laziest. And what's a legal paper, anyway, when you've got Trina crying on the phone—'Mommy says you won't let me do ballet.' What am I supposed to tell her?"

Nick had no answer. D.C. United took a corner kick, harmlessly cleared away.

"That paper's useless anyway." Luca had lost interest in the game. "It says I get the kids every Wednesday night, right? So a month ago, I buy these tickets for tonight. A month ago. We'll all have a nice time together. Then this morning I get a text—not a call, a text—from Yvonne, saying Tony messed up his homework so they can't come. I call back to argue with her, and she won't pick up."

"But homework shouldn't matter—you're supposed to get them Wednesdays anyway."

"Little brother, you're not getting it. She knows I bought the tickets.

There is no power on this earth that would make her let Daddy be the hero, even for one night, taking the kids to the nice soccer game where they can eat cotton candy."

A groan from the crowd. Chicago scored. Nick hadn't seen how it happened, because he'd removed his glasses, trying to use a shirtsleeve to mop some of the sweat off his pudgy face. Washington was in its fifth straight day over ninety degrees, and Nick was sick of it. His frizzy dishwater brown hair was dripping wet, but there wasn't much he could do about it.

"Well, thanks for thinking of me for one of the tickets anyway. You gonna get me some cotton candy?"

Luca shot his brother an evil eye, then turned his attention back to the game. United was playing with more catch-up urgency now, but still not penetrating the Chicago defense.

"You know, there could be a way out of this" mused Nick, a few minutes later. "Other than shooting her. A legal way. But weird. Front page weird."

"Oh yeah? Three years in law school, and you're just coming up with this now?"

Nick paused before answering, as he spied an oyster-sized glob of ketchup on his pants leg. His work pants, that he needed to wear to the office tomorrow. Was it hot water or cold that got out ketchup stains? He never could keep details like that straight. The fries had been worth it, though.

"Well, there's this case I saw. An idiot, really, not even a lawyer. But he came this close to winning, saying it was his religion that he shouldn't have to work double shifts, 'cause it wasn't healthy. He was a prison guard, see, and—"

"But he didn't win."

"No, he didn't win," Nick said patiently. "But that's 'cause he was an idiot. He didn't have a real religion. He just made stuff up on the fly, half-assed. Called his religion the 'Sun Worshipping Atheists.' He was the only member. But the court still took him seriously, and they laid out exactly what the test is for something being a religion.[1] And he

---

1. Novels do not normally have footnotes. But this one does, because truth is stranger than fiction. When you find yourself saying "Oh come on, that couldn't have happened," you can check the footnote to verify that it did. The case mentioned here is described at Travis Gettys's, "California court rules that

flubbed it. But it's not hard to pass. I could throw something together that would pass in a heartbeat."

"That gets me out of paying Yvonne?"

"Mmm... maybe," Nick said slowly, still thinking. "Yeah ... I could justify that, if the court buys that it's really part of a religion. Once you get that magic ticket, you win."

"You're nuts."

"The law's nuts, not me. I'm just—"

A roar from the crowd—United had scored. Once again, Nick missed how it happened.

Sun Worshipping Atheism is not a religion and requires no accommodation," *Raw Story,* March 26, 2015. http://www.rawstory.com/2015/03/california-court-rules-that-sun-worshipping-atheism-is-not-a-religion-and-requires-no-accommodation/. *Copple v. California Department of Corrections and Rehabilitation* (California Court of Appeals, Fourth Appellate District, Division Three, March 4, 2015). http://www.courts.ca.gov/opinions/nonpub/G050690.PDF

June 10: General
Services Administration

Monday morning. Bi-weekly staff meeting of Branch 7-D of the US
General Services Administration legal department, chaired by the
ever-phlegmatic branch chief, Richard Myers.

"Next matter. A warehouse lease in Austin. Who has time to turn
this around by next Wednesday?"

After two years on the job, Nick knew how to play the game. "I
could finish it by tomorrow if you really want," though true, would
be the worst possible answer. It might generate more work. It would
definitely show up his office mates. And if turning around documents
at a normal pace became standard procedure, it might suggest to
the budget gods that this branch of the GSA legal department was
overstaffed. On the other hand, not responding at all to Myers' request
would betray a poor team spirit. So Nick needed to play a little hard
to get. But not too hard, or somebody else might grab this easy one,
leaving him with either a suspiciously empty plate or, worse yet, an
assignment that might strain his brain.

"Wednesday? Well, I've got a training to finish up, but ... what the
heck, I can handle it."

"Great, Nick. Here's the file." Myers slid a half-inch file folder down
the scarred wooden table toward him. While other assignments were
being doled out, Nick snuck a peek at its contents. As he suspected, he
could safely put off starting this until the day before it was due. Even if
he hit an unforeseen snag, it would be easy to get a deadline extension.

As Myers droned on, Nick folded his hands on the table and
contemplated a C-shaped gouge in its surface. Had someone made
that with a knife? Had a fight broken out, perhaps over the proper
formatting of a notary block? Or had it just been the metal cleat of
an overstuffed briefcase? So many possibilities, each so vastly more
intriguing than the next ninety minutes of this godawful ordeal.

After keeping his streak intact of not actually dying of boredom
during one of Myers's meetings, Nick returned to the cramped half-
office he shared with Kyle. Kyle had rearranged a dental appointment
to coincide with the staff meeting, thus once again receiving no
assignment at all. Nick considered this strategy high risk, but Kyle

generally wiggled by with the story that he kept busy helping others with their work. Nick was a frequent recipient of his officemate's "help." So long as Nick met Myers's undemanding schedule, all was right with the world.

Nick checked the sports scores on his computer while savoring what he liked to call a "handcrafted" peanut butter and jelly sandwich. Crumbs disappeared into the spaces between the keys on his keyboard. Apricot preserves fouled the space bar, quickly spreading to locations Nick was sure he had not even touched, by some kind of Smuckers osmosis.

He then turned to more serious matters. A man of the world, an official representative of the United States government, should not be caught with his pants down not knowing about the latest congressman who had been caught with his pants down. Or what *The Onion* thought about it. This all took time, which was good, because something had to fill the void until 5:00 when it was safe to leave.

Having news items up on the screen in case Myers walked in unannounced was a whole lot safer than letting him see what Kyle's screen often displayed. For three beers, Nick had agreed to switch desks with Kyle, putting Kyle's behind the door to protect against this eventuality.

"How about a Nats game tonight?" asked Kyle. "Merriman's pitching."

"Nah, I don't think so. Costs too much."

"Aw, come on."

Nick wheeled to face Kyle, whose desk was piled high with files— none of which he knew the contents of, there solely because he wanted to look busy. "My plan, which I've spent a lot of time working out, is to watch Merriman pitch for the Nationals tonight. At home. For free."

"Fine, Mr. Moneybags. What're you saving all your pennies for? Your dream house?"

"Saving? I'm trying to get back up to zero, and I've got over a hundred thousand dollars to go." Nick raised his index finger to within a foot of Kyle's nose—in a space so small, this didn't require much of a stretch. "Unlike some people, I didn't have parents who could just write a check for four years of college."

"Actually, Nick, it was five and a half years. I needed to spend time finding myself."

"I could have told you where to look. How about the women's dorm?"

"Co-ed dorms, my man. These are modern times."

Nick could have ultimately bested Kyle in one-upmanship, but chose not to. He turned instead to more important matters, quickly passing over the top stories. Nothing had actually happened, but no one would admit it. Then on to his favorite part: the religion news. Things happened there all the time that never ceased to amuse and amaze. Nick had a dozen different sources he ran through, saving the clips that appealed to him. His clip files ran to over three million words now. If only he knew what to do with them.

Nick had been a comparative religion major in college. He chose this partly because he saw it as easy. Unlike, say, chemistry, with all those annoying "right" and "wrong" answers, religion was readily amenable to unalloyed bullshit. Nick's most treasured memento was a paper he had done, completely off the top of his head, ostensibly comparing saint ordination in Buddhism and Catholicism. The teacher's annotation read: "Interesting—I'd never thought of it that way."

Today's clip was a gem. American Sikh truckers were getting out of taking the drug tests every other truck driver had to take, because the test involved clipping and submitting a tiny lock of hair. What a shocking intrusion on their religious freedom![2] Over a quarter-million bucks shocking, once the company had to pony up for its sheer gall in asking them to obey the same rules all the other drivers obeyed. Nick copied this and filed it next to the story about the Muslim truckers who'd won a similar amount for their mental anguish over being asked to haul a load of beer.[3]

The thought of sharing the road with druggie truck drivers, though, made Nick almost happy he couldn't afford a car.

2.   Brian Melley, "Sikh truckers reach settlement in faith discrimination case," *Associated Press*, November 15, 2016 http://www.usnews.com/news/business/articles/2016-11-15/apnewsbreak-trucking-firm-settles-sikh-discrimination-case.
3.   "Jury Awards $240,000 to Muslim Truck Drivers In EEOC Religious Discrimination Suit," *EEOC Press Release*, October 22, 2015. https://www.eeoc.gov/eeoc/newsroom/release/10-22-15b.cfm.

June 16:
Guilder & Hersh Lobby

Little good news ever arrived in Nick's email. Mostly it was ads, or pesky work items—questions he'd already answered once, and if they didn't understand what he meant, that was their fault. This message was entirely different. An invitation to a reception at the prestigious K Street law firm of Guilder & Hersh, in honor of their newly added partners, former Senators Rosalynn Fenter and Jake Miller. "Former," Nick knew, as a euphemism for "defeated." The food and booze would be top drawer, but what froze Nick's eye was the sender of the message: Natalie Parks.

So she wasn't married yet. Maybe she was, and hadn't changed her name. But at the very least, there was no evidence that she *was* married, which meant there was hope. Besides, he kept telling himself, she had gone out of her way to invite *him*.

Nick had asked Natalie out several times back in law school. She had only accepted once, to a movie, the night before a spring break. Nick couldn't remember what movie it was—he'd been absorbed in the thrill of sitting next to Natalie, sneaking peeks at her shining black hair, and fierce cheekbones, dreaming about what lay beneath her baggy sweatshirt. After that, nothing. She was a very busy girl. The truth was, Nick convinced himself, that she really *was* busy. She didn't have the top grades in class, but she put in more hours than anyone else, by a wide margin. As far as Nick could tell—and he spied on her closely—he didn't have a serious rival, other than *Williston on Contracts*, but that was enough.

Then came recruiting season, and graduation. Natalie had landed at Guilder & Hersh, a firm with a reputation as a high-end sweatshop that could make its partners millions if they could survive the pace. Nick had wound up at the General Services Administration, bored out of his gourd.

And now this. Natalie, anxious to see him. The possibilities were endless.

*****

Nick was the second guest to arrive. He thought he was the eighth, but six of the people he saw were firm lawyers on meet-and-greet duty. Natalie was not among them.

He had tried to dress as well as he could. He had one decent blue suit, which he paid to have cleaned for the occasion. Perhaps he should have paid to let out the jacket a bit, if that were still an option, because buttoning it was now almost impossible. It looked fine unbuttoned, he decided. A trip to the barber had produced the same inane question as always: "How would you like your hair today, sir?" Someday, he would try the smartass answer: "Just like it is now, but six weeks' shorter." Instead, he gave more detailed instructions for how to handle the wispy frizz that no woman other than Mama could ever appreciate.

The round face and puffy cheeks he couldn't do much about. He had tried concealing his unpronounced chin with a goatee in college, but it itched too much so he'd given it up. Contact lenses would have obviated the need for glasses, but the thought of something touching his eyeballs was too gross to contemplate.

Nick made his way to the buffet, which did not disappoint. Were those really shrimp? They looked more the size of lobsters. After scarfing a plateful down, Nick concluded that they were shrimp, but not the kind that came out of the freezer bag like Mama used to buy.

To wash them down, Nick headed over to one of the three bars. "Nice and full!" he said to the bartender, stuffing a dollar into the tip jar, in the hope that his refill might be even larger.

The lobby where the reception was being held was enormous and ornate. It sported marble columns—not to support anything, but just to show off. Nick had a vague sense of the dollars per square foot charged for premium K Street property, and this lobby was a heck of a lot of square feet not being used for anything.

Senator Fenter strode into the lobby, entourage in tow. What were you supposed to call her? Still "Senator?" "Roz?" "Ex-Senator?" "Loser?" Enough of a crowd was surrounding her by now that it didn't really matter, because Nick would never get close enough to talk to her anyway. Even if he could think of anything to say to her, which he couldn't. He doubted she had any interest in fantasy baseball.

No Natalie yet. His glass, which had seemed so full, was empty now, so he headed back to the bar. The bartender didn't recognize him and gave him a portion at least a half-inch shorter than his first, according to Nick's well-trained eye. There was a dollar he'd never get back.

Elbowing his way back through the growing crowd in front of the bar, Nick overheard a young lawyer wearing a Guilder & Hersh name tag ask another, "So how many did you invite?"

"Three hundred and forty-two. Everybody I've ever heard of, and his dog. I had to Google half of them to find their addresses—took me all night. And I only got six RSVPs."

"Spillman's going to be pissed. He's keeping count, you know."

Wait—was that Natalie? Nick whirled and clattered into a woman holding a plate of stuffed celery sticks, nearly knocking her down. "Oh, excuse me. My bad. Here's one ... no, I guess I'll just throw it away. Sorry."

It wasn't Natalie.

A small cloud darkened Nick's sun. If that clown had sent out 342 invites, then Natalie would have sent 500. At least.

Nick stood quietly on the outer edge of a conversation about research tax credits. He moved from there to the outer edge of a conversation about the best places to stay near Machu Picchu. He carefully calculated the length of the line at the bar on the far side of the room, concluding that if he started now he'd be finishing glass number two right when he reached the front. This was one of the things Nick knew he was good at.

Halfway through glass number four—the portions were definitely superior on this side of the room—Nick found himself on the edge of another largely incomprehensible conversation, but at least this one was animated, with a tone less "oh-so-in-the-know" than Nick had found so nauseating elsewhere. "They're killing me," the man kept repeating. The same words Luca had used the other night about Yvonne. "You can't reason with these people. You can't even talk to them. All you get to do is listen. These damn EPA punks, they already know everything, so they don't need to listen."

The speaker wore a nametag that said "Earl," in big bold letters. He was sixty or so, Nick guessed. The string tie told you right away he wasn't from Washington, and didn't want to be mistaken for someone who was. Seventies-style aviator glasses sat on a pug nose in a round, brick-red face. Nick couldn't tell if it was red from anger, booze, or the sun. Probably all three.

At "These kids don't know a drill bit from a dildo," Nick saw Earl's listener purse her lips. She did not approve. In fact, Nick thought, she didn't seem to approve of much of anything Earl was saying. She gave a dutiful nod and an "Uh-huh" now and then, but didn't seem to mean it. Probably a tree-hugger, Nick thought. Bikes to work.

Tree-huggers ranked low on Earl's list. "And a lot of 'em are Muslimlovers," he growled. "That's their plan, see—kill off the American producer, so we keep buying more and more oil from the Arabs, so they can run the whole damn world."

"Uh-huh."

"Don't get me wrong, ma'am. I love the land. I would never hurt the land, least not in a way I didn't patch up later. But damn it, there's oil down there. Oceans of it! Just trapped in them rocks. All we got to do is squeeze it out." Those ham-sized fists Earl was clenching to make his point could squeeze out quite a bit of oil, Nick suspected. "But we cain't do it when every time we turn around, some pointy-head thinks up a new rule to stop us. Do they get some kind of bonus for this?"

"Uh-huh. Well, no. Oh wait—there's Senator Miller. Could you excuse me just one minute?" Her relief at escaping was palpable. This left Earl staring at Nick, who had been measuring out the line for glass number five, weighing that prospect against the possibility that too much more might not leave him at his tippy-top best if Natalie ever did turn up. But he now knew she wasn't going to, so what the hell. Still, Earl was expecting some sort of response from someone, and Nick was the only person standing there.

"Those regs must be tough, man," Nick said.

"Sure as hell. We don't even know what we're dealing with—they change every day. We spend ten million bucks complying with one, then they turn around and say no, you gotta do it different."

"Wow. Ten million bucksh I mean bucks—sorry." Nick dug a fingernail into his thumb, embarrassed at his slurred speech.

Earl leaned in. "You should see what we spend on senators. Then Jake here can't keep his zipper shut, so that money's gone."

There was a short pause. Nick later thought of it in terms of the three times the Trojan horse had bumped against the threshold while being drawn inside the city walls, but it really wasn't like that. Just a break in conversation, which a polite fellow like Nick should try to fill somehow.

"You know, there are ways around some of these rules," Nick said, concentrating hard on steadying his speech. "Ways that haven't even been tried yet. Creative ways."

"Like what?"

"Well, you know. Exemptions. Special rules."

"That's why I'm here, son. Ol' Jake, he says this law firm has plenty of brains, they can fix things for me. So whatcha got?"

At least it was a chance to talk, about something Nick knew a little about. "Well, you know. Like, Hobby Lobby. They got an exemption for being religious, so they don't have to do the same health care everybody else does."

"Health care! Don't get me started! That's another racket. But that's not where the money is, son. It's in the ground. I got to get it out. Ain't no religion in that."

"Not right now, maybe. But there are new religions popping up all the time."

"About oil?"

Nick couldn't completely read Earl's look. Maybe 90 percent skeptical, 10 percent curious. He glanced down, trying to see the oil, even though they were ten stories up. "Ok," he finally said. "Who put the oil down there?"

"Nobody 'put' the oil there, son." Earl seemed exasperated. "You're like one of these EPA brats. There was an ocean, see, with millions of little plants, and they—"

"No-no," Nick interrupted. "I know all that. But that's not the answer. The answer is, *God* put the oil there. And who told you the oil was down there?"

"I got the most expensive geologists in America. They know what they're doing. Trust me."

Nick shut his eyes and shook his head vigorously, clearing away a few cobwebs in the process. "No no no no no. *God* told you where the oil is. Maybe God worked through a geologist, but it was God who did it. Do you believe that? *Could* you believe that?"

Earl squinted, but Nick didn't notice him. Nick saw only one thing: the most beautiful woman God had ever placed on the planet, approaching Earl and smiling as broadly as she had when Nick snapped her picture with her parents back on graduation day.

"Mr. Matteson!" she cooed, holding out an exquisite, slender hand. "Natalie Parks. I work with Peter Spillman. We met at the convention in Denver."

"Hey," Earl grunted, then turned back to Nick. "So what if I believe that?"

Nick heard nothing. "Natalie!" He had worked out other, wittier openers, but this was all he could come up with right at the moment. He was a little too loud.

"Oh, hello, Nick. So delighted you could attend. You've met Mr. Matteson, I see."

Earl bent over to look at Nick's name badge, which he'd written in tiny letters, because he already knew who he was and didn't think anyone else would care. "Nick ... Fraternity?"

"No—'Fratelli.' Nick Fratelli."

"Mr. Fratellity here says you folks can get me out from under the EPA with religion."

"Oh," Natalie nodded. "Does he, now?" She shot Nick a quick look.

"How have you been?" Nick asked Natalie, ignoring Earl entirely. "It's so great to see you again. What's it been—three years?" Not suave. Have to start doing better, fast.

"What have you got, son?" said Earl "I'm all ears."

Natalie tittered warmly at Matteson, then turned expectantly to Nick, saying nothing at all about how she had been for the past three years. This narrowed Nick's alternatives. He wanted only to talk to Natalie, but her interest was entirely in Matteson. So Nick turned back to him.

"The thing is," he said, "that just like you say EPA changes its rules all the time, the rules on religious legal exemptions change all the time, too. They keep getting bigger. Now even corporations can have their own religion, like Hobby Lobby. Not just people. And if you pay attention to how the rules work, and you're careful, you can exempt yourself from almost anything. This 'God put the oil there, God told me to get it out' deal should be a natural—and I haven't even thought it through yet."

"Jake never told me about this," said Matteson. "You folks done this before?"

"Oh, Nick doesn't work here," said Natalie quickly.

"But we could work together," said Nick. "You'd need a big firm like this to pull it off. Natalie here, she's amazing."

It was Earl's turn to speak. He sipped his bourbon instead. Then a booming voice from the corner: "Ladies and gentlemen, thank you so much for coming. I want to welcome you all ..." "Blah, blah, blah" was all Nick heard for the next thirty minutes.

Nick's plan was to lose Earl, fortify himself at the bar, then close back in on Natalie. He'd given her a plug; she should at least appreciate that. The first two parts of the plan worked fine, but Natalie had disappeared again. Twenty minutes, crisscrossing the room methodically, with no Natalie in sight. The same damn movie as law school, Nick thought bitterly. He stuffed some freshly baked chocolate chip cookies in his pocket when he thought no one was looking, then headed home.

One more beer at his apartment and Nick nodded off, long before the ballgame he was watching ended. He woke with a headache, and barely made it to the office on time. Myers didn't like it when people were late. He didn't care a whole lot about what you actually did between nine and five, but he wanted you there. Nick's voicemail light was on, which was odd because he knew there were no messages when he'd left at 5:01 yesterday.

The message had been left at 7:16 a.m. "Nick, we've got to talk. I don't know what you told Mr. Matteson, but he wants the two of us out there. In North Dakota. Tomorrow."

June 17: Guilder & Hersh Conference Room

Nick listened to Natalie's voice four times. He would have asked Kyle for his opinion, but Kyle hadn't come in yet. Besides, when the inevitable disappointment came, he didn't want Kyle to have more ammunition to taunt him with. "Oh, run away with me, darling!" he could hear Kyle in falsetto. "The Riviera? Cozumel? No, more romantic than that—North Dakota!"

There were a few things Nick knew for sure. First, he wasn't going anywhere tomorrow. Myers wouldn't stand for it. Second, a door of access to Natalie Parks had swung wide open. This was no one invitation out of five hundred. Natalie needed him. Third, fourth, and fifth on Nick's list was the way Natalie had looked last night. Of course she'd been eye-catching back in the jeans and flannel shirt days of law school, but in her exquisitely tailored suit and stiletto heels, she was breathtaking.

Near the bottom of Nick's list was the disagreeable thought that this Matteson asshole would be involved, which could be a distraction from the main task at hand.

After a half hour of reverie, Nick decided he needed to pick up the phone and make the next move. Should he suggest meeting for lunch? Coffee? Dinner? Drinks? Lunch seemed the best fit, but where? A place to impress her, or a place he could afford? The key, he knew, was to lock in the next date after this one, somewhere a little more romantic.

He found Natalie's direct line at the bottom of her emailed invitation to the reception. But after four rings, it wasn't Natalie who came on the line, but a gravel-voiced secretary. "I'm sorry. Ms. Parks is on a conference call and will be on for some time. May I take a message?"

"Well, just tell her that Niccolò Fratelli called, and I've made lunch reservations for us at Maison de Lucien at noon."

"I don't think so," she replied. "She has an associates' meeting at lunch today. She says you are to meet here with attorney Spillman at two p.m. Do you know where we're located? ... Mr. Fratelli?"

"Uh, yeah. Will Natalie be in the meeting?"

"Excuse me, there's another call coming in. Is there anything else I can do for you?"

"No, but thank you very much ... Actually, what time was the meeting again?"

But he'd lost her after the "No."

Down but not out. The basic framework hadn't changed. Natalie still needed him, but now there was yet another obstacle in the way of his quality time with her. Nick looked up "attorney Spillman" on the Guilder & Hersh website, and found an impressive resume indeed. Groton, Harvard, Georgetown, clerkship for the senior judge on the Second Circuit Court of Appeals, chief counsel to the Senate Commerce Committee, a Fortune 100 client list that spilled onto a second page, and chair of the second biggest government affairs department on K Street. Photos of Spillman and George W. Bush, Spillman and Bill Gates, and Spillman receiving a bear hug from Harry Bertram, president of the United States. Not bad for a forty-nine year old who vaguely resembled Brad Pitt. He'd been married for sixteen years and had three kids. Nick hoped that kept him out of the running as competition for Natalie.

*****

Nick arrived at the reception desk of Guilder & Hersh at 1:47 for the 2:00 meeting. He had actually arrived at the building even earlier, but didn't want to look too eager. A stroll up and down K Street had chewed up a few minutes, but it was too hot to keep that up for long. A delivery man wore a wet towel on his head, which seemed like an outstanding idea.

"I'm here for the 2:00 meeting with Mr. Spillman."

"And you are ...?"

"Oh! Sorry. Fratelli. Niccolò Fratelli. Is Natalie com– I mean Ms. Parks. Is she on the list for the meeting?"

"I'm not seeing a room for Mr.—excuse me." She picked up the phone, which Nick had not heard ring, and explained to the caller that Ms. Doucette was still not back in the office, that yes she had given her both messages, that yes Ms. Doucette regularly checked her voice mail, and that no, she really couldn't think of any other way to reach Ms. Doucette.

Nick eyed the glass-enclosed conference room behind the reception desk. Rich black leather chairs, maybe twenty of them, around a pink marble table, with the home theater setup of Nick's dreams at the far end. The view, though, was unspectacular: another office building with an exterior nearly as dreary as this one's.

"I can just wait there in the conference room for Mr. Spillman and Ms. Parks," said Nick to the receptionist. Her name, according to the sign, was Tonetta James.

"Mr. Spillman hasn't reserved any rooms today," Tonetta replied, frowning. Nick wasn't sure whether the frown was directed at him, Mr. Spillman, Ms. Doucette, the conference room reservation software, or the last irate caller. "Just have a seat and someone will be with you shortly."

Two o'clock rolled by, then 2:15. The newspapers on the waiting room table were of no use to Nick: two *Wall Street Journals*, two *Financial Times* ("Why pink?" he wondered), and one *Roll Call*, to show off the firm's political savvy. Nothing useful in any of them about who was pitching for the Nats that night, or when if ever Murry might be coming off the DL. *Travel & Leisure*, *Southern Living*, the *Legal Times* top 100 American Law firms (listing G&H twenty-fourth) ... If Murry did come off the DL, Nick decided for the hundredth time, he would drop Castillo off his fantasy team in a heartbeat—batting .217 wasn't going to cut it.

Nick fidgeted away, wishing he had some sort of video game to keep his hands busy. He tried to revisit more carefully last night's conversation with Matteson, but mostly he just fretted.

"Mr. Fratangelo!" barked Tonetta. "I said Mr. Spillman would see you now. Not this conference room, but the southwest—down this hallway." Not much doubt about who her frown was for this time.

The southwest conference room, empty when he arrived, wasn't designed to impress clients. Its window displayed a blank cinder block wall, ten feet away. Eight chairs huddled around a scarred metal table, with little room between chair back and wall. Nick squeezed into a seat, while studying a whiteboard displaying a complex corporate structure left over from some prior meeting. "If I could figure out who A, ENG, Holdco, B REIT, R-tech, and that scribble on the bottom are," he thought, "I'd have some valuable inside information to sell. If I knew who wanted to buy it." Not a promising plan, but better than the wild goose chase he was now on.

After another ten minutes, Peter Spillman bustled in, with Natalie in tow. Spillman looked dapper in dark pinstripes with a collar pin propping up the knot in his tie, but Nick was searching for Natalie's fingers. Ringless! In his confusion last night, Nick hadn't thought to look. Natalie's hands, like the rest of her, were long, dark and lean. In an earlier time, she might have been dismissed as "too tall." The effect on Nick, though, was closer to "larger than life."

"Mr. Fratelli, how do you do? I don't believe we met last night." Spillman's tone was stiff and formal.

"Hi. No, I don't think so. You had a lot of people here! Hey Natalie, how you doing?"

Spillman gave her no chance to speak. "Yes, it was quite the occasion. So tell me, did you bring a memorandum outlining your proposal?"

"My proposal?"

"Yes. For Matteson Resources. Your regulatory strategy?"

"Oh. Well, no. I don't really have a memorandum. I don't even have a 'strategy,' like you do for a football game or something. I just, I was telling this guy Earl, the way all these crazy cases are going, you know, anybody can get out of just about anything if they call it a religion."

Natalie was focused intently on Spillman, cringing slightly.

Spillman's coldness could have frozen the Potomac. "No, Mr. Fratelli, I do not know. If I knew, you would not be here. What I do know is that you come to my reception, you accept my hospitality, you use the occasion to pitch my client, you suggest to him, perhaps not in so many words, that we don't know what we're doing, and when we attempt to do our duty for our client—Matteson Resources is still our client, you know—by analyzing your proposal, you suddenly turn coy. Is this how you do business?"

Nick's mouth hung open. It took a few seconds for words to tumble out. His violent head shaking filled the pause nicely, though. "I never—Natalie, you were there—I never said—I just told Earl that—"

"In this office," interrupted Spillman, "we refer to the president of Matteson Resources as Mr. Matteson."

Nick's brain didn't have time to formulate the precise expression "little prick" right at that instant, but that's where he was heading. Being humiliated in front of Natalie was not at all his plan. He met Spillman's glare with one of his own. "The man's name tag said 'Earl.' Excuse me. If you don't want people to talk to each other at your receptions, maybe you should put gags on them."

Natalie quickly jumped in. "Nick, we have a problem here. It isn't your fault. Nick really was very kind to us," she said to Spillman. Turning back to Nick, she said, "But Mr. Matteson gave us a hard time last night. He said he flew all the way to Washington to get some new ideas, and he thinks you have one. So he wants to talk to you. So if Mr. Matteson is interested, then we do want to work with you. What is it you have in mind? I will admit, I just didn't follow you."

That sounded better. "Natalie, honestly, I don't have any detailed plan. And I'm not being 'coy.'" He shot a stormy glance at Spillman. "I'm just fascinated with these cases of people getting out from under all kinds of rules based on religious exemptions. And either they win, or they lose just because they were stupid, and didn't plan things out right. I may not be a legal genius, but I can read a roadmap. And the courts have drawn a roadmap—a simple one—for what being a 'religion' means. Once you get something classified as a religion, which I know I can do, you're 90 percent of the way there. You just have to plan it out right."

"Which of these cases, Mr. Fratelli, allows an oil driller to circumvent environmental rules governing fracking?"

Nick shoved his glasses further up the bridge of his nose. "None of them do. Just like none of them allowed corporations to pick and choose which health insurance rules they felt like following, until *Hobby Lobby* came along. There's a first time for everything, you know."

"But *Hobby Lobby* involved a real religion. Not one some id—some*body* just made up."

"A 'real' religion?" Nick sneered. "Like how many people in this country really believe contraceptives are sinful?"

Spillman scowled, but didn't answer. "This is all quite extraordinary. And quite a rich source of potential embarrassment for Matteson Resources, if your pet theories turn out to be flawed. Be that as it may, you'll be meeting Mr. Matteson tomorrow out at his ranch, at his request. Not mine. He specifically demanded that you be present. It is critically important for this law firm to be kept in the loop. I have a call I need to go on, but Melinda has your reservations ready. She'll need your contact information."

"Um, I'm not going anywhere tomorrow."

"What?"

"I have a job. I have to put in for leave. I can't just disappear on a moment's notice."

Spillman exhaled disgustedly and raised his eyes to the ceiling. "But Nick," Natalie pleaded, "we told Mr. Matteson we'd be right on it. Can you please help us? It would mean a lot."

"The best I could do would be request leave for next week."

Spillman made no effort to conceal his scorn. "This just ... we're talking about the president of Matteson Resources here, not some peon. What does it take to get you there tomorrow?"

"I can't."

"Tomorrow is Friday," tried Natalie. "How about Saturday? You don't work on weekends, do you?"

"Well, no, but me and the guys ... Look, I don't even work for you. How much does this plane ticket cost? I don't even know this guy. Am I getting paid for this? Am I going by myself?"

Nick was pleased with himself for concealing the only real issue he had at the end of a stream of other questions. You never want to look too desperate.

Spillman softened his tone. "We're quite aware of the imposition on your time. Of course we're buying your ticket—first class. We can't pay you directly, because there are ethical concerns with your position as a government employee. But as everyone knows, this town runs on favors, and your doing this favor will not be forgotten. Besides, you and Ms. Parks will be staying at Mr. Matteson's home. Believe me, you won't be sorry you went. It's quite a spread."

Leaving on Saturday meant missing paintball. But Nick always lost at paintball, sometimes rather painfully, so it wasn't a great sacrifice. Then he caught the expression of eager anticipation on Natalie's face.

"Okay. But you have to understand—and Mr. Matteson has to understand—that I don't have any detailed legal plan."

"Detailed legal plans are not Mr. Matteson's forte," noted Spillman drily. "He gravitates rather quickly to the bottom line. I believe we're done here. You can find your way back out? I need to discuss one other matter with Ms. Parks. Could you close the door behind you, please?"

Damn, damn, damn. Not a moment with her alone. Well, Nick thought, he'd have a whole plane ride with her. And a fabulous weekend, with Peter Spillman thousands of miles away.

*****

After Nick closed the door, Spillman's face turned back to stone. Natalie tried to head him off. "I know, I know—damage control. I'll stay on top of this, I promise, and make it totally clear that anything crazy Nick says is Nick saying it, not us."

"That's not my question. My question is, what possessed you to invite this, this twit to our reception?"

"You—we were told—I thought the idea was to have a big crowd?"

"A crowd?" he snarled. Natalie was taken aback by how much scorn Spillman could pack into one little word. "A crowwwd? Did you offer milk and cookies to Miss Prendergast's kindergarten class to attract a 'crowd'? We're looking for clients, Ms. Parks, not crowds. People who will pay us money, that we can use to pay the ridiculously high salaries your crop of associates commands."

Natalie silently registered that he had said only "salaries," not "salaries and bonuses." That was troubling. Was everybody losing their bonus? Or just her?

"I'm sorry, sir. I'll do better next time."

"I'm sure you will." Peter leaned back, and twirled a pen through his fingers. "Now one other thing. Your friend's idea, whether or not it has any true merit, does appeal to Earl. Earl loves nothing better than to tweak the government, and he doesn't mind spending money to do it. There's that 'M' word again, Ms. Parks. Did you catch that? This can be a fee event. So when you say 'damage control,' what I'm asking for here—complex as it may sound—is for you to exercise a little judgment. Don't embarrass this law firm, but don't fritter away this litigation opportunity. Is that clear?"

"Yes, sir. Got it."

June 19:
Reagan National Airport

Nick was already at the Frontier Airlines gate Saturday morning when Natalie arrived. An enormous Danish pastry balanced precariously on a paper plate on his knee, while he stuffed an overambitiously large bite of another into his mouth. A small drop of cherry goo oozed down his lower lip, seeking his chin.

"Like some?" Nick asked, mouth half full.

Natalie glared at him disdainfully. "That's not the tie you're going to wear, is it?" she asked.

"Tie?" Nick responded, glancing down and reassuring himself that the paunch it appeared to rest on was purely a result of the way he was slouching. "Well, yeah."

"We'll have to get you another one. Look at that spot." Nick held up the tie and took a few moments to locate the spot. "You can barely see it. You should see my navy blue tie. Now that's bad."

Natalie shut her eyes. "Don't you know that Mr. Matteson, the man we're flying out to see, is a billionaire—with a 'b'? You need to make an impression."

Nick gazed up sheepishly. A look that always worked on Mama; maybe it would work on Natalie, too.

"With all respect, counselor, he's not going to be looking at my tie, at least not while you're in the room."

One point for Nick?

Natalie moved Nick's bag from the spot he'd saved for her and sat down. "Seriously, Nick, this is a big deal. We're staying at the man's home, for heaven's sake. All it takes is one little flub, one little impression that we're not serious, and we could lose him. You could at least have worn a suit rather than that old corduroy jacket."

Nick pushed his glasses back up his nose with his thumb. "I've got eighty-two pages of serious in this backpack. This is what's going to get Matteson his second billion. Not my tie."

Across the narrow aisle, a sour-faced matron with blue-rimmed glasses glanced up from her crossword at the mention of "second billion."

"Just wait here with the bags," said Natalie, bouncing up again. "There's a men's store on the concourse. I'll get you a tie."

Nick ogled Natalie's well-defined posterior, jangling left-right-left-right under the skirt of her charcoal business suit as she marched off, high heels clicking down the concrete passageway, ebony ponytail propelling her like a fish. He had actually bought a new tie yesterday for the trip, and thought he had put it on, but evidently had not. His head had been too full of appellate cases, tactical options, and visions of Natalie to manage mundane tasks like selecting the right tie.

Now he had a new puzzle to solve: what was he going to do with two new ties?

Natalie returned before he could finish the second Danish. "What eighty-two pages?" she demanded, thrusting a bag at him. The new tie was red with diagonal stripes like the one he had just bought, but the material was more expensive. Nick had hoped she might help him put it on, but she made no move in that direction. "You said you didn't have any written proposal."

"I didn't, then, but I've been busy. Spent all day yesterday on it. I tell you, these cases. I knew there was some weird shit out there, but when you put 'em all together, it's just overwhelming. The thing is, you've gotta—"

"You wrote eighty-two pages in one day?"

"No! I didn't write it. That's copies of some of the cases I read, and regs, and other stuff. I only wrote a few notes. But I'm telling you, if you do it right, it's there. There are loopholes you could fly that plane through."

"We do very thorough work."

"That's what I mean!" Nick started to throw out his hands, then caught the remaining half-Danish before it tumbled to the floor. "Look. You got these guys, like the Pastafarians, or the Satanists—"

"Hey, Nick, could we hold off a little bit? We'll have time on the plane." Natalie nodded slightly toward the woman with the blue glasses. Associating Earl Matteson publicly with "Satanists" wandered too far into "Don't embarrass the firm" territory.

"Oh, okay. Why don't we talk about you? You look terrific, but then you always looked terrific."

"I'm great. We're very busy. I've been lucky to be assigned to both government affairs and to regulatory, and I've been able to get involved in some litigation."

"So you go to court?"

"No, not yet. But all the document work, the discovery management, it's just a fantastic opportunity. It's starting at the top!"

Nick envied her success, but at the same time congratulated himself for avoiding that kind of pressure. "Sounds peachy. What about when you're not working?"

"Not working?" Natalie cocked her head wistfully. "I don't do much of that. I don't want to let these opportunities pass me by."

"That's what you used to say in law school."

"Well I'm still learning, really. It takes a lot of effort to get ahead. Except—hold on."

She pulled a cellphone from her oversized handbag. Nick had not heard it ring.

"Yeah?" she said. " ... Shit ... okay."

A woman of few words. None of which were directed toward Nick, as she furiously typed in some sort of message on the cellphone. Look at those luxurious fingers. No fancy manicure, though. Pointed nails would slow down typing, for sure. She also wore no scent that Nick could discern, but she looked so much like someone who smelled of lavender that she may as well have.

At a break in the action, Nick tried again. "So what are you—"

"Wait," she commanded, holding up her left palm at Nick's face while starting to type again with her right.

Nick waited for the next pause that seemed to last more than a few seconds, then tried yet another approach.

"Just think," he said, leaning back and draping his elbows over the chair. Blue glasses had left. "I could come out of this as head of my own religion. Pope Niccolò the first. Or I guess it wouldn't be the first, because they don't call the first guy the first. Like when they had the first Francis, he wasn't called the first. Just Francis."

Natalie had not looked up from her cell phone during this short history lesson. "Mmm," she said, seeming to sense a pause in the flow of Nick's words. Then she started pecking away again.

Ever quick on the uptake, Nick tried a different tack. "Of course, it wouldn't have to be me. It could be a woman. That would be different, for sure. It could be you! Wouldn't that be cool! You could be the, the what? The Popette? Nah, that wouldn't be good. The 'pet' part, I mean. We'd have to dream up something else."

Natalie clicked off her cell phone, closed her eyes, and drooped her head. At last, he had her attention.

"You know what I dream about, Nick?"

"What?" he said eagerly.

"I dream about your not making a total ass of yourself at this meeting.

I dream about G&H not losing a four million dollar a year client. Most of all, I dream about not getting fired, for making the incredible mistake of dredging up my law school list to invite to the fricking party. Now,"—she fluttered her lashes sweetly—"can you help me make my dream come true?"

Ok, Nick thought, so "irrepressible boyish" wasn't going to work. It hadn't worked all through law school, so why should it start now? It was the main role he knew, though.

His only other idea was to try "legal scholar." That certainly wouldn't work with most women, but Natalie wasn't most women. He ruffled through his eighty-two pages, trying to identify an issue he could ask her a question about that she couldn't answer, so that he could then offer a thoughtful conjecture that sounded smart. He was close to formulating something about a split among the circuits on standing requirements when, without looking up from her cell phone, Natalie quietly said "Empress. I could be an empress."

June 19: North Dakota

"So how do we get from here to Matteson's house?" asked Nick, as their flight descended into Bismarck. "Did you rent a car?"

"No," replied Natalie. "Melinda said someone would meet us at the airport and take us there."

"Maybe a limousine? Sweet! I've never been in one of those. A couple of guys rented one for our prom, but that was a little too rich for me at the time."

"They're okay," said Natalie, not looking up from her laptop screen. "Just a car with a little extra leg room, really. And a bar. And a TV. If you like that sort of thing."

"I could get used to it. This time next year, when I'm pope of my new religion, I'll have a whole fleet of 'em. What kind of TV? A big flat screen? I hate playing Halo on anything less than sixty inches."

Natalie looked up from her laptop and scowled. At least she looked up, which she had only done a couple of times since Washington. She'd been buried in some sort of reply brief due on Monday, which she couldn't even talk about because of confidentiality. Nick suspected, though he didn't come right out and ask, that she was billing this travel time to Matteson at the same time she was billing brief-writing time to the other client. That's how some lawyers got caught billing more than twenty-four hours in a day.

"This is no game, Nick. I hope you understand that. Maybe you've got nothing to lose, except your precious paintball match, but I do. Don't fuck this up, okay?"

He kicked himself for mentioning the paintball. She'd never want to play, even if she had the time, which she didn't. And if he ever did get her to play, she'd whip his ass, which would be embarrassing.

"I told you I couldn't promise anything. Especially on a day's notice. A day I spent using government facilities, illegally, working for *you*. And your big shot boss. Falling way behind in my own work, by the way, of which I do have some, thank you very much. So let's just give this a shot, okay?"

"Whatever," Natalie mumbled, without looking up.

"And if I have to get by with a smaller screen in the limo, then God's will be done."

Was that a flicker of a grin Nick saw her trying to repress? Probably not.

*****

Just outside the airport security zone, a tall, stunning woman with a tight sweater and flowing red hair held up a printed sign that said "Fratelli."

"Are you parked out front?" Natalie asked.

"Not hardly, sweetie. Come this way."

Doris, as she identified herself, walked them down the length of the airport and out an unmarked door in the rear. A hundred yards of blacktop later, Nick spied a gleaming white helicopter, with the "Matteson" logo—the T's shaped like oil derricks—emblazoned on the side.

Nick whistled. "Some limo! I've never been in one of these. Have you?" Natalie shook her head, while Nick wondered whether she was really as nonchalant as she looked. "I hope these things are safe," he added, somewhat dubiously.

Doris loaded Natalie and the bags into the rear seat, and Nick up front. "Is the pilot here?" Nick asked, now a bit past "dubious."

"She sure is," said Doris, flashing a beauty pageant smile. She walked around and leapt into the pilot's seat. Then she sat for a few seconds staring at the row of switches, finger to her scarlet-painted lower lip. "Now which one is the starter thingy?" she muttered, flipping a couple of them on and off, with no effect.

"Can you fly this?" Nick demanded, with genuine alarm.

"Oh sure! No problemo! Brad—he's my honey—he lets me fly all the time. On his lap!" she squealed. "I just gotta crank it up—if you know what I mean." She giggled again.

Nick craned his neck back to Natalie in panic.

"Tell me, babe," said Doris, a devilish gleam in her eye, "You like it smooth? Or *bumpy!*"—that last word delivered with a Jimmy Durante rasp, and a jiggle of her breasts. Before Nick could wail in response, the engine roared into life, drowning out all further conversation.

Nick would have voted for "smooth," which is exactly what he got. The takeoff was effortless, like being in an elevator. So was the landing; he wasn't even certain they'd touched the ground. Forty minutes in between gave Nick a good look at North Dakota. The best word he could come up with was "empty." He'd never been west of Pittsburgh before, and he found the endless open prairie mesmerizing.

"Uh, thanks for the ride," said Nick after emerging from the chopper and welcoming the firm ground. He tried to avoid Doris's eyes.

"I'll see you in in the morning, babe," she simpered. "And I do hope you'll still respect me then. Go see Gretchen up at the house, and she'll take care of you. Bye now!"

"Serves you right," Natalie hissed when they were out of earshot, "for staring at her like that. Act professionally, would you?"

"What was I supposed to look at? The ground?"

The staring danger reached a whole new level when Gretchen greeted them at the back door. Her supermodel looks made Nick forget Doris instantly, and nearly forget his own name.

She told them Earl was still out in the stables, and would return shortly. Until then, they could make themselves comfortable. There was a bar, just past the billiard room, if they were thirsty. There were two pools, one indoor and one outdoor. And a hot tub.

Nick was trying to keep his eyes fixed on Natalie, in desperation. He could tell from the anthracite in her eyes that the correct response was "No, thanks. Is there just a place we could spread out some papers? And plug in our laptops?" A response he duly delivered.

Gretchen led them to a handsome conference room, half again as large as the one at G&H, with a bar conveniently located at the far end. Matteson's mansion sat atop a ridge, and the view from the fifty-foot window seemed to go on forever.

"What kind of place is this?" he asked Natalie in a low voice, after Gretchen left them alone.

"Mr. Matteson has a ... a 'reputation' for his staff with the guys back at the office. I always thought they were exaggerating, but maybe not."

"Is that how you came to be working for him?" Nick had the good sense to merely think these words, not say them out loud. Instead he said, "You mean there are more?"

"Afraid so. You'll just have to soldier on as best you can. You should stay away from the kitchen, though. I've heard the cook is really something."

"Don't worry. After Doris, I don't want to be around any of them carrying sharp objects."

*****

A few minutes later, just as Natalie was settling back into her brief-writing groove, Earl Matteson bustled in.

"Howdy! Welcome to paradise. Bet you're glad to be out of that hellhole you live in. I hate the place! How was your flight? Did you meet Doris?"

Nick nodded ruefully. "Yeah, we met Doris."

"Hell of a gal. She flew seventy-odd missions against them ISIS bastards in Syria. It's a wonder they got any Muslims left."

For the first and only time in his life, Nick felt a twinge of pity for "them ISIS bastards."

Gretchen had clearly been telling the truth about Earl's being in the stable. He wore an old denim shirt with a torn pocket, and dirty blue jeans with brown splotches that did not look like mud. Nick made a mental note to tease Natalie later about her obsession with the spot on his tie.

"So whatcha got for me? You need a drink? Hell, what are we in here for? Let's go down to the bar."

Scientists teach that light is a physical particle. Nick could vouch for that, because he could actually feel the laser beams shooting out of Natalie's eyes when he allowed as how yes, a beer would be nice after their long journey. Natalie requested some ice water, which she didn't really need.

After settling in with a tall Coors, Nick launched into his spiel in earnest. At one point, yet another jaw-dropping staffer stuck her head in to ask if they needed anything. But Nick was in a groove, and barely noticed her. He told Earl and Natalie about the peyote-smoking Indians who took their case all the way to the Supreme Court, claiming the drug laws shouldn't apply to them because they were practicing their "religion." About how the Supreme Court threw them out, saying the drug laws applied the same to everyone, regardless of religion. About how the churches then began lobbying the Democrats in Congress, who were anxious to appease them. How they proceeded to pass the Religious Freedom Restoration Act of 1993, "RFRA" for short, which invalidated every single federal, state, and local law that anyone had a religious objection to, unless government bent over backwards to try to accommodate them.

"Damn Injuns," Earl chimed in at one point. "Nothin' but trouble."

Nick plowed ahead. This was the first time anyone had ever shown any interest in this, his pet subject. He'd chatted with Kyle back in the office about the more outrageous news items he ran across as he filled the empty GSA hours with his study of the foibles of government involvement with religion, but Kyle just turned everything into a wisecrack. Now here were two people—two intelligent, successful people—hanging on his every word. Even Natalie seemed to be taking him seriously. Probably an act, but an act she'd never bothered with before.

RFRA went too far, he continued, and a few years after it passed the Supreme Court threw it out. Not all of it, though. The court said Congress had no authority to make such a sweeping change to state and local laws, so RFRA could only apply to the federal government. That still covered a lot of territory, but not enough for the God lobby. They immediately started working on the states, half of which now had their own mini-RFRAs. And they got Congress to pass another law, called "RLUIPA," to subject state and local land use laws to the same exemption racket RFRA imposed on the federal government.

Earl was beginning to flag, but Nick was oblivious. "Now the weird thing about RLUIPA is that it was written to cover zoning, so that megachurches could plunk themselves in the middle of residential neighborhoods whenever they felt like it. But at the last minute they tacked on special privileges for prisoners, too. You wouldn't believe some of the crap murderers and rapists are able to get away with now."

"Who the hell's idea was that?" Earl bellowed.

"That's what's so bizarre! You remember Chuck Colson, one of Nixon's Watergate guys? It was him! He's the one who got his buddies in Congress to slip prisons in at the last minute. That's what RLUIPA spells out—the Religious Land Use and Institutionalized Persons Act. The 'insitutionalized persons' are the prisoners."

"Chuck Colson was a good man," Earl said defensively. "So was Richard Nixon. I thought you said this was Democrats' doing?"

"It's all of them. Pigs at the trough. You know that first law, RFRA? You know who were the two main sponsors of that? Teddy Kennedy and Orrin Hatch. How many times do you think they agreed on anything?"

"Raising my damned taxes, for one."

"Well, maybe. Anyway, it's exploded way beyond just RFRA and RLUIPA. There's religious carve-outs in Social Security, in discrimination laws, in health care laws, you name it. And now with *Hobby Lobby*—"

"Hold on, son. You're wearin' me down. Can I get you another beer?"

"No thanks. Just bear with me—one little story. You'll like this one."

"I'll like it better with another bourbon. Keep talking."

"Okay. This is all true, by the way. You can read it all here."

"Talk."

"Well there's this coal mine, see, in West by God Virginia. And the miners used to punch in and punch out on time clocks. And some of them, you know, they'd do favors for their buddies, punch each other in and out. So the company caught on, and put in a new system with a hand scanner. You stick your right hand inside a machine, like a bar code scanner, whenever you come and go. That made it impossible to cheat. But one guy, he doesn't want to do that. Why? Because in the Book of Revelation, it says something about the devil putting the 'mark of the beast' on the right hand of his followers. This guy said he didn't want any truck with the devil, so he wasn't sticking his right hand anywhere. Even though he admitted that the machine wasn't putting on any mark, it was just looking at the lines on his hand."

Even Natalie was smirking now.

"So the company says 'Fine. Just for you, we can re-rig the machine, so you can use your *left* hand instead. The Bible says it's just the right hand the devil's interested in, so you can stay cool with God. But the guy says nope, not good enough. A hand's a hand, and he's not sticking either hand anywhere."

"I'd have fired his ass."

"No, you couldn't have. Because he quit! On the spot, as soon as they offered him the left hand deal. And you know what's coming next. A lawsuit, like ten minutes later, claiming he's been harassed out of his job for his religious beliefs. Which, of course, he wins, socking it to the company for half a million bucks."[4]

"It's a crying shame, what the lawyers have done to this country. No offense, but—"

"That's the thing!" Nick interrupted gleefully. "It's not the lawyers! You know who brought this case? Not some quick-buck ambulance chaser, but the United States government, on this crazy miner's behalf."

"Crazy like a fox," Natalie murmured. It was the first thing she'd said since Nick had started on his monologue.

"Now when you get to the state level," Nick began again, but Earl cut him off.

"This is all very entertaining, but let's get to the point. You're saying all I've got to do is say God wants me to squirt chemicals in the ground to help me pull the oil out, and I can get the local EPAs off my back?"

Nick leaned forward to make direct eye contact. He spoke slowly

---

4.   Brian Bowling, "Former Consol employee wins nearly $587K in 'Mark of the Beast' lawsuit," *Pittsburgh Tribune-Review*, August 28, 2015. http://loganbanner.com/news/1878/former-consol-employee-wins-nearly-587k-in-mark-of-the-beast-lawsuit.

and clearly. "No, sir. Definitely not. If you do that, you will lose, and you'll look bad in the process. You probably don't really care how you look, but you could screw up some of the more legit—some of the more 'traditional' defenses Mr. Spillman and his team are using on your behalf."

Natalie nodded vigorously. She really was listening.

"Then what the hell is the point?"

"The point is, sir, that you can work your way up to it. You don't just punch a hole somewhere in the ground on a whim and hope there's oil there, do you? No, you work your way up to it. That's how the law works, especially something like this. The first, biggest step is to get it established that there's really a legitimate religious belief here. Not just a one-off. The people who come in and just say 'Oh, it's my religion to smoke pot' get shot down, because they don't have a, a comprehensive, legitimate-sounding tradition. Now if you think about what happened in the New Song cases—"

"Nick!" Natalie broke in. "The point."

Nick had been enjoying the attention so much that he hated to stop, but Natalie was probably right. "The first thing you need is a theology. Well-constructed, consistent, understandable. The New Song guys had a written document, but it was crap, and that ultimately did them in. You need it to be comprehensive—not just one issue, but lots of things, a whole view of life.[5] You need that not just for the substance, but to be able to attract followers—the more people you get signed on, the harder it is for the courts to ignore. Or the politicians, for that matter."

Earl's eyes were narrowed in rapt attention.

"Then you need a win. An easy case, that doesn't step on many toes, so the judge won't lose any sleep over saying 'Yeah, I guess that's a religion.' What you want to do with fracking, sir, is not that easy case. But that's huge, to have a court recognize in precedent that this theology you've put together is a legitimate religion. Then you need another win, in a different judicial district, on something a little harder. Then, maybe, a couple more intermediate-level wins. I don't know. It would depend how things are going. Finally, you spring it. You've pre-baked the religious justification for whatever it is you want to do with your fracking into all the documents that court after court has approved, that law after

---

5.   *Africa v. Pennsylvania*, 662 F.2d 1025 (3d Cir. 1981) http://openjurist. org/662/f2d/1025/africa-v-commonwealth-of-pennsylvania-s.

law has been bent to make way for. You've got 'em surrounded! They might not even fight!"

Nick was up, pacing about excitedly, flailing his hands to show what "surrounded" meant in case Earl didn't know.

"So what's this 'theology' you're talking about? Keep it short, please. I'm gettin' hungry. And what's this 'easy' case? And how much does it cost?"

Nick sat back down heavily and planted his hands on his knees. "I'll keep it short: I don't know. I know all the pieces of the puzzle are there, but I haven't put them together yet. I don't want to bullshit you."

"There's a first," Earl snorted. "You sure you're a lawyer?"

"I told these guys," Nick said, nodding toward Natalie, "that I didn't have a neat plan all laid out, but they said I should come out here anyway. So here I am. And unless you want to hear about the rest of these cases, that's all I've got."

Earl walked over to the window, saying nothing. Sunset was in full force over the mountains. He tapped a button on his cellphone, and asked whoever was on the other end when dinner would be served. "Half hour break ok with you folks?" Earl asked. Natalie headed straight back to her room. Nick tarried a moment to study a picture of an aircraft carrier. Earl sidled up and poked him gently in the ribs and nodded toward the doorway Natalie had just passed through. "Hey, just between us: how's Miss Saigon in the sack? I bet she's a tiger!"

Nick flushed with fury. "Hey! You leave her alone! In the first place, she's not Vietnamese. She's Korean. And second, her sex life is none of your business. You got enough around here—you leave her out of it. Plus, she's a damn good lawyer. None of this happens without her!"

Nick started to walk away, then turned back. The whole decadent scene, so utterly foreign to everything he was accustomed to, capped off by a money-grubbing lecher degrading his dream goddess was all too much for him. "In fact, none of this is gonna happen at all. I'm leaving."

"Now look, son—"

"And another thing. I'm not your fucking son. Quit calling me that. I'd puke if I had you for a father." The beers Nick had consumed may have been a bad idea.

"Now look, *Mr. Fratelli*. It's a long walk to Bismarck; if you start now, you might get there by Tuesday. So cool your jets, and we'll have some dinner. And here: I apologize. I don't do that often, but I'm doing it now. I shouldn'ta said that, and I'm sorry I did. I get in trouble for saying what I think—that's why I don't get along in Washington. But I'm not the only one who isn't perfect. Show you what I mean. Did you meet Gretchen?"

"Yeah."

"And the only thing you thought about when you met Gretchen was what a disciplined, well-organized personal assistant she must be?"

No response.

"So the difference between you and me is that I blurt things out, and you sneak around with 'em. And that makes you better'n me?"

"In some ways, yes. More respectful, anyway."

"Yep. But I'm trying to catch up here, make things right. I'll apologize to Miss Parks, too. Happy to do it. Go git her. I don't want you to go away mad, walking or otherwise."

Nick hesitated. "That won't be necessary." Earl stuck out his hand, and Nick shook it.

*****

Dinner featured the largest steak Nick had ever seen. He initially doubted whether he could finish it, but did his duty manfully. As the plates were being cleared by yet another distractingly attractive young woman, Earl asked Nick how much time it would take to put together a plan to get the job done.

"I don't know. I've never done this kind of thing before. No one else has, either."

"Well, I'm not too religious myself, but I seem to recall it took Jesus forty days in the desert to come up with his religion."

"Not exactly," Nick stammered. "Besides, Jesus didn't have a job. I do. Reading about religious craziness is just a hobby."

"What if this were your job?"

"My job?"

"How much you makin' now?"

"I ... that's sort of personal, isn't it?" Nick's mind had wandered briefly to the possibility that a conversation like this might occur during his preparation yesterday, but it seemed so farfetched he hadn't dwelt on it.

"I know what you make. Roughly, anyway. Third-year government lawyer, ain't much difference one to another. How about if I triple it? How long does this take then?"

Nick was stunned. "I've got ... benefits. I've got healthcare."

"Answer my question."

"I've got ... security. You know a government job, it's not that exciting, but—"

"Shit. I thought you might be different. You ain't. You're the same as all these other Washington boys. Security, my ass! You think this country got built on security? It got built on people standing up for what they believe. I don't understand everything you said, but I saw fire in your eyes, and I've made a lot of money working with folks when I could see that fire. You go on back to shufflin' your papers, and I'll find somebody else to take the gist of what you were telling me and work it up into somethin' I can use. That'll be another 'case' for you read about."

Natalie leaned anxiously in toward Nick. "You did sound awfully excited. Why are you holding back now?"

"It's just sudden." Another long pause. "I can't answer your question about how long anything would take. Forty days? I don't know. But ... say I do this. I up and quit and burn my bridges. And then you change your mind, or something happens, and even though I'm doing my part fine, I'm nowhere. I've got debts to pay."

"That's fair," said Earl. "I get it." Turning to Natalie, he asked for Peter Spillman's home number.

"He would be in the office now, sir."

"At this time on a Saturday night? Back east where it's two hours later?"

"Yes, sir. We're very busy."

Earl punched a speed dial button on his cellphone, then put it on speaker. Peter Spillman, who was anticipating the call, picked up immediately.

"Hey, Pete, we're all here. Gotcha on speaker. Here's the deal. You got a pencil? Do me up a new LLC, and an employment contract for Fratelli. Leave the salary number blank—he'll give it to you. One year minimum—got that? If he never shows up for a minute, he still gets the one year minimum."

"That's not standard."

"Shut up and write. You house him in your space. I know you got empty offices there. I'll cover the rent. You just watch him."

"Whatever you say. Might I ask what his job duties will be?"

"Now another thing. You watch him, but I want Miss Parks here running the details, keepin' things hummin'. Mad scientists on their own can't do shit. She's a sharp cookie, even if she don't talk much. How much you paying her? I don't care—whatever it is, bump it up. Out of your pot, not mine."

"I hardly think—"

"Now *that's* the first smart thing you've said in a long time. You don't think. You just stay in the middle of the pack, where it's safe. And I pay out the wazoo, and keep losin'. Now this boy here—" Earl caught himself, flummoxed for an instant. Politically correct did not come easily for him. "Fuck it. It's my money. This *boy* here, I think he's onto something. Plus he's got balls, if you stir him up. So we're gonna do things my way for a change. You got all that down? You write up a contract for Monday, and he'll come in and sign it. Or he won't. Up to him. G'night, Pete. Don't stay too late."

After a moment of stunned silence, Natalie was the first to speak. "Mr. Matteson, I don't think—"

"Good! You heard what I told Pete. Nick here does the thinking, you run him. Hard!"

"And you," he said, wheeling sharply toward Nick. "You got your fuckin' security. But I got mine, too. You know what that is?" His face contorted purple, his stubby finger stabbing an inch from Nick's nose. "If you rip me off, if you and your oh-so-clever Washington faggots take my money, and don't do your damnedest, and just play me for the big hick sucker, I will personally hunt you down and yank your nuts off. Comprende, amigo?" The twisting motion he made with his meaty fist implanted itself permanently in Nick's mind.

Earl sat back, beaming, and clapped the arms of his chair. "I think we're done here. This has been a good day. Enjoy the rest of your evening, and Doris will take you back to Bismarck in the morning." Earl rose and leaned in toward Nick. "I got me a little appointment with the cook. Time for my dessert!" With a stage wink, he was gone.

*****

Nick walked with Natalie outdoors to the deck. He'd never seen so many stars in the sky. He wondered if it were some sort of desert optical illusion.

"So," he finally asked, "is this what life is like in a big law firm?"

Natalie burst out laughing, "No! Not at all! I've never been around anything like this. Did I dream it?"

"If you did, then we both dreamt the same thing. You think I should take the job?"

Natalie reverted to her more customary scorn. "Oh, no. Go ahead and pass on it. You should spend the rest of your life boring everyone around you with what you could have, would have done if you had taken the offer, which wasn't good enough because it would *only* triple your salary and give you total freedom to pursue your pipe dream du jour. Who'd want that?"

It took Nick a little while to formulate an answer. "The thing is, yeah, I think it's all doable. Even a church that would legitimize fracking. But I don't like that it's doable. I hate it. That's why I study all these news clips and cases, so I can learn about this shit, and maybe do something about it someday. Get rid of all the special privileges, so everybody follows the same law. So nobody gets treated like they're better than me, or my family. I've just never had an idea how to begin."

With a little less scorn, Natalie replied, "The only way to begin is to begin. Get involved somehow, then look around. You'll never get this kind of experience at GSA."

Or, he reflected, the chance to interact with Natalie every day. "Plus, if I don't take it, you might not get your 'bump.'"

"Why are we talking about this? You know you're going to do it."

They both studied the stars for a while. Nick had spent several evenings before the G&H reception binge-watching movies with Asian starlets, trying to decide which one most closely resembled the Natalie of his dreams. Yao Chen, Smith Cho, Julia Ling? The younger Lucy Liu probably came closest. He'd take Natalie over any of them. "Hey, Natalie," Nick said, finally breaking the silence. "I've been trying to figure out some good way of finding this out, but I haven't been able to. So please, don't get mad, but ... do you have, like, a boyfriend?"

Natalie gazed at him earnestly, almost sadly. "No, Nick, I don't. And I can't. Not now, anyway. This firm will either spit you out or put you on top of the world. I want the top of the world. My parents worked in a laundry their whole lives. Do you have any idea what that's like? I'm not going to blow this chance on a boyfriend. So, I'm glad you finally asked, because we've got to be clear on that. Especially now, if I'm going to be supervising you."

Nick expected her to head back inside, replaying the hackneyed "Nick watching Natalie walk away" scene for the umpteenth time. But she lingered by his side a while longer.

"Nick," she finally said, "I heard your little tirade with Earl about me. Every word. And I appreciate what you tried to do. But let me fight my own battles, okay? I'm used to it. You're not, and you almost ruined everything. Don't do that again." With that, the familiar scene played out: Nick standing helplessly, watching Natalie walk away.

*****

When Nick and Natalie left the following morning, it became immediately clear that the grapevine had passed a message on to Doris. "Hey, Mr. Fratelli, I just want to say I'm sorry for messing with you yesterday. I know a first chopper ride can be scary for some people. It sure was for me. So I shouldn't have made things worse by teasing you, and I am sorry. No hard feelings, okay?"

Nick took her outstretched hand. "Sure, no hard feelings." Then, glancing down, he added "Well, maybe one."

Two of the three of them thought that was hilarious.

June 21:
The Library of Congress

Nick was startled by a limousine that nearly ran him down as he jaywalked across K Street, absorbed in thought about his eventful day. First thing in the morning he had cornered Myers to give him two weeks' notice of his resignation. Myers was none too pleased. Not that he had any special affection for Nick, but replacing him meant more work. As partial atonement, Nick volunteered for more projects than usual at the morning staff meeting. But he still knew he could get them done working only a couple of hours a day, giving him the rest of the time to launch his new adventure. Being seen at quitting time no longer mattered as much as it had before.

He left for lunch promptly at noon, not intending to return to GSA that day. Instead, wolfing down a vendor's hot dog as he walked, he headed straight for G&H.

Tonetta still didn't recognize him, but the office manager at least knew he was coming. She showed him to a secretary's cubicle with four-foot partitions, telling him this was where he would be temporarily assigned. "But we just passed two empty offices," he protested. "Can't I get one of those?" Still, the cubicle made the GSA space he shared with Kyle look classy by comparison.

"Those are for the lawyers," she said evenly.

"I'm a lawyer."

"Those are for lawyers who are employed by the firm. Mr. Spillman said we are simply housing you. I'm not sure what you'll be doing, but this is where you are supposed to be. Mr. Spillman also gave me this contract for you to sign."

"Is Natalie's office around here? Ms. Parks, I mean."

"No, she's on the eighth floor. Now, did you bring a laptop with you? You won't be able to use one of ours, for security reasons. But you can log onto our wi-fi, as a guest."

"Uh, no. Just this tablet. I can't do much work with this."

The office manager shrugged. "Here's a key to the men's room. The reception desk is staffed from eight to eight, six days a week. I can't give you an office key, so you'll have to come and go when the desk is staffed."

"For security reasons. Like I'm going to steal all your legal pads."

"I don't know whether you've been through an SEC investigation before, Mr. Fratelli, but I can assure you they are not pleasant. How would you propose we explain to the SEC that we allow unscreened non-employees to wander in and out at will?"

Screen me and hire me, Nick grumbled to himself. That would work. But he didn't need to antagonize her any more than he already had. Instead, he sat down in his stall and reviewed his contract, noticing Earl Matteson's faxed signature on the last page even though the salary line had yet to be filled in. The name of his new employer was simply "Company 1441, LLC," which was owned by "Company 248, Inc." How romantic! Every other detail of the contract was one-sided in favor of the employer. Part of Nick wanted to haggle every fine point to death, as he'd learned to do at GSA. But he was sick of that world, and had the sense that if he held up his end of the bargain and gave his best shot, Earl wouldn't wiggle out on any technicalities. Spillman might, but Earl wouldn't. So Nick signed, after filling in and initialing the salary blank and then writing in the margin on the same page: "Employee to be provided with a (new) laptop computer."

*****

There was little more to be done at G&H without a decent computer, and Nick's official starting date wasn't for two more weeks anyway. So after stealing an official G&H labeled legal pad, he headed out toward his other new workplace across town: the Library of Congress. Pondering what kinds of books he should order once ensconced there was what nearly got Nick hit by the limousine. He knew a great deal about the foibles of religion already from his college studies, and his continuing reading of the religious press after that. Nothing amazed him anymore, from the prodigious sums paid to certify Catholic sainthood to the even greater sums devoted to an object purporting to be the Buddha's tooth—which zoologists said was actually the tooth of a cow.[6] His greatest awe, though, was reserved not for the moneymakers, but

---

6. "Experts claim Buddha tooth relic in Singapore temple actually came from an animal," *The Nation*, July 15, 2007. http://www.buddhistchannel.tv/index.php?id=57,4484,0,0,1,0#.WMMMwzvytt4

for the scofflaws, who seemed to be able to get away with just about anything by pinning a religious freedom tag to it. His head-shaking rhetorical question, "How do they do that?" was now replaced with a more urgent "How do *I* do that?"

"Now this," thought Nick as he settled into the main reading room, "I could get used to." Soft light filtered down from the skylights, surrounded by statues of the great scholars of history: Plato, Gibbon, Newton. Every detail of the furnishings was luxurious, the better to impress the tourists who gawked from a balcony above. Thank you, taxpayers, Nick thought. I do appreciate the gesture. He didn't appreciate that, unlike most libraries, he would never be allowed to take a book out of the room, or even to look for a book on the shelf. He had to request a book by filling out a little form, and then wait for an hour or so until a silent librarian placed it on his desk. He could store books overnight, but not take them from the room. Still, it wasn't a bad place to cool your heels, and once he got rolling he could be studying one book while waiting for others to be delivered.

Then there were the free subscriptions to all the online newspapers and scholarly publications normally hidden behind paywalls—so long as you accessed them through the reading room's wi-fi. Nick wondered whether pay-for-porn websites were available free as well, but quickly discovered they were not. Oh, well.

He soon found enough relevant material online to keep him absorbed until his first stack of books arrived. He used that opportunity to bone up on the New Song saga he'd tried unsuccessfully to regale Earl with. A federal prisoner named Harry Theriault had founded the "Church of the New Song" (CONS for short), whose principal sacrament was steak and Harvey's Bristol Crème at five p.m. every Friday afternoon. CONS and its sacrament were legitimized and protected by federal courts for nearly thirty years—thirty years!—until the Eighth Circuit finally shut it down, having carefully analyzed the "scriptures" Theriault had written and spotting some "inconsistencies." Nick knew he was no genius, but he believed he was more sophisticated than Theriault had been, and could put together something without the same "inconsistencies."[7] Nor was Theriault the only imaginatively religious inmate. Matthew Hale, serving

---

7.   Marci A. Hamilton, *God vs. the Gavel*, Cambridge University Press 2005, p.163; *Remmers v. Brewer*, 494 F.2d 1277 (8th Cir. 1974) http://openjurist.org/494/f2d/1277

forty years for conspiring to murder a federal judge, had persuaded a different federal judge that his "Church of the Creator"—which didn't believe in God, but did believe in white supremacy—deserved recognition as a privileged church as well.[8]

Exploring all the nooks and crannies available free online kept Nick so busy that he was startled to hear the announcement that "The library will be closing in fifteen minutes."

"I thought you stayed open until eight p.m. on Mondays?" he asked the librarian.

"That's correct sir. In fifteen minutes."

Nick had worked right through his dinner hour without even noticing. Not once, in his twenty-eight previous years on earth, had that ever happened.

8.	Charlie Butts, "Convicted Felon Awarded Religion Decision," *OneNewsNow*, October 12, 2015. http://www.onenewsnow.com/legal-courts/2015/10/12/convicted-felon-awarded-religion-decision; *Hale v. Federal Bureau of Prisons*, D.Colo. 2015 http://cases.justia.com/federal/district-courts/colorado/codce/1:2014cv00245/145813/66/0.pdf

June 21: The White House

"Over here, Reverend," called the chauffeur.

Richard Henry Marshall perspired easily, and was happy that his walk to the limo door on this blistering Washington afternoon would be short. He paused briefly before entering, less to wave goodbye to the others than to confirm to himself that he was the only one not sharing a car. "A Catholic, a Mormon, and a Muslim crowd into a back seat," he mused, wondering what the punch line might be.

All in all, the meetings had gone exceedingly well. True, the time actually spent with President Bertram had been briefer than he'd anticipated, before they were all bundled off to staff. But he'd already spent hundreds of hours with Bertram, on the bus tours through Iowa, South Carolina, and New Hampshire, developing enough of a bond that the two could now communicate through shorthand phrases, even glances. Far more time than anyone else in the room had, for certain. It was Marshall who had locked in on Bertram's potential, some five years ago now. It was Marshall who had disdained the conventional "hedge your bets" political wisdom, putting all his chips on one number, then watching that number pop up. Not through dumb luck, as in a roulette game, but through the hand of God, working through his chosen.

Pride was a deadly sin, Marshall knew, but since November he had succumbed to it frequently. How could he not be proud today, he wondered, reviewing the private tour of the Oval Office conducted by none other than the president of the United States himself. "Now this desk," Bertram began, "was a gift from Queen Victoria, back in 1856. It's made of wood taken from the HMS *Resolute*, which was trapped in Arctic ice until it was freed by American seamen. Not the last time we bailed them out!"

Remington's *Bronco Buster* statue, in place since the time of Lyndon Johnson ... the bust of Churchill, restored to its proper place after being shunted off by Obama ... and best of all, the new carpet, boldly emblazoned with "In God We Trust"—Bertram's campaign slogan, first proposed by none other than Richard Henry Marshall himself.

"Now, I know you gentlemen did not come here today just to take selfies," Bertram began, as they settled into couches flanking the new carpet. "And I've got to excuse myself in a few minutes to receive some new ambassador from Lower Slobovia, or somewhere—I forget. But after the little hiccup we had with Rodriguez, it's important that we get this next nomination right. Which is why I want to consult with you first."

Hector Rodriguez had been Bertram's nominee as Secretary of Education. A good man, they all agreed, but with a more creative view of how to fill out a Form 1040 than the IRS had found amusing, by several hundred thousand dollars. Somehow this had escaped the attention of Bertram's crack transition team. Heads had duly rolled, but there was still the need to pick a replacement.

"Mr. President, we know you can't afford another distracting embarrassment, with so much you are trying to accomplish." This from Sunderland, president of the Presbyterians. Or at least what was left of them, after so many congregations had split off in protest against the national organization's liberal bent. "I would suggest you consider Governor Fitzgerald. He's a known quantity, at least. After that primary campaign, there's nothing the world doesn't know about him."

Such as that he's a weak-kneed loser, Marshall thought. Much of what the world knew about Fitzgerald had been unearthed by Marshall's privately funded opposition research teams, allowing Bertram to knock him out of the race early. "At least we know he's looking for work," someone else piped up, to general amusement.

"Snider's done a fine job in Utah ..."

"Brinkman over at Commerce is sound. He's already passed through the confirmation process. You could switch him over to this more important post, then promote one of the undersecretaries to take over Commerce ..."

"You only have one black cabinet member. And no gays. Shouldn't this be an opportunity to ..."

Marshall folded his hands on his lap, waiting for the babble to subside. "Mr. President," he finally began, in a powerful baritone that silenced the others. "You were not elected to take the safe and easy course. You were not elected to be politically correct. You were elected to give this country back to God. There is no more important choice you have to make than into whose hands you will entrust the direction of educating America's youth. Secretary of State, Secretary of Defense, what have you—these folks come and go. But the demise of Hector Rodriguez is a sign, sir. A sign. You must seize this brief opportunity of service that has been bestowed upon you. You must strike, sir, with the sledgehammer of righteousness, at the foundations of the corrupt edifice American public education has become."[9]

Marshall quietly gloried in the fact that the eyes of all these so-called leaders were as raptly fixed on him as any in the front rows at his weekly megachurch orations.

"I commend to you, sir, Mrs. Dorothy Hopkinson as our next Secretary of Education."

"Who?" asked Bertram.

"Is she Catholic?" asked Cardinal Klinger.

"Is she qualified?" asked Rabbi Goldstein.

"Mrs. Hopkinson," replied Marshall, pleased that surprise had been achieved, "is eminently qualified for this calling. She is an outstanding member of my congregation, of unquestioned character. She holds a doctorate in education. She holds a doctorate in Christian studies. But those are scraps of paper. Mrs. Dorothy Hopkinson has personally educated her five outstanding children in the privacy of her own home, shielded from the perfidy that pervades our cesspool schools. Her youngest daughter Betty, for example, placed third in the Virginia state spelling bee, and is now preparing to graduate with honors from Liberty University. And do you know what else? All five are good Republicans!"

"That's fine, Dick," said Sunderland after the polite laughter subsided, "but has she ever managed a large organization? DOE's a big outfit. If you don't know how to work a bureaucracy, they'll eat you alive."

"No lion ate Daniel," Marshall testily replied. He despised the name "Dick." "Dorothy, with support of the staff here, can hire technocrats to manage the details. She will be there to keep her eyes on the prize—our children. There is no way to cleanse the secular curse from our government-run schools, any more than there is a way to cleanse the salt from the ocean. Dorothy will hone in like a laser beam on all the government obstacles to the home schooling of our children, the only kind of sound education that can produce the men and women to turn this country around. She knows every regulation, every obstacle, from

---

9.   For a Christian view of public education, see Bethania Palma Markus, "Christians urge parents to save their kids from 'indoctrination' with an 'exodus' from public schools," *Raw Story*, September 8, 2015. https://www.rawstory.com/2015/09/christians-urge-parents-to-save-their-kids-from-indoctrination-with-an-exodus-from-public-schools/.

her personal experience. In a year—one year—*they will be gone.* And you, Mr. President, will have accomplished true, lasting change for America."

Marshall spotted Bertram gnawing on the tip of his eyeglasses as he held them in his hand. A clue that his brain was engaged, which was not always the case.

"That's very interesting," murmured Bertram. "But here," he said to the group, reverting back to glad-hand mode. "Let me show you a secret. You see that little light over the door? That means I'm about to run late for my next appointment. Now don't go telling the Russians about that! Thank you all so much for your time, and for your prayers. You go meet with the domestic policy boys now, and they'll give me a full report, and we'll get cracking on this. Now, let's see, Rev. Abercrombie, could you lead us in a short prayer before we part?"

He did.

Marshall held his tongue throughout the domestic policy staff meeting, while the others yammered away. He knew one key fact they didn't: that Bertram hadn't given him anything yet. He'd kept his powder dry the half-dozen times he'd been solicited for input, waiting for Education to pop up. But the same dim bulbs who'd failed to vet Rodriguez's tax history properly had failed to seek Marshall's advice on this one, and Marshall truly believed that God had a hand in Rodriguez's downfall. So long as Dorothy was found to be unblemished and well-spoken, as she surely would be, Bertram would give him this one. Besides, he knew how Bertram thought, and knew the folksy logic of her selection would appeal to him.

So all in all it had been a highly satisfying first visit to the White House. Now it was back to the Mayflower Hotel, where he would spend the afternoon preparing for tomorrow's meeting of the Religious Freedom Foundation board, which he had chaired for the past decade., His limousine lurched abruptly to avoid striking a lost-in-thought jaywalker crossing K Street, who Marshall never did find out was heading toward the Library of Congress.

July 4: The Mall

Nick's next two weeks were a blur of activity. GSA every morning, then straight to the Library of Congress nearly every afternoon. There was little point to spending much time at G&H, since he had no access to their computer network or the other resources available in their library. One day he did stop by, though, and found a high-powered laptop computer set up in his cubicle. "This machine belongs to the firm," the office manager told him, a bit coldly. "The one in the carton underneath the desk is yours to keep."

"I should have asked for a private office," thought Nick. "Maybe they'd have given me two."

Nick even worked on the long Metro rides to and from his efficiency in Silver Spring, at least when he could get a seat. Morning rides were a good time for collecting his news clips online; evening rides, when his brain was overflowing from what he'd learned during the day, were good times for random note-jotting. Once he reached his little high-rise apartment though, his brain shut down. Dinner—typically out of a can—a ballgame on TV, and maybe a little video game mayhem were all he could manage. He normally dozed off in his chair, before flopping half-clothed into bed.

On his last day at GSA, Nick decided to give Uncle Sam a nod and spend the whole day in the office. Uncle Sam would have been better off without him. Not only did Nick do no work at all, but he distracted his officemates from their own work with extended goodbyes. He was circumspect, though, in telling people what he would be doing. Not because of any pledge of secrecy, but just because it was all too hard to explain. He had told Kyle, of course, and even used him as a sounding board for ideas. But he knew Kyle was just being a buddy for listening, and that deep down he thought Nick had jumped off the deep end. Others he just told that he'd be working at G&H, "on special energy projects." A true statement, if a little misleading.

During a lull in the round of goodbyes, Nick sent Natalie an email:

> Are you going to be in on Monday? That's officially my first day, but the office is closed for the Fourth of July. Anyway, I really want to get some things moved in, and I know you work all the time, so could you let me in? They still won't give me a keycard.

Her reply arrived moments later. "I'll be here Monday, at least until the reception starts at six."

"What time will you come in?" he wrote back. "And what reception? Do I need to dress up?"

Natalie phoned back rather than writing. "I'm usually here by seven. Maybe a little earlier Monday, because we have to quit early for the reception. But you are not invited. It's on the roof, for people to watch the fireworks. There's only room for seventy-five, including clients, so they do it by seniority. Last year was the first time I was allowed to go."

"Okay. I guess I don't have much seniority before I even officially start. I might not be there right at seven a.m., though. More like noon. I'll call up from the street, and you can let me in."

Monday dawned, brutally hot. It had never really cooled off even the night before. Nick arrived at Guilder & Hersh around eleven, lugging three boxes on a dolly he'd borrowed, hoping against hope that he wouldn't have to stand around long waiting for Natalie to let him in. One of the boxes had fallen off as he wrestled the dolly off the train onto the Metro platform; it was a good thing he'd taped it securely shut or papers would have flown everywhere. By the time he reached the office he was drenched with sweat. "I wonder if they have AC on holidays?" he thought. "This could be a problem."

He needn't have worried. In fact, over half the lawyers were toiling away, though all the staff were gone.

"It's too bad you're stuck at this lousy reception," he told Natalie as they rode up the elevator. "I'm taking the guys to my secret spot. Best place in Washington to see the fireworks, guaranteed."

"We get a good view from the rooftop."

"Not like this, you don't. Your neck gets sore by the end, because you're practically looking straight up. What I do is, I lie flat on the grass. The booms are so loud, they shake the ground, and you get to feel it through your whole body."

"Really?"

"Yeah, really. But that's ok. You go party with the bigshots. Just remember to look up from your schmoozing around nine, so you don't miss 'em. You might not be able to hear them start from here."

Natalie stuck her tongue out at him as he rolled his dolly off the elevator.

Once Nick settled in, he tried to sort the papers he'd brought into some useable order. This proved too difficult, though, so after a while he gave up. Instead he spent most of the afternoon cleaning up, elaborating, and arranging the notes he'd been jotting on his Metro rides into something coherent: the early glimmerings of what Nick was already calling, in his head, the Secret Plan.

Around four o'clock, he was surprised to see Natalie poking her head over his cubicle wall. He was even more surprised to hear her ask whether his fireworks offer was still good.

"Sure! Absolutely! Why?"

"I got bumped," she said sourly. "Senator Miller, who has brought in exactly zero business so far, invited some of his old, out-of-work staff without telling anyone. Said he didn't know about the seventy-five limit."

"So you have to slum it."

"Hey, if you don't want me to come—"

"No! I'm sorry. Just teasing. This'll be great! Except ... my friends, you'll be meeting, they're a little ... you know ..."

"I can only imagine."

"Not sure you can. Anyway, what about food? I was just going to pick up some chicken on the way down to the Mall."

"Sure. Chicken's fine."

"Say ... any chance you could liberate something from the reception before it gets started? A pile of those big shrimp would be nice. After you got bumped, and all. It's the least they could do."

Natalie looked pointedly up at the ceiling and walked away. "See you in the lobby at five. Don't stay any later than that—they want the place cleared out for security. There may be some cabinet members here."

"Hey, Natalie, one more thing," Nick called out just as she was turning a corner. "Important." Wagging his finger, he said, "This spot we're going to, it's secret. I don't want to come back next year and see it filled up with ten thousand tourists so I can't get right up to the fence. Agreed?"

As Natalie turned away again without responding, Nick wondered whether, as a matter of contract law, she had implicitly agreed to accept this condition by her mere attendance, even in the absence of explicit assent. Interesting question. He probably shouldn't have cut contracts class that day back in law school.

*****

At 5:10 p.m., as Nick was dissolving into a puddle of sweat outside the building door in what Weatherbug said was ninety-eight degree

heat, he fretted that he'd pushed the teasing too far. But no worries—
there was Natalie, holding a large paper bag. "I do carry some pull
around here," she beamed, pulling out a six-pack of Heineken. "Not
shrimp, but something, no?"

Poor naïve girl, thought Nick. In the first place, there was security
screening to get anywhere near his spot on Mall, and a six-pack of
beer would be impossible to sneak through. Maybe she didn't know
that. But she should know that by the time they got to the Mall, the
beer in these cans would be not just warm, but downright hot. Even
by Nick's low standards, hot beer was problematic.

"Wow, fantastic!" he said. It's the thought that counts.

"Let's take a break and have a couple of these before they get too
warm," Nick said after they'd walked a few blocks.

They plopped down under a shady tree outside a public building.
Heat shimmered off the sidewalk they'd been on.

"So how are things going?" asked Natalie. "I need to start supervising
you tomorrow. What, exactly, are you doing?"

A harder question than it sounded. "Where to begin.... That's the
problem, really: where to begin. It's not like there's a Wikipedia entry
on how to gin up a new religion to exploit exemptions. I do know there
are two separate tracks: the legal track, of what kind of exemptions we
could realistically shoot for. And then the theology track, of what kind
of religious belief it might be that would justify all sorts of different
exemptions."

"We just want the exemption for Earl's fracking."

"Well you can't get just that, remember? You'll get laughed out of
court. Or worse. You need a much bigger umbrella. Preferably something
with a little tradition behind it, at least arguably. The problem is, I go a
little way down the theology track, then I think no, I need to do more
on the exemption track. Then I go a little way down that, and think no,
I need more theology to justify this stuff and tie it together. It's like a
Rubik's Cube. And I never did solve one of those."

Natalie said nothing. Nick popped open another beer, which was
already up to room temperature. "And the big thing you need is that
first, easy case. The one nobody cares about, so it's as easy as possible
for the court to bless whatever this is going to be as a real religion. But
most of the laws I'm looking at, somebody does care about. Otherwise,
they wouldn't be laws, would they?"

"I guess. I never really thought about it."

"Me neither. Go ahead and Google 'Laws nobody cares about.' You won't find much."

They sat for a while longer, neither one anxious to step back out into the broiling sun. Nick hoped he could get to a third beer before they heated past the point of no return.

"I may at least have a clue about a direction for the theology. Do you know anything about Quakers?"

Natalie shook her head. "We were Methodist. At least on Christmas. My parents just work—not much time for church."

"Well, some of the Quakers were into the idea that everybody has his own private channel to God. Not just priests or ministers. You went to a meeting, and somebody would get inspired by God, and then tell everybody else what to do. That's why they called them 'Quakers'—'cause sometimes while they were getting inspired, they'd shake all over."

"So what happened if two different people said they were inspired, and said opposite things?"

"Beats me. Maybe they flipped a coin. Anyway, when you look at all the different possible exemptions, and try to figure out something plausible to tie them all together, I'm thinking something like tweets from God straight to individuals might be a way to do it. But then I bounce back to what exemptions I'm really trying to cover, and get tied up in knots again. But I've got a year, so I think I can do it."

"You've got forty days."

Nick looked up sharply. "Oh, come on, I never promised that. My contract says a year."

"No, it doesn't. I wrote it. It says you get *paid* over a year, not that you have a year to ponder your navel. If you don't have solid progress, with a big shiny light at the end of a short tunnel in forty days, well—"

She reached up and made the same twisting motion in front of his nose with her silky hand that Earl had made with his beefy, calloused one.

"I haven't even officially started yet. Isn't it a little early to be getting on my case?"

"Forty days. Four-zero. That's August 14, giving you the benefit of the holiday. Let's go. This beer was supposed to be for your friends, by the way, not just for you."

Twenty sweat-drenched minutes later, they caught up with Kyle and his friend Brigitte outside the Mall security entrance.

"Natalie brought these for you," said Nick, shoving the now hot-to-the-touch cans into Kyle's hands. "I've already had mine—the rest are yours."

*****

Most of the conversation, once they were inside, froze Natalie out. Facebook friends, reality TV shows, the local music scene, softball—none of this had any connection with the pleadings, client development, and firm committee assignments that made up Natalie's life. Nor did it help when, as darkness began to fall, Kyle pulled out a plastic baggie filled with marijuana and a packet of rolling papers.

Natalie eyed the bag as she would a dead cat.

"It's all good," said Kyle. "This is DC. Land of the free, home of the brave! We're legal—here, try some."

Natalie leaned away. "No, thank you. And isn't the Mall a national park? Are the laws the same here?"

Kyle thought that was the funniest thing he'd heard in ages. "Nobody's getting in trouble here. Trust me." He and Brigitte then busied themselves with constructing their joints. Nick declined their offer, partly because of Natalie's unease, and partly because he half expected Kyle to ask him for money later, which he didn't feel like paying.

"Is this the same shit you brought over last week?" asked Brigitte, after her first drag. "This sucks. Where'd you get this?"

"I don't know. Rooney. Where he gets it, I don't know."

"Tastes like dirt. Does he sweep it off the floor?"

"I told you, I don't know. This is so stupid," Kyle added, turning to Nick. "Why can't you buy grass like in a package, at 7-11? You can buy potato chips, soda—shit that's actually bad for you—and you know what you're getting. You buy grass, which never hurt anybody, and you gotta find somebody who knows somebody, or says he does. Legal to smoke it, but not to sell. How much sense does that make?"

"Why is that?" Natalie asked. Finally, conversation about a law— something she could talk about.

Nick jumped in, hoping to sound erudite. "A few years ago, they had a referendum in DC. But all it did was repeal the possession crime. It didn't set up any sort of regime to regulate sales."[10]

---

10.   Ian Simpson, "Pot fans, foes fume as Washington DC tests limits of high life," *Reuters*, February 8, 2016. http://www.reuters.com/article/us-districtofcolumbia-marijuana-idUSKCN0VH0YH. Massachusetss is similar: Scott Malone, "Massachusetts tiptoes into pot legalization; OK to smoke, not to sell," *Reuters*, December 15, 2016 http://www.reuters.com/article/us-massachusetts-marijuana-idUSKBN144195.

"Why not?"

"Dumb fucks!" Brigitte chimed in, starting to giggle. Evidently Kyle's batch had some kick, after all.

"So it's technically against the law to sell marijuana in Washington DC, but since it's ok to possess it, no one cares about this law?" asked Natalie.

"Correctamundo!" said Kyle, tickled with his own wit.

"A law, which nobody cares about." Natalie rotated her head majestically toward Nick, and rested her case.

The fireworks started a few minutes later. Nick had exaggerated only slightly; the best way to view them from this spot really was flat on your back, and the ground shook with each boom. Nick savored the experience of lying next to Natalie, the only time in his life he figured this would ever happen. To the other side, between booms, Nick sensed that Kyle and Brigitte were starting in on their own private fireworks. As the grand finale commenced, Nick reached out his hand to rest it on top of Natalie's—maybe she wouldn't notice. But her hands were clasped tightly over her ears.

July 10: Victory in Jesus

Richard Henry Marshall despised doing business on Sunday mornings. Not only was it wrong in God's eyes, but it violated his routine of proper mental preparation for his weekly performance. NFL stars didn't negotiate contracts on Sunday mornings while psyching themselves up for the afternoon's combat—Marshall shouldn't have to, either.

Still, some things couldn't be helped. His lawyers had been butting heads with the Bartimaeus lawyers all week, including a four-hour call yesterday, and still there were half a dozen issues unresolved. Arbitration procedures for disputes on referral origination ... indemnification procedures for state insurance commission complaints ... and four other problem spots with more legalistic syllables than Marshall cared to contemplate. Exhausted, both teams of lawyers agreed that the principals would have to get involved to finish off the deal—or crater it.

"Ray," Marshall boomed into the speakerphone at precisely nine a.m., the scheduled time for the final, make or break call. "How are you on this fine day of the Lord?"

"I'm a little peeved, I have to tell you," replied Rev. Raymond LaPelletiere. "I thought we had a deal."

"And so we shall," said Marshall. "God's will be done."

"Not with those lawyers of yours, it won't. My folks tell me you're fighting tooth and nail on every little comma."

"Interesting. That's the same thing I hear from my lawyers about yours. A fine world we live in, isn't it?"

"This is serious, Richard. You said the rollout was to begin today. We've staffed up in anticipation of that, and it's really going to hurt morale if we have to let people go after we just hired them."

"The rollout will begin today. In two hours' time. Now, let me tell you how we are going to resolve this. The lawyers, God bless 'em, tell me there are six issues still in play. Is that what you're hearing?"

"Yeah, six. That's only down from the eight they had on Tuesday. Now, we just can't have any wiggle room on this indemnification clause—"

"Hold on, Ray. Hear me out. If you have no room, you have no room. I understand that. Now the lawyers, they think you and I are going to hash things through, then you'll get your way on three items and we'll get our way on the other three. Right?"

"Yes, but I'm telling you—"

"I asked you to hold on." His tone was a little more peremptory. "Let's not do that. Let's look back to the original deal. We get a base fifteen percent commission on all the premiums, before the remarketing adjustments—sorry, not premiums, but *contributions*—we send your way. Let's modify that, in one of two ways. Your choice. Either you get what your lawyers want on every one of the six items in question, and we get a seventeen percent commission, or we get the language our lawyers want on every one of the items, and our commission drops to thirteen percent. And I'll let *you* choose which way to go. Right now. Then I'll go in front of my congregation at noon, and start the rollout. I have faith in you to make the right choice. The choice God wants."

"Seventeen percent! You're moving the ball."

"Then make it thirteen. The ball's in your hands to move, not mine. Do what you believe God wants."

A long pause ensued. Marshall knew that LaPelletiere was likely to have been cowed by his lawyers into thinking that all the legal boilerplate actually mattered, and didn't have the courage to overrule them. That's why Marshall had instructed his lawyers to be so intransigent, right up to the brink of the cliff. So he wasn't surprised when LaPelletiere accepted the seventeen percent choice. Winning an extra two percent of what could turn out to be hundreds of millions of dollars annually was worth a little disruption of his Sunday morning routine.

"You won't regret this, Ray. I promise you won't. Bartimaeus is going to take off now—make sure you have those telephones manned first thing tomorrow morning! You're not even going to notice that two percent, you'll have so much new business rolling in."

"I believe you, Richard. That's why I want to work with you. We'll make a fine team."

"You, me, and the Lord."

"Amen."

*****

Marshall sat alone on a hard plastic folding chair, just offstage in the wings of his massive Victory in Jesus megachurch, awaiting his moment. He riffed through the pages of his script, which he wouldn't really need.. This would be easy. No tricky theology, just red meat. If anything, he needed to avoid too many specifics, and just let 'er rip.

First, there had been the music, if you could call it that. Then one of his dough-faced assistants had delivered the gospel reading and lesson. Marshall normally kept these kids on a tight leash, but this week he'd been too preoccupied with the Bartimaeus negotiations to supervise closely. Nothing he was hearing caused any concern, though.

Then more music—no, scratch that—more cacophony from the "Christian Rock" bozos he so despised. The lead vocalist, Marshall was certain, was a faggot. Marshall loved the hymns back in his father's little church in Georgia, out of tune as they always were. But the consultants had shown him all their charts and graphs about what it took to build a church up to six figures in the twenty-first century, and Marshall couldn't argue with results. God's work needed cash.

Finally, the racket ended. Marshall's producer let the lights swirl for a few long moments, giving more folks time to get back from the john. Thirteen other Victory in Jesus simulcast venues had to be considered as well.

Marshall's smartwatch buzzed with a signal from his producer, and he strode deliberately to the podium as the congregation roared. Some of his hipster rivals preferred to strut around the stage unencumbered, but traditionalist Richard Henry Marshall valued his podium. Like his father had.

He opened quietly, with the story of Jesus healing the man born blind. "Blind" created an easy segue to the bureaucrats in Washington, who thought they knew everything, but actually knew nothing. Of the many things they knew nothing about, your family's health topped the list.

Marshall worked the crowd expertly. He wound them up with how much they were paying for Washington's insurance, and what else they could use that money for. Mission work in Africa would be one use for part of it, he opined, but maybe folks had some other ideas too.

That little tease set them up for the final push. The whole event had been set up by a week's worth of advertising that Rev. Marshall would be unveiling something new this day.

He glared at the right side of the auditorium, and slowly swept his head to the left. "Christians: Do you want to pay for someone else's AIDS? Someone who does not, you can be sure, practice Christian morality?"

"No," the crowd responded.

"I can't hear you!"

"NO!" they shouted obediently.

"Well you are! That's why your health insurance bills are so high. Because that's what our insurance has you paying for. Let's try another. Do you want to pay for someone else's syphilis?"

"NO!" The audience was beginning to feel the rage.

"Hepatitis?"

"NO!!"

"Cirrhosis of the liver?"

"NO!!!"

"Do you want to pay the medical bills of radical Muslims, who have illegally entered our fair country to cash their welfare checks, while they seek to destroy our Christian way of life?"

"NO!!!"

His voice fell to a hush. "Now let me ask you, Christians. Think before you answer. Ask Christ Jesus to help you with this one. Look into your hearts, and tell me, truly: Do you want to pay your hard earned money, to take bread from the table of your children," — his voice steadily rose—"and use it to MURDER a tiny baby girl before she's even born?"

"NO! NO! NO!" they chanted.

He was roaring now. "How about that tiny baby's great-grandma?! She's old now. She's in the way. At least, that's how her grandchildren make her feel. In the way! Does Jesus want you to pay to snuff out great-grandma's life, before the man upstairs is good and ready to call her home?!"

"NO! NO! NO!"

Marshall clasped his hands in prayer, closed his eyes, and stood in silence. A good thirty seconds passed. Some in the audience began to wonder if he was all right.

"Christians," he began slowly, "there are many thousands of you listening to me today. Some are here at Victory in Jesus, and many more are watching at our sister churches. I don't expect every one of you to agree with me on everything. That's ok. Some of you are deeper in your faith than others. I understand that. For those of you who enjoy seeing your money spent coddling those homosexuals who God punished with AIDS, or the illegal Muslims trying to take your jobs away, or who are all for murdering little baby girls, and great-grandma after that, your choice is easy. Your choice is one word. You know it. That word is *Obamacare*." It mattered not that after years of congressional tinkering, "Obamacare" was a pale shadow of the ambitious program originally passed. The word still polled negatively among the evangelical base, which was all Marshall cared about.

"All you have to do is go with the flow. Go right ahead! Pick item A or item B or item whatever off the list. Doesn't matter. Every one of them will kill those little babies dead. Have at it!"

"But for those of you who don't want to pay to prop up a homosexual lifestyle, who don't want to buy that killer cocktail to finish off great-grandma, Jesus has a word for you. That word is *Bartimaeus*."

Marshall paused for effect here, wiping the perspiration from his upper lip. He knew most of his audience had no idea what Bartimaeus was, but they would learn.

"In the book of Mark, you may recall, Jesus finds Bartimaeus by the highway. Blind. Begging. Not willfully blind, as seculars today who will not see, nor willfully begging, as seculars today who will not work, but blind and begging because of the power of the Prince of Darkness." The word "seculars" polled well also, and lent itself to hissing.

"And Jesus said to him, 'Go thy way; thy faith hath made thee whole.' Thy faith hath made thee whole. Not thy insurance company. Not thy Washington. Thy *faith*."

The giant telescreen behind the podium, which had been showing only Marshall speaking, now glowed with the words of gospel of Mark, superimposed over a backdrop of praying hands.

"And do you know what happened then, my friends? Do you know what happened then? You do know, because God *tells* us what happens when people have faith. 'Immediately he received his sight, and followed Jesus in the way.'"

On cue, the telescreen showed a short dramatization of Jesus laying a hand on the bowed head of a handsome blonde actor, kneeling in first-century garb. Slowly, he removed his hand that covered his eyes, and gaped with wonder at the world now on display for the first time.

"Insurance didn't do that!" Marshall boomed, pointing back at the screen. "Obamacare didn't do that!" The preacher paused, inhaling and exhaling a deep breath for dramatic effect. "*Faith* did that. Faith in Jesus. The faith that leads Christians today to join with their fellow Christians in Bartimaeus, the Christian health-cost sharing ministry."

The screen showed the Bartimaeus logo, with the 't' cleverly styled as a crucifix.

"I will not give you all the details of Bartimaeus today. But I will tell you what you need to know. Bartimaeus is Christians helping Christians to pay their medical bills. That's it! That's all it is. Bartimaeus is for people of FAITH. If you have no faith, do *not* join Bartimaeus. In fact, if you have no faith, Bartimaeus will throw you out, and you can go right on back to Obamacare, paying double what you'll pay for a simple cost-sharing plan among Christians."

Double, Marshall knew, was an exaggeration. But it made the point.

"See, it costs a lot more when you have to pay for abortions, when you have to pay for murdering grandma, when you have to pay for the consequences of the homosexual and drug addict lifestyle. When you have to pay for atheists and Muslims and welfare cheats and everybody else. When it's just Christians helping Christians, that leaves a lot more money for your family. *That's* what you need to know about Bartimaeus. The rest is fine print. Go ahead and read it. Read it two or three times. But I just told you what you need to know."

"Who will join me today? Will one of you—just one person—join me today in saying NO! to the abortionists, NO! to the grandma-killers, NO! to Obamacare, and YES! to Jesus, as Bartimaeus himself did? Please, just one of you, come down here to the front, and pray with me. Tell me that you will help to share my medical bills—they're not large, praise the Lord—and I will help to share yours. And then we'll both tell Jesus what we've done! One person? Anyone?"

Several pre-arranged plants in the audience stood and began striding toward the stage. One clapped his hands over his head, but the telescreen operator knew to focus on the one with tears streaming down her face, courtesy of a quick dab of menthol under her eyes. The aisles were quickly jammed with people.

"Father in heaven," Marshall intoned, "bless thy people of faith. Give us health when thou wilt, and give us the joy of sharing our burden when inevitable suffering comes. For thine is the kingdom, and the power and the glory. Amen."

Watching the video feed, Raymond LaPelletiere still resented the last-minute pressure job, but silently agreed that this was going to be a beautiful relationship.

July 18: Peter Spillman's Office

Fourteen days later, not forty, Nick had immersed himself sufficiently in the law of religious drug exemptions to present what he'd learned to Peter Spillman and Natalie. This time they met in Spillman's corner office. It was larger than the conference room where they had first met, and far more luxurious—a stark contrast to the rest of the building, whose function-over-form interior matched its Soviet-style façade. The distinguishing feature, in one word: wood. Nick had spent a weekend helping his father install Lowe's paneling in the basement, which he felt made him something of an expert on the subject, and he determined that the floor-to-ceiling mahogany paneling in Peter Spillman's office was the real deal. The hand-knotted Persian carpets showed just enough fabric wear, without color fading, to be genuine antiques.

Spillman and Natalie sat in a corner living room area, replete with a high-end leather couch, easy chairs, and two television screens.

Nick sank down into the couch and started talking. "So you see," he concluded after fifteen minutes, "the results just by themselves don't look too promising. The Rastafarians have always lost, and the potheads who've dreamed up marijuana churches have lost, except in Minnesota, and in some other countries.[11] Even the Indians smoking peyote lost in court, until Congress came along and bailed them out."[12]

"So you've discovered, after two weeks of intense study, that illegal drugs are illegal," said Spillman. "Profound."

"Except where they're not. That's the point. That's what no one has tried before."

---

11.   Olivia Lavecchia, "Minnesota Supreme Court Will Not Hear Rastafarian Drug Paraphernalia Case: Rastas Win," *Minneapolis Star-Tribune City Pages,* December 11, 2013 http://www.citypages.com/news/minnesota-supreme-court-will-not-hear-rastafarian-drug-paraphernalia-case-rastas-win-6537380. The court's opinion is available at https://www.scribd.com/document/190936303/JJMA-Opinion. Gopal Sharma, "Shivaratri Festival In Nepal Includes Temporary Lifting Of Marijuana Ban," *Huffington* Post, May 11, 2013. http://www.huffingtonpost.com/2013/03/11/shivaratri-festival-nepal-mairijuan_n_2851875.html.
12.   42 U.S. Code § 1996a - Traditional Indian religious use of peyote. https://www.law.cornell.edu/uscode/text/42/1996a.

Nick's eyes shone. "Here's how RFRA works. Every federal law that gets in the way of the exercise of religion is invalid. Kaput. Every one. The only way the government can do anything to rein in what someone can call the exercise of religion is if it has a 'compelling interest' in doing so, and if it chooses the 'least restrictive means' of achieving that compelling interest. Otherwise, they can't do anything."

"Now, the courts have all found that government has a compelling interest in keeping people from getting high. Except on alcohol. And there can't be any 'less restrictive means' of keeping people from getting high than, well, keeping people from getting high. At least that anybody outside of Minnesota's thought of. Because the guys who bring most of these cases aren't rocket scientists. They're potheads."

"So how does the Fratelli rocket work?"

"No compelling interest! People can get high here in DC all they want. The law's cool with that. The people voted for it, and Congress let it slide through. So if there's no compelling interest in keeping people from *using* pot, then what's the compelling interest in keeping people from *selling* pot? Huh? You tell me."

Spillman didn't respond. After a moment, Natalie said accusingly, "But how are you going to test this in court? According to your friends, nobody gets arrested for selling marijuana in DC. So how does selling contraband to Kyle set any precedents we can use? This isn't making sense."

Nick leaned forward, face flushed with excitement. "I'm not selling anything to anybody! You know what I'm going to do? I'm going to start a little not-for-profit corporation. Maybe name it Religious Pot Sales, Inc. That's got a nice ring to it. But instead of something vague like "to conduct lawful business" at the top of the certificate stating the purpose of the corporation, mine's gonna say, 'For the sole purpose of selling marijuana, at cost, for Nick's cool new religion to his members in the District of Columbia.' And then I'm going to walk it over to the corporation office, with my forty-dollar filing fee and a little sticky note pointing right at those words. And just to be sure, I'll ask the clerk, 'This is ok, right?' And what's he gonna say? He's gonna say, 'I'm sorry sir, but we cannot accept this. We can only accept corporations formed for a lawful purpose.' He's got no choice. And what I'll do next is go to court and challenge his decision not to accept my filing. Actually, you'll go to court, because I don't know how to do court. But you're gonna fucking win. Because there's no way the government has any compelling interest in keeping my church from distributing marijuana at cost to my believers, who have every legal right to possess it. And then I've got a court-approved religion, and we're off and running!"

Nick leaned back and rapped the arm of the couch triumphantly. He considered throwing his feet up on the intricately carved coffee table, then thought better of it. He waited for Spillman's praise. Which was not forthcoming.

"May I see a copy of your memorandum?"

"Haven't got one. Been movin' too fast for that."

Spillman pursed his lips. "In this office, we record our analyses in memoranda. With proper citations. Now explain again—excuse me, explain for the first time—what any of this has to do with religion? And how it relates to the drilling techniques employed by Matteson Enterprises, which is paying your absurdly generous salary?"

Nick suspected that part of Spillman's distaste for him had to do with the way he was dressed. Maybe Spillman didn't need to shop at Walmart, but Nick did. Debt was debt, after all.

"Well ... uh ... I haven't been doing as much on the theology part, because I've been going on the drug cases and the corporate purpose laws. But like I was telling Natalie, there's Quaker stuff, and I think I can work it up—"

"What?" Spillman cut in. "You have nothing? Whose chain do you think you're jerking here?"

Nick was more surprised than annoyed. He thought he'd moved mountains to come this far this fast. "I can only do ... I've got forty days ... This was the trickiest part ... the theology is the soft part, and I'm moving on it, I just—"

"Ms. Parks," Spillman interrupted again. "How much revenue is Earl losing every day because of the EPA restrictions on his operations in the Munster field alone?"

"He says it's over $350,000 a day."

"How are your math skills, Mr. Fratelli? Perhaps you could try a calculator."

Nick had been waiting for this moment for weeks. "I thought you said he was referred to as 'Mr. Matteson' in this office. You just called him 'Earl.'"

Spillman ignored the gibe. "I don't know what you think you're doing during all those hours you claim to be spending at the Library of Congress, but I would suggest you try a little pastime we in this office like to call 'work.' Anything else?"

Nick looked to Natalie for moral support, found none, and stormed off. After he left, Spillman said to Natalie, "This holds promise. I've done some reading on RFRA, and it does seem rather open ended. Keep pushing. Speed up the memorandum, double check all the citations yourself, and make sure he hasn't glossed over anything."

"I will, sir."

Spillman looked annoyed. "If he's right, then these cases are far too easy to win. Any idiot can do it. It's demeaning to the profession."

July 31: Paintball

Thick skin was not one of Nick's stronger points, emotionally or physically. That's why he avoided both Spillman and Natalie for the next couple of weeks. He was damned if he was going to put up with more humiliation until he had something solid to offer. And it was why he sometimes regretted playing paintball—those little suckers really stung, especially for a player as clumsy as Nick.

Every now and then, though, he was able to nail an unsuspecting foe. The sweetness of those moments made the pain worthwhile, so long as he didn't keep score too carefully.

A close-range shot Nick had taken above his kneecap had him limping slightly as he trudged back to the car with Jay Gimenez, Nick's frequent paintball companion and best buddy from grade school. Jay, who still lived with his parents, had borrowed his mother's car.

"What was up with the green dudes, man?" asked Jay. "There were like fifty of 'em. Did you hear them calling that guy 'colonel?'"

"Maybe they're really soldiers, just doing this for fun."

"Well I hope they're our guys. If ISIS is that organized, we've got problems. And hey, next time I ask you to cover me, how about something more than just a blank look, ok?"

"Wouldn't have mattered," said Nick. "They had you anyway."

"So you've got no scoops at all for me?" asked Jay as they rolled down the highway. "All that time at GSA, rolling in waste, fraud, and abuse, you never feed me one little tip. And now you're not even there anymore."

Jay was now a freelance online reporter. Rather, that's what he wanted to be. He'd sold precious little material, and his parents' patience with his still living at home at age twenty-seven was starting to fray. Anyone who counted on making a living by cultivating "sources" as out-of-the-loop as Nick Fratelli faced an uphill struggle.

"No scoops yet. I'm telling you, though, once this Project X hits, it's gonna be huge."

"But you won't tell me what it is."

"No. I can't. But I do want to bounce some things off you. So could you turn off the NPR, and just listen for a while? Totally off the record?"

"Off the record" paid none of Jay's bills. And keeping up with NPR was part of his modus operandi, or so he figured, because it might help trigger some saleable story ideas. But it was a long ride back to DC, so he put up no resistance.

"I'm trying to create a new religion," said Nick, flipping off the radio. "And I think it sort of hangs together, but I can't really talk to anyone about it, because ... well just because."

"You're creating a religion? Terrific—'Atheist Dumb-Ass Starts Religion.' Sure, I can sell that. You had any miracles yet?"

Nick ignored him. "Most religions are top down. I don't want that. I want something that can change and grow, and lets the believers come up with their own meanings. Now, there are Quakers, who sort of did that, but they're not the only ones. There's Sufis. And Jews, at least the Kabbala guys. All the big religions start with Jews. Except they started with Zoroastrians, so go figure. Anyway, the Kabbala guys said that God was like too big to fit in the universe, so he sort of busted up, into all these divine sparks. You catch a divine spark, that's like a piece of God. And you can't argue with God, right?"

"Not me. Especially if he's wearing a green uniform."

"It's all in here." Nick pulled a pile of wrinkled papers out of his knapsack. Partly out of irritation at Jay's cold shoulder, he said "I'm going to read the whole thing to you."

"What! How long is it?"

"Seven thousand four hundred and twelve words. Counting the title. Here we go." Nick overrode Jay's protests by simply shouting over them. "'Doctrines of Inspired Spirituality.' That's the title. 'In the beginning ...'"

Jay dropped his head in resignation. Nick droned on as the highway rolled monotonously by. Jay listened, because he was given no choice. He interrupted only once.

"Whoa, hold on. You're saying to be in this religion, people gotta pay to watch you on Youtube, once a week?"

"Neat, huh? I need to have a continuing congregation, plus a revenue source, to be a real religion. It's all in a bunch of IRS guidelines, which aren't too tough.[13] Hell, even John Oliver got a tax exemption for a fake church he made up.[14] This uses the technology God has given us,

---

13.   IRS Publication 1828, "Tax Guide for Churches and Religious Organizations." https://www.irs.gov/pub/irs-pdf/p1828.pdf
14.   Leonardo Blair, "Comedian John Oliver Lampoons Televangelists on 'Last Week Tonight' Show; Opens Our Lady of Perpetual Exemption Church,"

through inspiration, to spread the word nationally. Without paying for brick and mortar."

Jay fiddled with the vents, trying to squeeze out a little more cool air somehow. Nick vaguely sensed that he was commanding something less than Jay's complete attention.

"So this is your plan to make money? Who's gonna pay to watch this, besides maybe your mother? Until your dad finds out, and then you won't even have her."

"You'd be surprised," Nick replied, trying to sound mysterious.

"Yeah, I definitely would be. And you keep calling God 'it.' What's wrong with 'he?'"

"Feminists. They'll eat it up. Besides, it makes sense. If there's no she-god, how can there be a he-god? What's the point?"

Jay didn't know what the point was, so Nick resumed reading. When he finished, he asked "So what do you think?"

Jay turned on him sharply. "I think you've lost your mind. Did you fall and hit your head or something?"

Nick wished Jay or his mom would clean the interior of the car more often, to do something about that stale Dorito smell. But it was too hot outside to roll down the window and let out any of the precious AC. "You're not helping. I've gotta get this right. You want scoops someday, I've gotta get this right. Were there any inconsistencies that jumped out at you? Did it make sense at all?"

"There are no scoops in that, Nick," Jay said angrily. The speedometer shot up to eighty as he roared past a double-trailer truck that had been frustrating him nearly as much as Nick's bullshit had. "It's just gibberish. With some platitudes tossed in here and there. 'The Divine Spirit speaks through our hearts, if only we give it space'? Christ, where do you get this shit?"

Nick was taken aback by Jay's vehemence. He wouldn't have launched into his recitation if he hadn't been proud of his work. He didn't expect Jay to appreciate every nuance, but it wasn't *that* bad. Especially compared to the "gibberish" in other religious texts like the Koran, or *Dianetics*. If L. Ron Hubbard could sell Scientology, then "Doctrines of Inspired Spirituality" ought to be a slam-dunk. But Jay

Christian Post, August 17, 2015. http://www.christianpost.com/news/comedian-john-oliver-lampoons-televangelists-on-last-week-tonight-show-opens-our-lady-of-perpetual-exemption-church-143003/.

wouldn't have gotten that either, Nick told himself.

"Was there anything at all that you liked?" Nick asked, grasping for a straw of encouragement.

"Yeah," Jay said, after reflecting for a moment. "The end."

Nick brightened, and flipped through his pages. "Oh! You mean 'Thus has the universe unfolded from the beginning, and thus shall it flourish, now and forevermore'"?

"No. I mean the part after you stopped talking. Look, I gotta get the car back so I'll just drop you at the Metro. But look, can you ask some of your buddies back at GSA, and see if they've got any stories for me? Things are a little tight."

"Uh-huh," said Nick, absorbed in the page. He was thinking that "unfolded" maybe wasn't such a great word. He wasn't carrying a pen, so he stuck his fingernail through it, as a reminder to run it through thesaurus.com to see if he could find something better.

November 5: The Tune Inn

Peter Spillman's tan always puzzled Nick. How could anyone work so many hours indoors and look like he'd just stepped off a surfboard? That three-thousand-dollar suit, crimson power tie, and monogrammed shirt hadn't been riding any waves, though. "PDS," it read. It was a good thing, Nick thought, that Peter's middle name wasn't Michael.

"Melinda should be getting the opinion from the clerk any minute now," Spillman said as Nick entered his office. No need to waste time on "Hello," or any other such banality.

"Is Natalie coming?"

"Yes. As soon as the clerk sends over the opinion, Melinda's going to call it right in," he said, tapping his conference phone. "But we've got it, my friend. Cannot miss. Then we're on to phase two!"

Spillman seemed positively bubbly. Nick hadn't experienced this side of him before, but the man evidently liked winning. His brilliant teeth glowed like LEDs. The conference phone, though, is what riveted Nick's attention. Not just because it would momentarily deliver a breathless paralegal's report, announcing that he'd lost his key first case and wasted everyone's time—or that he'd won, which could be worse, because it would force him to put up or shut up on his Secret Plan. Or worse yet, some asinine nuanced middle ground, that he couldn't make heads or tails of, leaving him not knowing what to do. He'd already obsessed over those possible outcomes for days on end. No, what struck him about the conference phone was how much it looked like a spaceship. Gently curved to power itself off intergalactic gamma rays, standing on three feet for easy landings on any alien terrain ... The hatch where Nick would enter, if he could make himself small enough, must be located near the power cord, and it would be necessary to disengage the cord before blasting off. Then, assuming the office door remained ajar, Nick could be outta here. But he'd want to bring Natalie, and she hadn't arrived yet.

"Hey, Nick." Natalie leaned on the doorframe. "Any word yet?" Her suit skirt was longer than Nick would have preferred.

"Hi!" Nick tried to stand, struggled with the heavy chair, and sat back down. "I think they're still looking up adjectives for what a great brief you wrote, and that's holding things up."

The flattery earned Nick a flicker of acknowledgement. Her half-smile might have been bigger, Nick decided, if it weren't for the fact that Natalie was as nervous as he was. Or if Gestapo-boy Spillman hadn't been there, complicating everything.

"Where are we on the Rubenstein response?" said Spillman, glancing at Natalie but not *seeing* her, as Nick felt she deserved to be seen. She seemed flush with anticipation, a temporary change from her more typical pallor from so much screen-staring.

"We're, um, we're ... tonight," she said. "I'll have it tonight, and on your desk in the morning."

"It was supposed to be yesterday."

"Yes. It was. But Paul had me on those deposition summaries, and—"

"I don't really care about your excuses, Ms. Parks. Do whatever Paul tells you—fine. You said you'd have the response yesterday."

"YYYes, but Rubenstein isn't due for two weeks, and Paul—"

"Ms. Parks. Tomorrow. Seven a.m. The response. This desk." He jabbed his index finger down, to erase any doubt about which desk he meant. His teeth were nowhere to be seen.

"No problem. Thank you, sir."

Nick, no dummy, inferred from this exchange that any celebrating he'd be doing tonight of his glorious victory—or any licking of wounds—would be done without Natalie Parks at his side. Again. Not all the blow-offs he'd gotten from her were faked—she really did work all the time. But tonight! He pictured the two of them together, maybe with champagne at Fredo's, or on the romantic walkway around the Tidal Basin, and then maybe—

"OOGLE OOGLE OOGLE." The conference phone spaceship was erupting. Urgent message from home planet: Destroy Earth at once. Get Nick out of this.

But it was not the home planet. It was the dreaded Melinda.

"The opinion just came in. Three pages. After the boilerplate at the top, it just says—here, let me read it—'that Reverend Fratelli—'"

Nick hated that. Worst idea he'd ever had. Well, one of the worst. No time to rank order them now. But the thought of Kyle, and Jay, and the guys at paintball, and everyone, really, snickering "Reverend Fratelli" as the ultimate, unanswerable put-down whenever he might otherwise fleetingly have the upper hand, made him want to kick himself.

"That Reverend Fratelli has satisfied—"

Shit. We won, thought Nick. Life would have been a great deal simpler with a loss. Secret Plan, here we come.

Natalie covered her mouth with both hands. Spillman signaled "Touchdown!" Melinda continued.

"—has satisfied the court that the doctrines of the Church of Inspired Spirituality ("CIS") qualify under the *Africa*[15] standard as a religious belief. They are comprehensive—in fact, sweeping—and not limited to a single issue."

You have no idea, thought Nick.

"And the external elements of the church—the elaborate prayers, liturgy, and sacraments—all evidence a belief system which, though new, compares favorably with any Abrahamic or Eastern religion."

And beats the hell out of the damned Indians or the oh-so-precious Wiccans, Nick told himself, beginning to feel the charge of victory. His religion could whip those assholes any day of the week, twice on Sundays.

"Having established that the Church of Inspired Spirituality (CIS) is a legitimate religious belief, we turn now to the plain meaning of the Religious Freedom Restoration Act of 1993 ('RFRA'). It is the amply documented religious belief of CIS that its members may partake of marijuana, and may distribute it in any form to other members of the church. CIS scriptures, in fact, go on at tedious length to this effect."

Nick winced at the low blow. Tedious?! There was careful theological progression for everything he had written. If the judge didn't see it, shame on her.

On and on the opinion droned, ticking off the elements of RFRA one by one and noting with some reluctance how CIS complied with each. Just like Nick had planned, and Natalie had executed. Finally, Melinda reached the crescendo: "There is no compelling interest of the government to prohibit distribution of a substance that its citizens are fully entitled to possess. That prohibition is the legal equivalent of one hand clapping."

Now it was Natalie's turn to grin. That was her original line, straight out of her brief.

"Therefore, the court grants plaintiff's motion for summary judgment, and hereby orders the Department of Licensing and Regulation to approve the incorporation of Church of Inspired Spirituality Distribution, Inc. as a nonprofit corporation under the terms of its proposed charter."

---

15. *Africa v. Commonwealth of Pennsylvania*, 662 F.2d 1025 (3d Cir. 1981) http://openjurist.org/662/f2d/1025/africa-v-commonwealth-of-pennsylvania-s.

"That's it," Melinda said. "You want anything else?"

"No, that'll do," said Spillman. "You can get back to work now."

*****

Peter Spillman seemed to float above his chair. "A most excellent result," he gushed. "Most excellent. We can be quite pleased with how we've done here. Earl will be pleased as well, when I tell him."

"We?" thought Nick. This guy sure switched pronouns in a hurry. He was also intent on keeping Nick as far removed from direct communication with Earl Matteson as he could manage.

"We need to get moving on the wellness case," Spillman continued. "That's the next step, before we can spring the environmental surprise. Having CIS established as a religion is important, but not sufficient. Having it established as a religion for *corporations* is the key. A motherhood-and-apple-pie issue like wanting to make your employees healthier is the ideal way to achieve that."

Nick tried to crush the lip of the table between his thumb and forefinger. This was the plan Nick himself had laid out. Spillman was now lecturing him with his own idea, like a biology student explaining to Darwin what evolution was all about. At least the guy can read, Nick thought.

"We've identified a company in Toledo ready to go. In fact, they're up against an audit response deadline that sets up quite nicely for us. They want you there on Monday."

"I don't know," Nick said, glaring at Spillman. "Toledo? It has to be Toledo? You don't have any clients in, like, Hawaii? Or Hollywood?" What he didn't say was that the Matteson plan and the Secret Plan would have to begin diverging at some painful point, and a meeting with a businessman in Toledo might well be it.

Natalie's victory smile disappeared. Her left eyebrow arched high enough to carry up the whole side of her face. "Nick, this is no joke. Not everyone is willing to go out on a limb just because you had a cute idea. You'll like these guys. They really do care about their employees."

"I could make it Monday if you come, too."

Spillman stood, all five-and-a-half feet of him, and indicated it was time to end this. "Monday. Melinda will get your ticket. They just want to meet and greet, but they're already on board. The case will then be filed as soon as Ms. Parks here finds the time to get a petition drafted, which she cannot commence until she completes a number of other projects that have been piling up."

Which would not be piling up if you hadn't laid off half the associates last summer, Nick could hear Natalie grumbling, just assuming the lucky survivors would absorb all their work without missing a beat. He'd heard that complaint from her often enough. Out loud, he heard her correct response: "The draft will be ready Sunday. Not a problem, sir."

"Good. Back to work, then!" Spillman's radiant face looked to Nick more like someone who had just announced: "Time for dessert!"

*****

Nick followed Natalie into the hallway. Not a terribly private spot, but at least little Napoleon was out of earshot.

"I guess we're on our way," said Nick.

"Yeah. It's a little scary."

Time for bravado. Nick squared his shoulders. "It'll work. We're past the hardest part. Once you've toppled that first domino, the rest fall by themselves." Nick swept his arm out to indicate the falling of dominos, and accidentally banged his hand into the wall.

"But we haven't stepped on anyone's toes yet," said Natalie. "DC wasn't prosecuting small marijuana sellers anyway, so they didn't put up much of a fight."

"Exactly. Which is why we started here, remember? Anyway, where do we go to celebrate?"

Natalie turned away. "I'm sorry. You heard what he said. I'm not going to be a victim in the next great profits-per-partner purge. I'll be lucky to be home by midnight."

"Well, what about this weekend?"

"What about it?" she snapped. "You think this petition's going to write itself?"

Natalie's face softened. "Look, Nick, this is my first win, too. First big one, anyway. And I have to hand it to you—you're onto something here. So I'd love to just savor it with you. But now isn't the time. I'm really sorry."

"Well, then, I guess we're all 'back to work!' Yippee!"

*****

Back to work, in Nick's view, did not mean heading back to his cubbyhole. It meant a leisurely stroll outside on this warm autumn afternoon, to work up a thirst he could deal with appropriately, in a venue far more conducive to creative thought than a law office. He window-shopped briefly at an electronics store. Once the dinero started rolling in, he thought, but before the Secret Plan started complicating things, he'd be buying the biggest flat screen TV they'd ever made. And a bigger apartment to fit it in.

Watching people go by on K Street, Nick mused that most of them were probably losers. Low-level bureaucrats, as Nick himself had been until last summer, or stressed-out lawyers, doing the most soul-crushing work imaginable. The kind of crap Spillman kept piling on Natalie. But none of them had the spark—the vision—to spot the flaw that well-meaning people had let creep into the legal system. Or the guts to do something about it.

For the hundredth time, Nick reminded himself of the story of the young Voltaire, starting out life as a penniless writer in eighteenth-century Paris. He had wangled an invitation to a fashionable dinner party, where a mathematician joked about the weakness in the city's new lottery scheme. It seemed the way the winning combinations worked, if someone could succeed in buying up every one of the lottery tickets, he would be assured of winning a fortune, at the city's expense. Everyone at the party thought this was terribly amusing. Everyone except Voltaire, who quietly left to begin putting together a syndicate to buy up every lottery ticket in Paris. The scheme worked, and Voltaire was financially set for life.

As he reached the door to the Tune Inn on Capitol Hill, Nick wondered whether Voltaire ever felt the same queasy feeling in his stomach that Nick was having about his trip to Toledo. This adventure had started as a half-joke at a cocktail party, then taken on a life of its own. It was one thing to snicker through an essentially meaningless pot case in DC, but quite different to meet a business owner in the Midwest—real America—and try to sell him a fraud. That could prove quite disagreeable. He couldn't really stop now, though, could he?

*****

Nick arrived before Friday night happy hour began at four o'clock. Jay and Kyle would be stopping by later, the two little words "on me" having worked their customary magic. Nick didn't mind getting a head start, even if that meant buying a couple of full-priced beverages. A little time to himself to drink it all in, so to speak, wasn't the worst idea. And this was by far the most congenial place to pull his thoughts together: a former speakeasy whose décor had simply darkened, not changed, over the decades. Comfortable as your favorite old slippers, with a clientele ranging from congressmen and yuppie lobbyists to cops and aged artists struggling to stretch their Social Security checks to the end of the month. From a pair of antlers high above the center of the bar hung a strikingly large, strikingly purple brassiere. Nick had heard more than one patron ask how it had gotten there, only to be met with a shrug.

The older clientele, when you could draw them out, all had stories. CIA, USAID, USMC, RNC ... Nick suspected half the war stories he overheard pushed "exaggeration" into "falsehood," but they were entertaining nonetheless. Someday he wanted his own war stories to tell, and he knew that now was the time to lay their foundation.

One thing seemed clear: he needed to start getting his act together. He used to be a hard worker, always at the top of the class through grade school and high school. He was the first Fratelli to go to college, and he'd picked a small and expensive private school rather than the University of Maryland, as his father had urged. But a light flickered out there. He may have had an IQ as high as these rich suburban kids, but he didn't have the polish. Their dads didn't drive buses; they didn't even ride them. Their moms shopped at boutique delicatessens; they didn't stock the shelves. And none of them worked as part-time janitorial assistants, as Nick had. They made jokes Nick didn't get. Some were at Nick's expense, especially when he got too earnest about something.

The course of least resistance, Nick had eventually decided, was to hunker down. Just get by, with high enough grades to get into law school. Which he did, barely, at a state school nowhere near the top of his wish list. There he'd found the competition an order of magnitude greater than in college, and he was further burdened by the need to work a heavy schedule to pay his basic rent and grocery bills, which his family was unable to subsidize. Every nickel of his tuition was borrowed money, six figures worth of it. He actually failed a course for the first time in his life, sparing the world the grief of one more tax lawyer. The mundane courses that led to plentiful employment opportunities—tax, torts, evidence—Nick found insufferable. First amendment law was where he excelled, despite the advice of his counselor that the competition for the glamor jobs in that field was fierce. No matter. Nick had almost always gotten what he wanted somehow, and he'd find a way to build a career in something interesting as well.

Except he didn't. Not for lack of trying, but he never even got a callback from his targeted résumé mailings. There was one First Amendment-related nibble from a Catholic hospital chain, but Nick wasn't quite ready to flip to the dark side yet. A legal job where he could work *against* the vested interest of the God industry, rather than for it? Good luck with that.

With a few months to go before the first tuition loan payment would come due, Nick broke down and started applying for any legal job he could find. He grabbed the first offer that came in from GSA, even though he knew the low-level government contract work there would be stultifying. After all, it would just be a few months until something sexier turned up.

Except, once again, it didn't. A few months turned into a year, then another year, and a third. The rejections wore him down, and he started sending out fewer applications. Nick mastered the art of getting by in the bowels of GSA, earning just enough to be able to spend a little on entertainment after rent and debt payments. He never completely abandoned the hope that something interesting would pop up, but he found himself thinking less and less about it, and more and more about what surprises the next hot video game might hold, or how on earth he could spend so much time studying baseball statistics without ever managing to nudge his fantasy team above third place. Did those clowns above him use paid informers?

Now his ship had come in, as he'd dreamed it would. A federal judge, a *player*, saying "Yep, Nick my boy, you were right. Everybody thought you were just a fuck-up, but you're not. You, Mr. Fratelli, have just punched a hole in the system, a little hole that's bound to become a big one. You're a *somebody* now." Not in those exact words, but that was the gist of it.

To be somebody meant acting the part. Which was good and bad. It was very unlikely to benefit his fantasy baseball team, which now had a solid young core and with some careful attention might soon become a real contender. It was also unlikely to do anything for the level of comfort in his daily wardrobe. He chafed at the thought of having to dress like Peter Spillman every day.

"Another beer?" the Tune Inn barkeep asked, interrupting Nick's reverie.

"Ok. No, wait. Uh, what kinda wine you got?" That wouldn't do. "Could I see a wine list?"

The bartender wordlessly tapped the plastic holder sitting right in front of Nick. It proudly displayed all six wine varieties on offer, even though it said "Amstel" at the bottom.

"Oh. I'll have a glass of the house red. No, wait. I'll have the Pinot Noir." That's one small step for man, one giant leap toward celebrity cool.

Not enough of a step to guarantee prompt service, though. While he waited for the bartender to finish rearranging his tray of glasses before getting around to pouring the first drink of the rest of his life, Nick thought back to the gut religion classes he'd taken to inflate his GPA. "I bet I'm the only one who's ever made a nickel off any of that shit," he thought. "Dumb fucks." They'd never won anything. All it took was a little imagination, a little patience. Wait for your opportunity, then grab it.

*****

"Hey, reverend!" It was Kyle, somehow breezing in fifteen minutes before GSA's normal closing time. "Yo!" he shouted at the server, fifteen yards away. "Pitcher of Heineken down here. On him!" He smacked Nick on the back, a little harder than the occasion called for.

"So you beat the fuckers," he bubbled, settling on a stool. "Damn! I didn't think you had it in you. That anybody had it in them, I mean—not just you."

Nick nodded indulgently. "I know what you mean. Thanks. You know, you read about people making law, making things really happen, and it's always like somebody else doing it. To have it be me, you know, my idea, it's really gratifying."

"I thought it was Natalie's idea," said Kyle, with a hint of accusation. "I was there, remember?"

"Well, yeah," Nick said, shrinking back an inch. "She was involved in a piece of it. But the whole big picture—I started it. She just, she's just helping, you know? There wouldn't be anything without me."

Kyle's pitcher arrived, but Nick's wine was still AWOL.

"But she wrote the brief," said Kyle. "Her name's on it. I didn't see yours anywhere."

"Where'd you get the brief?" Nick didn't think Kyle had ever read a brief in his life, even though he'd been practicing law—make that, been employed as a lawyer—a year longer than Nick had.

"Online, man. Where do you think? I've been reading the whole filing, all afternoon, ever since I got your text. What do you think, I just goof off all the time?"

"You, goof off?" Nick smirked. "I take it that religious exemptions from the drug laws now fall within the purview of the General Services Administration?"

"Well," Kyle grinned, "it's still law, right?"

"True. Nothing at all like XXX Swedish Hotties, or whatever it is you spend most of your time studying."

"Speaking of which," said Kyle, "that Natalie is one hot chick. Are you two, uh ...?" Kyle waggled his fingers.

Nick winked. "We get along." Technically, that was true. Nick was getting better and better at the Washington game.

"Once she dumps you, gimme her phone number, ok? You know, I could follow most of what she wrote in the brief. Made sense. I gotta tell you, though, buddy, that attachment—the one you wrote—that's some deep shit, man."

"You mean the *Doctrines of Inspired Spirituality?*"

"Deeeeeeep shit." Kyle shook his jowels on the "Deeeep."

The bar was starting to fill up now. A guy with a gray ponytail wearing a worn leather Desert Storm jacket chatted with a younger, heavyset man in a yellow polo shirt. Another pair at a table had a laptop between them, conducting some sort of business like an insurance sale. A group of three fiftyish women gossiped animatedly.

"You didn't like it?"

"Like it? I haven't the faintest fucking idea what you were talking about."

"So what you're saying is," said Nick smugly, "you could attribute almost anything to it, and make a case that it really means that? Sort of like the devil being able to quote scripture for his own purposes? You think this wasn't planned?"

"I guess. Like I said, I haven't the faintest fucking idea what you were talking about. I mean here and there, yeah, I can get what this sentence or that sentence means. But when you put the whole thing together, nada."

Nick downed another mug of beer before his wine finally arrived. What Kyle saw as confusion, Nick saw as flexibility, allowing his theology to roll with the punches, to take advantage of exemption opportunities yet undreamed of. He was spared the difficulty of trying to explain this to Kyle by the arrival of Jay.

"All hail the hero!" sang Jay, raising his hands above his head and bowing to the waist. "And thank you, thank you, thank you for the scoop! I mean it. You don't know how important that is, to be even a half hour ahead of everyone else. My stock with a dozen editors just shot up. Some of them might even remember my name now—who knows?"

"Did it shoot up enough in value for you to pick up the tab for this guy?" asked Nick playfully, jerking a thumb in Kyle's direction.

"No," replied Jay firmly, without missing a beat or looking at Kyle. "It did not. I'd need a lead on something like the president's mistress to justify that kind of expense. Especially for somebody who's never fed me a single scoop, the whole time he's been at GSA."

While Kyle mimicked a flapping mouth with his fingers, Nick said, "Be grateful for what I can do for you now."

"I am," said Jay, nodding vigorously. "Seriously. So what exactly is it you can do for me now? In twenty-four hours, this case is old news. Whatcha got next?"

"Chill out, dude," said Kyle, handing him a full mug. "Work's over."

"A bureaucrat may work from dusk to dawn, but a reporter's work is never done," Jay replied, after draining half the mug.

"You could do a background piece on me," Nick suggested. Joking, mostly. "My childhood, how I struggled, how I was influenced, how I—"

"How many times he whacks off every day," Kyle interrupted. "What's your personal best? The world wants to know."

"Guys!" Jay said sharply, "that tract or whatever it was you read to me in the car. Is that what you used in this case?"

"Pretty much. I tinkered with it, right up to the last minute, but that was basically it. And the judge, obviously, didn't think it was so bad."

"Well I couldn't stand it, but I do remember there was a hell of a lot in there besides weed."

"Deeeeeeeep shit," Kyle added.

"Uh, yeah," said Nick trying to ignore Kyle. "It's a whole, self-contained theology. You see, you start with the premise that God—"

Jay threw his hands in front of his face to protect himself from the onslaught. "Spare me. I heard it already. Plain English: you got more cases coming, right? What are they?"

"That's classified." Nick Fratelli, Man of Mystery. He fit right in at this bar.

"Off the record."

Nick worked his jaw back and forth. Spillman had told him flat-out to keep what they were doing quiet. Partly for client confidentiality, partly to keep their options open, partly because there was more downside than upside to letting the press twist what you were trying to do. This fight would be won in the courts of law, not in the courts of public opinion. The last thing you wanted was to let the people decide whether there ought to be one law for everybody, or a mish-mash of special exemptions for special pleaders.

"Well?" Jay demanded.

Nick took another swig. Spillman probably wanted to keep all the press glory for himself. "We" indeed! Besides, Jay was a friend. He wouldn't screw him.

"What do you mean, 'off the record?'" Nick finally asked. "If it's really off the record, there's no point to it."

"Sure there is. You're trying to do something bigger here. I get that. I can do a better job reporting it—and get you more coverage—if I have some idea what it is in advance."

Nick took another long gulp, and gently shook his head.

"Of course," Jay continued, "if you're not really calling the shots ... if you're just some kind of pawn here, is there somebody important I could talk to who knows what's going on?"

Alcohol molecules had congregated at busy intersections inside Nick's brain, disrupting the normal electron flow. The cortex network that was trying to say "Juvenile trick—don't fall for it" was stalled in a traffic jam. An evolutionarily older "fight or flight" lobe broadcast a simpler message that found its way through: fuck Spillman.

"You might want to read up," Nick said quietly, "on the Department of Labor regulations governing corporate wellness programs."

"Huh? Corporate wellness programs?"

"Yes." Nick nodded gravely, as though he had just revealed the dark secret that Jay was Geraldo Rivera's love child.

"You mean like weight loss and quitting smoking?"

Nick continued nodding, eyes closed.

"What the hell has that got to do with religion? No, wait," Jay added quickly. "I didn't say that. Don't start on the doctrines again. Look, there's something going on here, and I'm not getting it. So just one more question, in real plain English, that even he can understand." He pointed at Kyle, without breaking eye contact with Nick. "Who's paying for this? It ain't weed sellers, 'cause nobody needed you for that. It ain't corporate wellness, whatever the fuck that is. Who's paying you, really?"

It would have taken a great deal more alcohol to penetrate Nick's defenses on that one. Another small network of neurons even began to grapple with the notion that Peter Spillman may have had a point about not talking to reporters. Especially smart, hungry ones.

Nick waved his empty glass at the bartender who was passing by.

"Could I get a refill here?" Turning back to Jay, he said: "The time has come for us to talk about... shortstops. You've got Benny Coughlin, I want him. What's it gonna take?"

Another pitcher of beer came and went, with the conversation steered in a harmless direction. No fantasy shortstop deal was struck, though numerous combinations involving as many as eight players were discussed. Kyle struck out twice with nearby women. As they rose to leave, Kyle made his way to the restroom, prompting a thoroughly buzzed Nick to lean over and speak into Jay's ear, as softly as he could while still making himself heard above the din.

"Bathrooms. Transgender bathrooms. You think Kyle wants to stand there and pee next to some dude in a miniskirt? Or some dyke in a butch cut? Not that she could ... Just read up on it, ok? Word to the wise."

Jay's face lit up like sunrise. "Now *that's* something I can use!"

Nick wagged a finger three inches in front of Jay's face. "Totally off the record, ok? Just be ready."

*****

Peter Spillman had placed his first call to Earl Matteson immediately after Nick and Natalie left his office, only to be told he was in the field, out of cellphone range. He tried again right about the time Nick was stumbling out of the pub, with the same result. He pinched the bridge of his nose. No use putting it off. Back to the numbers.

He had hoped that wangling a promise of an additional retainer from Earl for the next phase of the CIS campaign might make the financial projections a little less bleak. It never ceased to amaze him how a law office that charged such obscenely high rates, to a clientele that could so easily afford them, managed to lose money. It seemed less amazing once he grumbled through the latest monthly expense reports. The sums these lawyers took home were staggering. So was the rent, especially for all those empty offices of laid-off associates. He'd been the one who had to dish out the bad news to them. And he'd been the one who devoted all those non-billable hours to helping each of them find other work. Not jobs that paid as well as Guilder & Hersh—nobody paid that well—but decent jobs. Most firms didn't do that, but Peter had been around Washington long enough to grasp how insular it really was, and how a small kindness or a small slight from twenty years ago could come to matter again when you least expected it. Not that he got any credit from the remaining associates for his efforts. Maybe they'd have preferred the whole place to shut down?

An ever-increasing pool of lawyers chasing a finite amount of work. That was the fundamental problem facing the profession. That, and the lack of loyalty. The latest headache was the banking law group threatening to move across the street unless G&H would match the offer they'd received. An offer not out of line with their revenues, but an offer he couldn't match because of the need to divert funds from other practice areas to make up for the disaster in the government relations group. Listing a stable of prominent ex-senators on the stationery looked oh-so-glamorous, but it was Spillman's DC office budget that took the hit, especially when seven-figure partners didn't pull their weight.

Well, he'd match the banking group offer. He had no choice. Not only would more empty offices send his lease-to-revenue ratio into record-breaking absurdity, but the loss of confidence such a defection would generate could easily lead to collapse. He'd just have to find more paying work somehow, somewhere, to plug the gap. The same thing thirty other Washington managing partners were staying up late that Friday night trying to figure out how to do for their own firms.

"Excuse me, sir. I have the draft of the Rubenstein response for you." A baggy-eyed Natalie Parks stood in in his doorway, holding a file folder. A ship's clock on Spillman's wall read 9:45.

"Oh. Thank you. Uh, please, come in. Have a seat."

"I think it's strong," Natalie said. "There's a Third Circuit laches case right on point."

"I'm sure it is. You've had quite a day today."

Natalie shrugged. "We had a strong case, Mr. Spillman. Even if we hadn't won at summary judgment, we'd have won at trial."

Which would have generated a lot more fees, Peter thought ruefully. But perhaps there were more to be had. It was time for a world-view shift, to accommodate changing circumstances.

"Natalie, people who win groundbreaking cases in district courts of the United States, or achieve similar success, normally call me 'Peter,' rather than 'Mr. Spillman.'"

"Ookaaay."

"Not 'Petey,' or 'Pete.' Those terms are reserved for use by billionaires."

Natalie nervously returned his smile. This was the first attempt at humor she'd ever heard from him.

"Another thing. I want you to go home now. Then—"

"I still have those summaries to do, and—"

Peter held up his palm in a "Halt" signal. "Let me finish. I'll speak to Paul and have him find someone else. You're too valuable for that. I want you to go home, and I want you to sleep in tomorrow, or go shopping, or do whatever it is you do on Saturdays. Then I want you to work on the Toledo petition, and nothing else. I want your full, refreshed attention on that. And I don't need it Sunday. I need it by Tuesday, when Nick returns. But I need it to win. That I need, if we're to keep Earl happy. Any confusion?"

"No, sir. Peter."

Spillman leaned back, vaguely worried that he'd revealed a hint of desperation to one of the troops.

"Your friend, Mr. Fratelli. His master plan could involve a great deal of litigation, on numerous fronts, couldn't it?"

"I suppose so ... Peter. But it all seems so farfetched. So many things have to break the right way. One slip, and we could be done."

These kids, Spillman thought. The only thing they care about, other than running up the hours, is not being wrong. Wrong means embarrassed. Wrong means fired. But not taking a little risk now and then meant that his "Expenses" number would continue to exceed his "Income" number, at least for another six months or so, until everything screeched to a halt.

"But we don't 'slip,' do we? We do thorough, top quality legal work. That's why our clients pay us so much. And why we pay our attorneys so much. So we don't 'slip.' Am I right?"

The top quarter of the Washington Monument was visible over Spillman's shoulder, red lights blinking on and off as a warning to aircraft. "No, sir, we don't slip," she said. "It just seems so ... outlandish. The kind of world that would result if everything Nick runs on about were to happen, I just can't picture it."

"The world can take care of itself. It always does. But we can be paid just as much in the process of tearing it all down, someday, as we're paid for building it up now. Do you agree?"

Natalie froze. A "no" meant disagreeing with her boss. A "yes" meant setting herself up for blame if things didn't work out. She studied her nails. "I've never done anything like this before."

Spillman leaned in to share a secret. "Well, that puts you in good company. I haven't either! The one vulnerability I can see though,"—he rubbed his knuckles together—"is our fearless leader. Your friend, Mr. Fratelli. Is he... ?"

Peter Spillman was rarely at a loss for words, but wasn't sure which one to use for Nick. Sane? Stable? Trustworthy? Super-flake? A sound bet for the future of this law firm? This was all way, way too easy. Winning an exception to a federal rule, even a little one, was supposed to require ex-agency insiders, generous PAC contributions, carefully orchestrated constituent pressure, meticulously wordsmithed compromise. Not some slob blubbering "Dude, it's my religion." Still, it was the postmodern age, and change was the only constant.

Natalie rescued him. "I know what you mean, sir. And I can't answer that one, either. All I can say is, if Nick weren't Nick, we wouldn't even be having this conversation, would we?"

November 8: Toledo

Melinda had pulled together an itinerary to get Nick to Toledo, Ohio, and back in a single eighteen-hour day, saving the expense of a hotel room. He finally pulled his rental car into the parking lot of a shabby, half-empty industrial park west of downtown a few minutes late for his 1:00 p.m. meeting, hoping someone would have the decency to take him to lunch.

"Trabicor Systems" read the sign on the door, with a geometric logo offering no clue as to what its systems might do. No one greeted him at the receptionist's desk. The woman who finally responded to his third effort at the buzzer informed him that Mr. Nielson would be back from lunch shortly.

When Bruce Nielson finally did turn up, he didn't fit Nick's image of the midwestern manufacturing tycoon. He was wiry and intense, with a short-cropped beard. Nick guessed his age at forty-five, ten years too low. Nielson took him on a quick tour of the headquarters—the human resources department, the finance department, the marketing department. Metal desks, computers, binders, stacks of papers, photos of children, and nothing whatsoever to indicate the point of it all.

"So what do you guys actually do?" Nick finally broke down and asked when they got back to Nielson's office—the same as all the others, but with a wooden desk instead of metal, and a soft couch.

"We make precision instruments. Sort of like GPS, on steroids. One of our boxes is up on the space station right now."

"Awesome! So you do a lot of work for NASA?"

"No, NASA doesn't have that much of a budget. Most of what we do is for the Air Force, and the Space Command."

"Do you make all your stuff here in this building?"

Nielson warded off the question with two palms. "Sorry. If I told you that, I'd have to kill you. I guess you've heard that one before. Anyway, the point is, we employ a highly skilled, highly specialized work force. We can't outsource to China—we have to do everything here in the states. We pay our people well, and we demand a lot. 'Oops, it broke' isn't acceptable where our boxes are being used."

"I guess not."

"So we keep our people happy. And we need to keep them healthy. It's bad enough when someone slows down production because of sick days—but it's even worse when they drag themselves in with a fever, or a hangover, and do sloppy work. We had an 'oops' on one of our boxes four years ago that almost brought down a bird and put us out of business. We traced it back to one inspector who let a bad weld slip through, the day before he called in sick with the flu."

Nick nodded absently at the thought of the quality issues that could arise while working through a hangover.

"That's why we started the wellness program," Nielson continued. "So we can do better work. And because, well, we're not softies, but we're sort of a big family here. We look out for people, try to get them to take care of themselves. Weight management, quarterly phone consultations, vaccinations, cardiac testing, medication reviews—a Cadillac program. It's good for business, and good for our people too. Is this such a crime?"[16]

Adjusting his glasses, Nick replied, "Well, it's not a crime, but I know the Department of Labor doesn't like it if it's mandatory. They think it interferes with people's privacy."

"Yeah, right," Nielson scowled. "No rules. Just a Karl Marx worker's paradise, where everybody does the right thing and sings a song while they're at it. Worked out dandy in the Soviet Union, didn't it? Tell me, Mr. Lawyer, has DOL ever actually made a product? One that better damn well work right?"

"I doubt it."

"So why are we in trouble? Tell me. We've got investigators crawling all over us, trying to interview employees—which they can't do, by the way, because of Air Force rules—and threatening us with huge fines if we don't shut the wellness program down."

Nick suppressed a stomach growl. "Well, Mr. Nielson, I'm actually not here as your lawyer. I mean, I'm a lawyer and all, but I'm not working for you as a lawyer. If you get what I mean. I'm just here on my own time as a representative of the Church of Inspired Spirituality, to see if Trabicor would like to join. We have some doctrines applying to

---

16. Daniel Wiessner, "Obama administration releases rules on wellness programs," *Reuters*, May 16, 2016. http://www.reuters.com/article/us-usa-wellness-idUSKCN0Y71ZK. Reed Abelson, "AARP Sues U.S. Over Rules for Wellness Programs," *New York Times*, October 24, 2016. http://www.nytimes.com/2016/10/25/business/employee-wellness-programs-prompt-aarp-lawsuit.html?_r=1.

wellness programs that could help your position."

Nielson shook his head in disgust. "It's like I told Peter already. We're a business. Businesses don't have religions."

"Oh, but they do! Sure they do. What are you, personally—Catholic?"

"Lutheran."

"Ok. Well I don't know how Lutherans work, but I know for Catholics, for example, there's a diocese of Toledo. And it's got a bishop who runs it. And that diocese, legally, it's a corporation. It can own property, it can go bankrupt—like plenty of them did, to worm out of paying their sex abuse victims. And it's got a religion, right? It's Catholic."

"But we're not a church."

"You don't have to be. Think of, like, Notre Dame. That's not a church, it's a college. But it's still Catholic."

"We're a business—we're nothing like that."

In the distance, Nick heard what must have been a large piece of equipment turn on. Clunk-clunk-cricket-clunk. Clearly they manufactured something at this facility. If CIS didn't work out, maybe he could become an industrial spy. That could be cool.

"Believe me, Mr. Nielson, when you owe as much money as I do for student loans—college is a business. But it doesn't matter. The Supreme Court said that every business, of any kind—manufacturers, retailers, you name it—can have a religious belief. And then you're golden. The government can't make you do *anything* that goes against that religious belief, unless they bend over backwards first to try to find a way to accommodate you. Accommodating you here would be a piece of cake—just help any employee who objects to the wellness program find a different job. Has anyone ever objected?"

"Not if they know what's good for them."

Nick squirmed in his seat. "Ahh. We may need to fine-tune that answer a teeny bit. Just a simple 'no' would be good, if a DOL investigator ever asks."

Nielson's chair creaked as he leaned back. "Look," he said. "I read the memo Peter's assistant sent. I understand—"

"She's not an assistant," Nick interrupted. "She's a highly accomplished lawyer. The fact is, we can get you what you want, if you just have Trabicor join the church and then follow the plan we laid out. No guarantees, but frankly I think you'll win without a fight. This'll tie DOL up in knots. They won't want to deal with it. There's much lower-hanging fruit for them to pick."

Nielson only half concealed his irritation over being interrupted.

"As I was trying to tell you, I read the memo. I get the whole *Hobby Lobby* shtick." He leaned forward over the desk. "But here's what I don't get, which is why I asked to meet you in person. *Why?* Why are you doing this? I can understand what makes tech nerds tick, and lawyers, and if I try hard I can even understand DOL investigators. Don't like 'em, but I understand 'em. But you, and this whole corporate religion mishmash, I don't get. And I have trouble signing up my business for something that I don't understand."

Peter Spillman had known Nielson well enough to anticipate the question, and had coached Nick on a pablum answer any congressman would have been proud of. "We truly believe ... power of individual inspiration ... a new departure ... a new beginning ... even the odds against big government ... the ground floor of something big ... " Which was a good thing, because a more candid answer may or may not have resulted in the signature Nielson ultimately affixed to Nick's paperwork. And it most certainly would have delayed Nick's lunch, because his explanation would have had to start a full decade back in time.

Ten Years Before Toledo: Rockville Dining Room

What Nick didn't explain to Bruce Nielson happened on his first trip home from college.

Nick's parents were lapsed Catholics, and Nick had only ever been in church for weddings, his grandpa's funeral, and a classmate's bat mitzvah. When he arrived home from college at Thanksgiving of his freshman year, knees aching from a six hour bus ride, his father had been unimpressed with his choice of major: comparative religion.

"What the hell are you going to do with that?" he growled. "Luca, get some more chips." Nick's father was seated in his reserved spot on the end of the couch, close to a television tuned to Georgetown basketball. Three empty Miller Lites sat on the end table, but Nick couldn't pinpoint their time of consumption.

"Well, lots of things. It's a liberal arts degree, Pop. It's not voc-tech. It doesn't really matter that much what the major is. It's just a well-rounded education. You can go into business, or government, or ..."

His father snorted. "You're gettin' well-rounded all right! What, they don't got intramurals at that college? Maybe you're doing comparative beer drinking instead of comparative religion. Hey Luca, how you like that? Comparative beer drinking!"

Nick reddened. He was, in fact, deeply engrossed in comparative beer drinking. He and his witty dorm buddies even called it that. That his oaf of a father could have the same clever idea, and turn it against him, was irritating.

"When I was your age," he went on, "I was skinny as a rail. I was maybe 130 pounds."

"Yeah, Pop," Luca cut in. "That's when you were walking twenty miles to school from your log cabin every day. Before you worked your three full-time jobs every night."

Big brothers had their value.

"Okay, smartass. Look, Nicky. All I'm saying is, you didn't go to Maryland, like you coulda. You went to the fancy school up north. And you're gonna get outta there up to your eyeballs in debt. I ain't payin' it. Your Mama ain't payin' it. Smartass Luca, you payin' it?"

"Not me, Pop."

"So you just gotta think, Nicky. Whoa, did you see that! Criminy! Call 'em both ways, asshole. Hey Luca: how much's it take to bribe a referee? Five hundred? Five thousand? What's the going rate?"

"Don't know, Pop."

"He crushed him with the elbow," Nick chimed in, and the subject was officially changed.

Nick's mother was more supportive. But then, baby boy could have said he was majoring in gobbledygook, and she would have said the same thing: "My son, the professor." She equated all college men with professors, never having known any professors. "I remember when you used to play teacher."

Nick had played teacher exactly once, to his best recollection. His play habits would have better predicted a career as a Ninja Turtle.

"I don't know about being a professor, Mama. There're plenty of other things I can do once I graduate."

"You know best, Nicky. You're the smart one."

Christmas break was different. Nick had eased off the comparative beer drinking, and instead begun to lose himself in the whirl of the material he was studying. Never having been properly exposed to spirituality, Nick found the surrender to pure emotion heady and gratifying. Instead of trendier choices like Buddhism, Nick gravitated toward the religion of his ancestors: Catholicism. He was attracted to the rigidity—you were on the bus, or you were off the bus. You were part of an army whose legions were all pushing in the same direction. Maybe not always the right direction, but shoulder to shoulder nonetheless.

On Christmas Eve, Mama baked her ham and her famous scalloped potatoes. Luca was there with his then-wife Yvonne, six-year-old Jonas, five-year-old Monica, and the baby Tony. Nick's dad wore a white shirt, just for the hell of it. Nick had lugged wrapped presents for everyone home with him on the bus. He ate only two plates full of food, less than his normal quota, while anxiously awaiting the right moment to spring his announcement. Never having witnessed such an announcement from anyone before, he was uncertain what that right moment would feel like.

"You know, I've been reading a lot of the apologetics—"

"Jonas!" barked Yvonne. "Quit playing with your peas."

"Let him be," muttered Luca. "He's eaten most of them."

"Oh yeah? Since when did you become the great father? Maybe he can just eat ice cream all the time?"

"Jonas," said Luca wearily, without acknowledging the outburst, "just have a little bit more, and we can get back to having a nice dinner."

"Do you want more ham, honey?" said Mama, pushing a plate toward Nick.

"What are you apologizing for?" Nick's father asked him. "You're not the one busting up Christmas dinner."

This felt like a good moment. Everyone around the table, except perhaps Yvonne, seemed ready for any conversational direction other than continued marital bickering.

"It's not apologizing. That's just what they call it when people write to defend their religious belief."

"So why do they call it that?" asked Luca, seeming to enjoy freezing Yvonne out of the conversation.

"I ... don't really know," said Nick. "Anyway, I've been reading a lot of it, and, you know, it's starting to make sense to me. And I've been spending a lot of time with Father McIntyre, taking some private instruction. And, well, if I keep it up, Father McIntyre says in a couple of months I can get baptized as a Catholic. Which is what I'm going to do."

Nick had expected his father to harrumph, his mother to beam about her son the bishop, Luca to ask what all was involved, and Yvonne to splash her personal brand of acid on whatever anyone else said.

What he did not expect was for Mama to gasp, drop her forkful of scalloped potatoes onto her plate, burst into tears, and leap from the table, knocking her chair back into the highboy. He wasn't aware his mother could move that quickly.

Nick had expected his father to be negative. Pop could be negative about a sunny morning in May. This was way past run-of-the-mill grumpiness, though. This was sorry-I-wrecked-the-car level fury. "You fucking moron," he growled. Then he headed off in pursuit of Mama.

"You fucking moron," Yvonne repeated. This was the most surprising reaction of all—the first time Yvonne had agreed with Pop about anything, ever. Monica wasn't sure what a fucking moron was, but she was sure that whatever had made Grandma cry was serious enough that she should join in. Yvonne swept up the baby in one hand, Monica in the other, barked at Jonas, and headed in the opposite direction from her in-laws.

That left Nick alone with Luca, whose hands were raised skyward. "What the fuck? What're trying to do?"

Nick thought it was perfectly obvious what he was trying to do— tell everyone he was going to be baptized as a Catholic. He hadn't the faintest idea why that should have caused such an explosion.

"Don't you know?" demanded Luca.

"Know what?"

"You don't know." Luca's voice dripped with contempt, as it would for someone who didn't know that sticking his fingers in an electric outlet was a bad idea.

Every word that Nick had uttered so far had only dug his hole a little deeper, so he was done talking for a while. He just looked at Luca expectantly.

"You don't know," Luca repeated. Less contempt, more astonishment.

It was now firmly established, beyond any second-guessing, that Nick didn't know. If Luca didn't tell him, no further progress would ensue.

"You're what—eleven years younger than me? D'j'ever think about that?"

Nick stuck to the no-further-words-until-it's-safe plan.

"They wanted more kids, okay? Pop wanted a little girl, who'd look just like Mama. Mama didn't care, she just liked babies. But something wasn't working with the pipes. Try and try—you know Pop—no baby."

Luca paused, looking for a flicker of recognition. Nick didn't move.

"So they went and did the test-tube thing. Pop kept whackin' off, and the third time around, it worked. You didn't come from no stork."

Nick ran a quick internal body scan, to see if he felt any different given how weird he now realized he was. He didn't feel like a test-tube, or any sensation of being surrounded by petrie dish gel. He just felt normal, but resolved to investigate the matter more carefully at a later time.

"But what's that got to do—" Nick immediately regretted breaking his vow of silence.

"You fucking moron." (All three aligned now—a red letter day.) "The rector found out, and gave 'em hell for it. That's why they had to move out of Baltimore—all their friends from the parish froze them out. They pulled me right out of St. Francis in the middle of the year. And now you—Mr. Walking Sin himself—decide you're gonna be a Catholic. Well lah-di-dah."

Nick knew all about the church's doctrine against in vitro fertilization. He didn't think that the sin extended to himself as the end product, and even if it did, it would theoretically wash away with the baptism. Still, he could only imagine what both of his parents' reactions must have been to sanctimonious bullshit from a priest against what they were trying to do. Wasn't the church supposed to be *pro-life*?

Nick had lots of other thoughts over the next few days, all crammed together. As always, he sought to pin the blame for his problems on someone else. Why hadn't anyone ever told him? He couldn't quite picture how such a conversation would have gone, though. Touchy-feely talk was taboo in the Fratelli household, especially when it dealt with sex, and most especially if it suggested some sort of "inadequacy" on the part of his parents. Luca could have told him—*should* have told him—but by the time Nick was old enough to understand things, Luca was off in the army. The bottom line of Nick's thoughts was an additional vote for the "fucking moron" column.

Thus ended Niccolò Fratelli's brief flirtation with organized religion. And thus began his fascination with every flaw he could find, every contradiction, every money grub, every pompous demand for special privileges, from the bastards who'd hurt his mother. The Fratellis were assimilated, yeah, but there was still a little Italian left in him.

Three Months Before Toledo: Rockville Patio

Had Nick told Nielson all about that Christmas, and had Nielson let him finish the story, he might have said something like, "So what? Lots of people your age aren't religious. You haven't answered my question. If you're not religious, then why are you selling me on a religion? Especially one as phony as this?"

It was because of the "Secret Plan." That's the term Nick used with himself. Secret, as in he couldn't tell anyone about it, a constraint that was already making life increasingly difficult. He certainly couldn't tell Natalie, or Spillman—God no. All they wanted to do was make money off his idea, not hear how about any hidden agenda that would screech their gravy train to a halt. He couldn't tell Jay, because Jay was press—rather the opposite of keeping a secret, no? He couldn't tell Kyle, or Luca—they wouldn't give a shit. The best listener he could think of was his father. And that hadn't gone too well.

Nick had taken the long Red Line ride from Silver Spring to Rockville one Sunday afternoon, a few weeks before the marijuana case was filed. He needed to tell his parents about his new adventure. About what had possessed him to give up the nice government job Pop had been so enthusiastic about him landing. Unfortunately, Mama had to fill in at the deli for someone who'd called in sick, so Nick and Pop had to make do with leftovers.

"Thirty years," Pop was fond of repeating. "That's all you've gotta do for the feds. Me, I gotta drive that bus till I'm sixty-five. Two more years, if my back holds out. That'll be forty-one years behind a wheel. Maybe eleven more years don't sound like much to you, but believe me, with this back, it's a lot."

Nick had heard some variant of this spiel at least half a dozen times now. He didn't dispute its basic logic, even though, technically, thirty years no longer had the federal pension magic it once had. Maybe the process of explaining to Pop why he'd chosen to abandon the security of government employment could help convince himself he'd made the right choice.

After they'd polished off a reheated half a tuna fish casserole, Pop retired to a plastic lawn chair outside, puffing an oversized cigar. Nick made some headway with the argument about how high a salary he was pulling down now. "Triple" was the magic word he kept falling back on, that Pop could understand. "And if it doesn't work out long-term, I can go back. Maybe not to exactly the same position, but somewhere, maybe even higher, because I'll have had private sector experience."

"It's a big risk, Nicky."

"Not that big." He admired the flagstones on the patio he'd helped his father put in. Suckers were heavy. The patio project, back when he was fifteen, had helped persuade him to direct his education toward some sort of desk job.

"Anyway, there's more to it. I think I can do some good. In sort of a backwards way. But that's the only way to do these things, because trying to go in the front door, it's too hard. There's too much money and power at stake. The only way to win is to use trickery. Like judo—use the momentum of the other guy against him."

"What in the world are you talking about?"

"The whole religion thing," he said fiercely. "Those guys make me sick. Bertram, and those sanctimonious snakes who got him elected president. I hate 'em. You didn't vote for him, did you?"

"Nah. I sat this one out. Didn't like either one."

"I didn't either. But especially Bertram. And the whole rest of the Christian crowd behind him—Marshall, and those guys. Make my skin crawl. I just think I can use this, this fluke that fell from the sky, as a chance to put 'em in their place. At least bug 'em a little. Like that pastor back in Baltimore who gave you and Mama such a hard time. I heard about all that. What was his name?"

Pop held eye contact for a few seconds, like the parent who discovers that junior has picked up a version of the facts of life on the playground. "That was a long time ago, Nicky. He's dead now, anyway. And the folks at the parish, it's all forgotten. We're not looking for revenge."

"It's not just what happened to you. It's all this thinking, and acting, like these religious pricks are so much better than us. I keep up with all this stuff. I'm gonna show 'em. I'll beat 'em at their own damn game."

Pop relit his cigar, but the pause didn't help him make any more sense of what Nick was saying. "But you said you're *making* a religion. I don't see beating somebody by joining up with them."

Nick hopped up and started pacing around the patio, gesticulating as he spoke. "That's the *only* way to do it! Like I was saying, with judo. You've gotta use the power and momentum of the other guy against him." Nick flipped an imaginary attacker to the ground, then sat down again. "I saw this documentary about Muhammad Ali once. He was talking about black separatists. Back in the sixties, some guys were saying, just split off some southern states, and give 'em to black people so they could have their own country. Do you remember that?"

He didn't.

"Anyway, Ali thought that was stupid. But I guess he didn't want to say that straight out. So he said it's like the bull and the locomotive. They're steaming down the tracks, straight at each other, and everybody says 'My, what a brave bull!' And then they meet, and the bull gets turned into hamburger, and everybody says 'Boy, what a dumb bull!'" Nick's knuckles hurt when he rapped his fists together a bit too vigorously.

Pop grunted.

"But what if the bull—not that a bull could do this—but what if the bull just bent the rails a little? Into empty space? Sent the whole train, using its own momentum, to its own destruction? Wouldn't that be cool?"

"You're losing me. What's a train got to do with religion?"

His father could be so dense. "Well, not exactly like that. Just the trickery part. Look, here's another one. You know Murphy's Law, right?"

"'If anything can go wrong, it will go wrong.'"

"Right. Well I saw this list of sayings that are corollaries to Murphy's Law. One of them was, 'If you fiddle with something long enough, it will break.' *That's* what I'm trying to do." He pulled his chair a foot closer to Pop, so he could speak conspiratorially. "I'm trying to push the whole idea that religion gets special privileges too far. Fiddle with it so much—it breaks. Like that fishing reel I tried to take apart. Remember that? So I could clean it after I dropped it in the salt water?"

"You fucked that one up good."

"Exactly! Everybody's good at something, right? If I push hard enough on the idea that religion deserves special treatment, I can show how stupid it is. I can fuck up religion as bad as I fucked up that reel. That's my 'Secret Plan.' What I call it, anyway. That's why I want to do this. At least, to see if it works, before I have to go back to being bored again."

Pop looked dubious.

"Not all of religion," Nick added quickly. "I wouldn't even want to do that. If believing in fairies makes people happy, good for them. But I do care about the big shots, all high and mighty, telling everybody else what to do. Then saying they get to pick and choose which laws they're gonna follow, when you and I gotta follow all of them. That sucks."

"Whatever, Nicky. You say if you go back to the government, you don't lose those three years toward your thirty, right?"

"No."

"Good." Pop stood up and stretched, then headed head back into the house. As he was opening the door, he turned back, winked, and said "Until then, give those priests a kick in the nuts for me, ok?"

November 17:
DVH Productions

Two for two. A fair summary of Nick's CIS record so far, with a win in court and a success at his first corporate conversion. His next trip to the plate should be easier, since he had no opponent but himself.

Nick arrived at DVH Productions early. A few more minutes walking in the same direction, he mused, and he'd be at Nationals Park. But with opening day still months away, there was no point to that. Still, since he'd be coming here every week or so for the foreseeable future, he should arrange matters so that his recording sessions would wrap up thirty minutes prior to game time. Or maybe even earlier than that, to give himself a chance to eat something first without paying those crazy ballpark prices. Planning: that was the name of the game.

"Mr. Fratelli? Hello. I'm Shawnay Jefferson, your producer. Won't you step this way?"

My producer, Nick thought. Me and Ryan Gosling. We've both got producers. He didn't know what producers were supposed to look like, but whatever it was, Shawnay Jefferson wasn't it. To Nick, producers were white and male, either a little older than Jefferson if they were senior and respected, or a little younger if they were the Next Big Thing. Shawnay Jefferson looked more like a social studies teacher than a producer.

"Do you use a prompter?" she asked, as they walked back through a cinderblock hallway smelling of damp concrete and through a heavy metal door marked "QUIET!"

"You mean like a teleprompter?"

Her shoulder sag made Nick regret having asked such a dumb question. "I guess. I don't really have it memorized. I was just going to read it off here, though," he offered, unfurling some pages he'd rolled into a telescope.

Shawnay's eyes narrowed to slits. "We'll set up the prompter. Do you have the script on a thumb drive?"

He didn't. It took another fifteen minutes to get an electronic copy sent over from the office. In the meantime, while Nick suffered through the application of makeup, Shawnay told him he'd need a different tie. "I have a red one with thin white diagonal stripes, and a powder blue.

Which would you prefer?"

Media star or no, Nick was losing patience. "I'll keep this tie, thanks. It's new, it's clean, and I like it. So this is what I'm going to wear. Now let's just get on with this."

Shawnay snorted. "Suit yourself. We'll see how it looks on the first take."

First take? As in, more than one? This was beginning to sound less like fun, and more like work.

Finally, Nick settled into the armchair in front of the green screen that would be used to superimpose background images. It took a few more minutes to fiddle with the lights. From what Nick could tell, after several repositionings, they wound up exactly where they had started.

*****

"Hello," he finally began. "I'm Niccolò Fratelli, founder of the Church of Inspired Spirituality. Welcome to our first weekly sermoncast. Thank you for logging in, and for paying your weekly stipend. I know that a dollar a week is much less than other churches request. But the Divine Spirit wants us to reach as many people as possible to spread its message, and we know that many of you belong to and financially support other churches as well. We seek not to replace your other form of worship, but to supplement it. We are unique in that regard."

And pretty damn clever, too, he thought. Why try to dislodge people from the religion they were brought up in, if you don't have to? Belonging to more than one church was the latest fad.[17] Besides, what he needed most at this point was head count, not dollars. There were plenty of ways to make money, if he could get to a critical mass of followers.

"Our fundamental message couldn't be simpler. The Divine Spirit speaks to us—to me, to you, to all of us—if we will only listen. And then obey, once we have heard. There's no point in talking to someone who won't do what you say, right? So we must listen, then discern what is truly the word of the Divine Spirit, then obey."

"This isn't new. Moses listened. Gautama Buddha listened. Jesus

---

17. Harriet Sherwood, "York Minister criticised for allowing Buddhist meditation," *The Guardian*, May 17, 2016. http://www.theguardian.com/world/2016/may/17/york-minster-criticised-zen-buddhist-meditation-grounds.

listened. Muhammad listened. Guru Nanak listened. Joseph Smith listened. L. Ron Hubbard listened," Nick paused, noting to himself that pictures of each would be added in the editing phase. "And I have listened, too. Now, I'm not claiming to be another Jesus, or another Joseph Smith. Far from it! I'm just me, Nick Fratelli. But I've listened. And what the Divine Spirit told me was simple: that you must listen, too. Listen. Discern. Obey. That is all you have to do. But that is what you *must* do."

The lights were so hot that Nick's underarms were starting to run. If his face began dripping, that would be bad. The good news was that he had worked on the script long enough that he'd nearly memorized it, with little need for the teleprompter. This accomplishment was put in perspective, though, when Shawnay held up a sign saying "Slow Down."

"Now, some of you may be thinking ..." Nick slowed, more suddenly than the teleprompter operator, and now he was out of synch. There was an awkward pause.

"Just start up again one sentence back," Shawnay advised. "We can patch things up in the edit."

"Can I wipe off some of this sweat?"

"Not without smearing, you can't." A stagehand materialized, and patted down his upper lip.

"Now, some of you may be thinking," he continued, "that the same Divine Spirit must not have been talking to Moses, and Jesus, and Gandhi, and so forth, because their religions all teach different things. Well, so what? You can't put the Divine Spirit in a box. You can't insist that it say the same thing to every different person, at every different time in history. You're not bigger than the Divine Spirit. It's bigger than you. And me. And all of us put together. So don't tell the Divine Spirit what to do. Just do what it tells *you* to do."

Nick droned on for a while about Guru Nanak and the others, then got back to the main point.

"But the first step is to listen. Again: you don't tell the Divine Spirit what to do. It doesn't always speak at mass on Sunday mornings, or at synagogue on Friday nights, when you're ready for it. It speaks when it wants to, whether you're ready or not. So you need to be tuned to the proper channel! You need to maintain the calm, the serenity, to hear the Divine Spirit when it chooses to speak."

"Now take Martin Luther. The Divine Spirit spoke to him, did it not? It certainly did. When? When he was on the toilet, that's when. Alone. Quiet. Released, for a moment, from workaday stress ..."

Nick prattled on a little longer without ever getting to a "therefore," then closed with his benediction: "May the Divine Spirit bless and inspire you all the days of your life." He was vaguely concerned that his attempt to look beatific at the close would just look goofy instead. As he rose and pushed his armchair back, he managed to knock over a light stand.

"Well, whadja think? I thought it was pretty good."

Shawnay shrugged. "Let's take a look." She led Nick in the direction of a cozy editing cubby, with room for only two chairs in front of a broad display screen.

The first thing Nick noticed was that instead of the blank green wall he'd been sitting in front of, the background image was now the beautiful sunrise he had selected. Corny, maybe, but not more than any other religion. Future weeks would feature stained glass, peaceful oceans, galaxies, whatever he could come up with. The second thing he noticed was his tie. More precisely, the lack thereof. He glanced down quickly, to confirm that he was still wearing it. But as he leaned in to squint at the screen in puzzlement, he saw that not only was there no tie, there was nothing there at all! Including him. Just a trapezoid-shaped hole in his chest, with the beautiful sunrise peeking through.

"Hey! What's going on?" He jabbed the monitor with his index finger.

"That's the green screen, hon. The software ignores every green pixel, and replaces it with a pixel from the sunrise picture. Including all the pixels from that green tie you wore."

Nick glowered at her. "Well, can you fix it?"

"Sure can. On the next take. Now, do you want the red tie with the white diagonals, or the powder blue one, like I asked you nicely when you came in?"

December 1: Grand Cayman

Richard Henry Marshall sat on his ocean view balcony, waiting for the weekly update call from the Religious Freedom Foundation's general counsel. It was hot for December, even for Grand Cayman. The pool six floors below looked inviting. He'd promised Christine her first swimming lesson, and was as anxious as she was to get on with it. But she was still at the mall with Judy, getting her first taste of real civilization after arriving from Nigeria. Such an amazing little girl, those black eyes widening in astonishment at every new experience outside the slums of Lagos. Judy had been dubious about adopting another child at age forty-eight, but now the two were inseparable.

Marshall's swimsuit revealed his paunch in a way his five thousand dollar suits concealed. Those fifteen pounds he'd picked up on the campaign trail stubbornly refused to budge. Next year, he'd bear down. He sipped the lemonade Judy had made. The real lemon kind, not the powdered substitute. Maybe he'd ask her to try a sweetener other than sugar in it. Have to start somewhere.

Back in the office, he would have been annoyed that Bickerton's call was now ten minutes late. It was hard to work up any rancor on a day like this, though, with the sun glistening off the waves and the scent of gardenias wafting up to the balcony.

Finally his cellphone buzzed. "Sorry I'm late, Richard," said Todd Bickerstaff. "Some sort of motorcade tied up traffic on K Street—I've been stuck in a cab just six blocks from the office for the last half hour."

"The Lord gave you legs to walk, you know."

"Not in this rain, he didn't. Anyway, I know you have better things to do down there, so let me get on with it. The hot item right now is nativity scenes, as you can imagine. Towns put 'em up, secular humanists try to take 'em down. We've got four cases pending, in various stages. First there's Clarkton ..."

Marshall cut him off. "Same old same old. What about the home school regs? How's my gal Dorothy doing?"

"Secretary Hopkinson is doing great, sir. The regs will drop right after the first of the year, pretty much the way we wrote them. They cut off all school funding for any state that tries to require testing of Christian homeschool students, and they give a preference to homeschooled applicants for federal jobs. Would you like me to shoot you a copy?"

"No, hold off on that. Let's save it for when I get back—something to cheer me up after I get back to Richmond weather."

"It will warm the cockles of your heart, I can assure you. The only other item I have is this toilet case, sir. We're not in it yet, but it looks intriguing. Some women in Denver are claiming they have a right to use their employer's restroom with no men in it—transgender or otherwise."

"Well good for them!" Marshall boomed. "About time somebody took the gay lobby on. Would you want your wife sharing a restroom with perverts?"

"No, I wouldn't. The funny thing is, though," said Todd, "they're doing it on free exercise grounds. EEOC."

Marshall understood the shorthand. The civil rights laws prohibited employment discrimination based on "religion," as well as on race. But since the time of George W. Bush, the federal Equal Employment Opportunity Commission had created employment for armies of lawyers by pushing the law way past the drafters' original intent: cracking down on employers who resisted hiring Catholics or Jews. Now, employers had to "accommodate" their employees' religious practices as well. Like stopping assembly lines so Muslims could pray five times a day, or the "Mark of the Beast" case Nick had regaled Earl with back in North Dakota.[18]

Marshall, though, was puzzled. "What's religion got to do with, um, you know... ?"

"Heh. 'Pee in peace.' That's what their Facebook page says. They say they get their inspiration from God in the john. Like, um, like they say Martin Luther did. Don't want any extra stress, or it might interfere with the signal somehow."

"What are they?" asked Marshall, trying to erase the image from his mind. "Some sort of Pentecostals?" Marshall didn't care for Pentecostals. Once you start speaking in tongues, who knows what might spill out?

"Uh, sort of. I guess sort of Quaker, too."

Marshall cackled. "Todd, if you can't tell the difference between a Pentecostal and a Quaker, you may be in the wrong line of work."

---

18.   Lucy Schouten, "Are employers required to grant prayer breaks to Muslim employees?", *Christian Science Monitor*, May 25, 2016. http://www.csmonitor. com/USA/Society/2016/0525/Are-employers-required-to-grant-prayer-breaks-to-Muslim-employees.

"It's a little complicated. They're not even really Christian, per se. See, they're not just into bathrooms. They're the ones who did the marijuana case in DC last month. And—"

Marshall's face darkened. "You have kids, don't you? You want them shooting themselves up with drugs?"

"It's really not like that, sir. Using marijuana was already legal in DC, but selling it wasn't. It didn't make sense."

"Not much does there. We're just starting to turn things around. But what do drugs have to do with privacy in restrooms?"

"I'm not sure I can answer that. I can complicate the question a little more, though, by adding that the same church is also taking on a corporate wellness case, in which a business wants to require its employees to do things to stay healthy and the Department of Labor wants to block them from doing that."

"Really? *Bertram's* Department of Labor?"

"It's a position they've had for a while, sir. Left over from Obama days. Even Hercules took a little while to clean out those Augean stables."

Marshall gnawed gently on this thumb for a moment. "Sounds like a personal freedom deal. Is that what they're doing?"

"It could be, sir. Unless you're an employee who doesn't like reporting in to the wellness police. Then it's your personal freedom versus the company's."

Without warning, two clammy hands clapped over Marshall's eyes.

"Uh oh, Todd. I've got an emergency here. I think I'm being kidnapped. Hold on."

Marshall spun back toward the sound of the squealing. He gave Christine a quick tickle in her armpits, producing a shriek. "You promised, Daddy! Let's go!"

"Did I promise to teach you something very important today?"

"YES!"

"All right, then go get your Bible and I will teach you another verse."

Christine's eyes did their widening thing, but she'd been prepped. "Mommy already taught me my verse today," she announced proudly. "'And he shall spread forth his hands in the midst of them, as he that *swimmeth* spreadeth forth his hands to *swim*.' Isaiah twenty-five eleven!" She wheeled her arms in a swimming motion that needed a good bit of adjustment.

Marshall had trouble maintaining a serious expression. "Your mother picked a very appropriate verse. But you can't go into the water dressed like that. Did you and Mommy just buy you a new swimsuit?"

Christine nodded vigorously. "It's pink. And Mommy got one, too."

"I'm sure she did," said Marshall. "Now you go put yours on—slowly—and by the time you're done, I'll be ready to go. See, I've already got mine on."

Christine sprinted off the balcony, disregarding the "slowly" part.

Todd had overheard most of this. "Sir, do you need any assistance? I could call the White House to send in the marines."

"No, I don't think they could help. Here's what I want you to do. Go ahead and prepare an amicus brief, or whatever you call it, on behalf of whatever case they're bringing on the bathrooms. Stay away from the drugs. And maybe we should meet these folks, do you think? Do they have some kind of pastor?"

"Yeah. Nicholas Farini. Something like that."

January 7: Syracuse

Jill Matzack nearly skidded her Ford Fiesta into a snowbank as she jerked into the Safeway parking lot. There she found, as expected, half the spaces still piled with week-old blackened snow, and the other half taken. Two other cars crawled the lanes ahead of her, waiting for a space to open up.

Fifteen minutes later she finally made it inside, where her shopping experience failed to improve. What was the point of the pullout ad for the fifty cents per pound special on navel oranges, if in fact they had no navel oranges to sell? They probably had piles of them ten minutes ago, she fumed, if she hadn't been beaten to that parking space. Why did the idiot babbling on his cellphone about what kind of flour he should get have to stand directly across from the other idiot, studying the coffee selection like it was a Rembrandt painting, blocking her way through the aisle? Why were both of them deaf to her normal voice saying, "Excuse me," and both then offended at her outside voice?

On to the meats. She glared at the sirloin for a full minute. Eugene's favorite. Tomorrow was his birthday, and he'd be expecting to come to her apartment to be fed. And, since the timing was right, to get a little personal service present as well.

This is so stupid, she thought. This relationship is going nowhere. But do I want to end it on his birthday? That's harsh. She picked up a sirloin steak, examined the price, then replaced it with a cheaper one that she slammed down into the cart.

Passing the frozen food cases, she eyed her reflection in the glass. It needed work. If she had to go back out on the market—again—she needed to let her hair grow out and pay for more frequent highlights. It would be an excuse to buy some new clothes, but she couldn't afford new clothes. Damn him anyway.

The last time she'd seen Eugene, two nights ago at his place, had been the same routine. She was definitely in the mood, and had brought along a bottle of cognac and a diaphragm. "But Jill," he said, as she began to rub up against him while they were drying the dishes, "isn't this too soon? Your period only started twenty days ago. We should wait a couple of days. *Star Trek: Insurrection* is on tonight, if you want to watch."

The only man in America still on the rhythm method. She'd accused him once of tracking her bodily functions on a Google calendar. Eugene denied it, but she didn't believe him. Long ago she'd given up trying to argue with him about contraception. He was the philosophy professor and she the mere human resources assistant at the Catholic college where they both worked. She wondered sometimes how he could be so adamant about avoiding the sin of contraception, while showing no compunction about that other premarital sin that made the contraception necessary in the first place. Some questions were better not to ask.

Not that Eugene was the world's greatest catch. Most of his hair was gone, and she'd meant to look up whether it was possible for surgery to do anything about that grotesque Adam's apple. But he was bright, and steady, and funny sometimes, and her friends had done a lot worse. He'd even helped her get the job, which was far better than the tollbooth where she'd worked before.

At least, it *had* been better. Now she wasn't so sure. Promotion seemed out of the question. They weren't supposed to be discriminating in favor of Catholic employees, but it sure seemed like they were. Then they had circulated a new employment contract, which they expected everyone to sign. With morals clauses. She had to promise no gay sex, no abortion, no IVF or artificial means of reproduction, no membership in any atheistic organizations, or anything else contrary to Catholic teaching. It didn't mention contraception—they needed to have at least a few employees, after all. Still, Jill balked at signing right away. A hesitance that was duly noted, from a non-Catholic employee who could be easily replaced.

Jill pushed her cart past the baby food aisle—her least favorite part of the store. Instead of turning her head the other way, as she usually did, her neck betrayed her and she stole a glance. A mistake for the ages. There she stood. An economics lessor Jill recognized, ten years younger and far prettier than Jill had ever been. Wearing a coat several hundred dollars more expensive than Jill's best. And at least eight months pregnant—ready to burst. Twins, maybe. Though maybe it was just her slim shoulders that made her look like a light bulb on stilts. She exuded a mischievous glow as she studied a jar of mashed peas, the one that supposedly had Humphrey Bogart's baby picture on it.

Jill could have shot her. Except she'd have missed because of the tears in her eyes.

Your ovaries only produced a few hundred eggs, Jill told herself, all of them back at puberty. You squirted out one a month. Eugene's little calendar made sure hers washed down the toilet. One a month, every month. How many did she have left? A hundred? No, a few more than that. But not that many more.

Marriage would solve both problems. Sex when you felt like it, not when the alarm rang. A baby to love. Maybe more than one. Live it up! Marriage to a professor would improve her precarious financial position as well. She'd gotten impatient waiting for Eugene to ask, so she'd raised the subject herself. "Marriage is a very serious step," Eugene had solemnly intoned. Oh, really? "Not to be taken lightly. Not lightly indeed. Marriage must last forever. Too many people rush into marriage, then rush into divorce. We're better than that. Aren't we? Let's just give this some time. If we do choose to marry, we won't regret having been careful and thoughtful first."

That was fourteen eggs ago.

Jill daubed her eyes. She wheeled the cart around, and funeral marched back to the meat section. There she retrieved the sirloin from underneath a five dollar bag of kale in her shopping cart, and placed it gently back into the cooler.

*****

Eugene's influence might have helped her save her job despite her reluctance to sign the new employment contract. Then again, he probably wouldn't have thought that proper. None of that mattered now, because Eugene was about to be history. And she wanted to hang onto those paychecks long enough to find herself something else decent, and not be tossed back into the tollbooth prison. Or waitressing, worse yet. She'd picked up a few insights working in HR, the most important of which was the deathly fear employers had of appearing to fire someone in retaliation for attempting to assert a religious right. Her HR training had covered the case of the tech support employee who'd won eighty thousand bucks from her former employer after she refused to provde service to a video game company whose games were, in her Christian view, "an abomination in the eyes of God."[19]

She had an idea.

---

19. Eve Tahmincioglu, "Reconciling Religious Beliefs With Work," *MSNBC.com*, September 30, 2007. http://www.nbcnews.com/id/20973408/#.WG7eM_krI2w.

After dinner—kale with a sprinkle of dry chicken, the first salvo in what promised to be a long siege—Jill curled up on the couch with her iPad. She lit a Newport, which Eugene would never have tolerated, and Googled "toilet church." The Church of Inspired Spirituality popped up instantly. Eugene had made her sit through the entire CIS YouTube oeuvre to date. He was in a "publish or perish" panic, toying with the idea of a compare and contrast between the *Doctrines of Inspired Spirituality* and the *Summa Theologica* of St. Thomas Aquinas. Or, as Eugene put it, between the rigorous beauty of intellectual discipline and the roll-your-own-rubbish of this depraved age.

The bits that Jill had picked up while working on her crossword puzzle hadn't seemed all that trashy, though. And the pastor was kind of cute, in a goofy way. At least compared to Eugene, though that wasn't much competition. She scanned the CIS page quickly, hit the big "Contact Us" button, and began to type.

*****

Normally, Nick wouldn't have noticed the question Jill posted. Traffic on the site had exploded after the "Toilet Splash," as Nick liked to call it. They'd have to start outsourcing the response function to some sort of service. Do they do that in India too, he wondered. The thing was, he hated the pregame chatter on TV, so while waiting for the Hoyas to take the court he spent a few moments on his couch flipping through the website. Where he saw Jill's question, the moment it arrived.

He hit the mute button on the remote and munched on a fistful of barbecue chips. This lady might be onto something.

Tap, tap, tap. "Thanks for writing, Jill. You are absolutely right. Sex is part of spiritual life. A major part. Look at the Prophet Muhammad, Peace Be Upon Him. How many wives did he have? And Joseph Smith. He was a busy guy. And you're right about the evil of undue stress associated with sex. Why should it be necessary to endure the risk of pregnancy, of a poor little baby having to grow up in an orphanage, when the Divine Spirit has inspired us with so many scientific ways to easily avoid that? How can anyone concentrate on opening their channel to the divine spark while worrying about an unplanned pregnancy?"

Nick lifted up the nearly empty chips bag, tipped his head back, and shook the last few crumbs into his mouth. God or no God, whoever had come up with barbecue chips had some sort of special inspiration. Nick just wished his own powers of prophecy had been sufficiently refined to have thought to pick up a second bag.

"Jill, if you belong to CIS, you have every right to use contraception, whenever you choose. Yes, it is part of your religion. Absolutely. And if your employer won't accommodate your religious belief by including contraception in your health care plan, shame on them. The law says companies have to accommodate their employees' beliefs. That's how Muslims and Sikhs get to ignore company dress codes.[20] You're not even asking for any special treatment like that. You're just asking for your health plan, that you've earned by your hard work, to cover the contraception your religion requires you to have."

Red barbecue powder was smeared all over his keyboard now. Not enough to be worth licking off, though.

"Stick to your guns, Jill! We'll help you if we can. Everybody, contribute to the Jill Fund you'll see here on the website, starting tomorrow. Support religious liberty!!!"

This, mused Nick, is how pretzels are made. Legal pretzels, anyway. The Supreme Court had said in the *Hobby Lobby* case that corporations had the religious freedom right to keep contraception out of their health care plans. But it had also repeatedly said they had to bend over backwards to accommodate their employees' religious practices, no matter how bizarre. And the DC Court of Appeals had said that employers have to offer healthcare plans to accommodate their employees' religious practices.[21] Not this particular practice, but principles are principles. So what if you had two exactly opposite religious practices between the employer and the employee? Nick remembered reading a Superman comic about the Immovable Object versus the Irresistible Force. He couldn't remember which won, probably because the writer finessed it somehow. Let's see the Supreme Court finesse this one. The brain-twisting might give one of those old farts a stroke.

Actually, it was easy to predict who the winner would be: Peter Spillman, raking in every nickel contributed to the Jill Fund.

---

20. *EEOC v. Abercrombie & Fitch Stores, Inc.*, 575 US. ___ (2015) https://www.supremecourt.gov/opinions/14pdf/14-86_p86b.pdf. David Alexander, "U.S. Army eases rules on beards, turbans for Muslim, Sikh troops," *Reuters*, January 5, 2017. http://www.reuters.com/article/us-usa-defense-religion-idUSKBN14P2AD.
21. *March for Life v. Burwell* (Dist. Ct. D.C. 14-cv-1149, August 31, 2015) http://web.law.columbia.edu/sites/default/files/microsites/gender-sexuality/march_for_life_v._burwell.pdf

Nick glanced at the television, and saw that Georgetown was already fifteen points up. Which was a good thing, because if the game had been tight he might have forgotten to hit the "Post message" button.

January 20: The Palm Room

Nick needed a vacation. The last time he'd gone anywhere, other than the beach for a long weekend, had been with his family to Florida when he was fourteen. Other than lounging at home during winter and spring breaks when he was in school, he'd been working steadily ever since. He wanted at least a week of sun, fruity drinks with little umbrellas, and randy chiquitas. Not much was going on with the church right now, as they waited for the Trabicor case to come to a head. As he shuffled down K Street toward the Mayflower, Nick struck a deal with himself. "If this meeting goes ok, I'll do it. I'll go somewhere. Somewhere warm."

He was heading into the lion's den alone, largely because he was still ticked off at Natalie from two days ago. "You need to be more of a team player," she'd said, during a rare visit to Nick's desk.

"A what?"

"A team player. You can't just haul off and launch major new campaigns without running it by someone first. You are being irresponsible."

"Whoa—whoa—whoa. What are you talking about?"

"You know what I'm talking about. Your bathroom thing, and now this latest brainstorm with contraception. You're just running off with no plan, no control."

"You gotta be kidding me. Did Spillman put you up to this?"

Natalie said nothing.

"What a chicken shit. What, is he afraid of me? Big bad Nick. What am I gonna do, condemn him to hell?"

"Peter just thought you might listen to me more than to him."

Nick didn't bother trying to conceal his contempt. "I'll listen to you, or to him, if you talk sense. I can't believe you have a problem with keeping men out of the ladies room. How can you have a problem with that? Or contraception. You have a problem with saying women have a right to contraceptive coverage in their health plans, regardless of whom they work for? Seriously?"

Natalie studied the carpet. "No, I don't. If we'd just talked about these things in advance, I wouldn't have had a problem then, either."

"Yeah," said Nick bitterly. "Like anyone gives a shit what you think. It's whether Spillman and Mr. Moneybags have a problem that matters. You just carry water for them, like you're doing now."

Now it was Natalie's turn to flare up. "We consult on everything around here. That's how we do business. So we don't have loose cannons putting everything at risk."

"You'd 'consult' any new idea I had right into the ground. You guys still have no clue. It's grow or die. It can't be just a tidy little fracking deal, or it won't work. I've told you that! All this time, everything I've done, has been right on track. We're pushing six figures now on Facebook likes, and after two days—two days!—the Jill Fund is up over $60,000. Why? Because people *like* contraception, and they *don't* like men in the girls' room. Is this complicated?"

Too complicated, apparently, for Natalie to respond.

"All of which goes into whose pocket? Yours. And then you bitch about me being a loose cannon."

"Just talk to us, ok? It's not a lot to ask." She flung her impossibly shiny black hair back over her shoulder and briskly exited.

So he'd emailed her only an hour ago about meeting with the Religious Freedom Foundation board, when it would be too late for her to change her schedule and join him. Besides, he'd be busy enough dealing with one set of assholes, without worrying about how whatever he might say would play with the assholes back home.

*****

Nick pushed through the revolving doors and into Washington history. Trying to redirect his anxiety the night before, he'd read up on the Mayflower Hotel, deemed "the second best address in Washington." John Kennedy's mistress Jill Exner had hung out here. So had Clinton's Monica Lewinsky. Elliott Spitzer had wrecked a career here with his two-thousand-dollar hour with Ashley Dupré, and a Nazi spy had made his way here after being dropped off by a submarine on Long Island. Most famously, J. Edgar Hoover and Clyde Tolson had lunched here nearly every day. Planning their ball gowns, perhaps?

Nick elbowed his way through a lobby full of chattering hospital administrator conventioneers and finally slipped into the much quieter Palm Room. Most people were dazzled by the chandelier, which couldn't have been wedged into Nick's apartment even if all his interior walls were removed. And dazzled he was. But he was also hungry, and the tableful of pastries on the far wall quickly drew his eye from the chandelier. There sat dozens of Nick's favorites: chocolate-covered, *and* cream-filled, *and* honey-glazed delights. He now regretted arriving fashionably late to avoid unnecessary mingling with what he figured would be a hostile crowd. A few cold glares would have been a small price to pay for a couple of those babies.

"Mr. Fratelli, I presume?" said the man at the head of the long boardroom table blocking Nick's access to the donuts. Nick instantly recognized him as the illustrious Rev. Richard Henry Marshall, maker of presidents and chair of the Religious Freedom Foundation executive committee that had summoned Nick to this monthly meeting. He looked ten years older than his picture.

"Yeah," replied Nick. "Sorry I'm late." Only two of the thirty chairs around the table were unoccupied. One was right next to Marshall; the other, which Nick chose, was next to a four-hundred-pound minister who Nick would swear was wearing a pint of cologne.

On the wall behind Marshall was a fresco of a gazebo in a sunny pasture. If I could just slip past him and into that scene, Nick thought.

"Welcome, Mr. Fratelli," said Marshall. "We've had a little trouble arranging our mutual schedules so we could meet. I'm glad something finally worked out."

In truth, nothing Nick had been doing over the past two months would have prevented him from attending this meeting previously. "But," he'd told Natalie when the first invitation had arrived, "I think I want to play a little hard to get. You're the all-time champ at that. Could you give me some pointers?"

She had replied with a from-the-gut groan. "You wear me down."

"Yep. Another thirty, forty years, and I'll have you eating out of my hand."

Nick had daydreamed about wearing a suicide vest to the meeting. That would get attention, for sure. A terrible plan, though, even aside from being utterly immoral. Because even if he wiped out this group there were guys lined up six deep behind every one of them. Guys younger and sharper than they were. Guys smart enough to play the martyr card for all it was worth. It was the *idea* that these guys deserved special privileges Nick needed to blow up, not this sorry gang. And he was halfway home to doing just that. A quarter-way, at least.

"Mr. Fratelli," Marshall was saying, "thank you for joining us today. We're all here because we believe deeply in the cause of religious freedom. I'm Richard Marshall. I'm afraid we'll have to hold off on all the other introductions, as we're running a bit behind schedule. I do want to introduce you to Wink McCarthy, seated to your left, who is counsel for the US Conference of Catholic Bishops."

McCarthy, somewhere around forty, had probably been heavily freckled as a kid, thought Nick. Only a few traces remained. The auburn hair, now thinning, had probably been bright red. Maybe the nickname had come from a black eye. Nick knew the name, though, and knew that McCarthy's law firm—which exclusively handled religious exemption cases—had cleared over $70 million last year.[22]

"Wink was just noting, while we awaited your arrival, that today marks the first anniversary of the inauguration of President Bertram. And what a glorious year it has been! From the new home school regulations to the coming Supreme Court nomination, we're making rapid progress on so many fronts. And to see fresh new faces getting involved, with ideas that are, well, innovative - heh, I think everyone would have to call them innovative—just adds so much excitement."

"An attorney?" Nick asked, jerking his thumb at McCarthy. "I had thought this was a meeting of religious leaders."

"You, Mr. Fratelli, are an attorney, are you not?" replied Marshall evenly. "And a pastor? Or a spiritual mediator, I think you call it."

"I don't think of my members as sheep. Pastors are for sheep, right?"

Not the most politic thing to say, Nick realized. The reaction startled him, though.

"He's a damnable fraud, is what he is."

Nicks ears reddened. He'd expected some friction, but not so vehement, so fast. The speaker's name card read Rev. Adonius Richardson, Second Methodist Church of Nashville. Nick didn't recognize the name. Richardson was the only black person at the table, football huge, and looking angry enough to wreak some highly un-Methodist mayhem.

"Now, Adonius," said Marshall. "We have invited Mr. Fratelli here as our guest. I'm sure that once we've had a chance to chat, we can work out whatever little misunderstandings may have cropped up."

By the age of nine, Nick had watched enough television to recognize a good cop/bad cop routine. That was the best these clowns could do? He felt insulted. He was trying his damnedest to be dangerous, and they were dissing him with this crap? Maybe someone would pull out a plastic gun and threaten to shoot him.

"When we first contacted you," Marshall began, "we were curious

---

22. Patrick Gregory, "Social Conservatives' Legal Juggernaut," *Bueau of National Affairs*, October 5, 2016, http://www.bna.com/social-conservatives-legal-n57982078295/

about your Trabicor case, and excited about what you were doing to try to roll back the homosexual agenda with your restroom litigation. I thought it was downright ingenious. It's high time we started to fight back against those troublemakers. Creatively, as you're doing."

"We're not fighting against trans people, sir. They have rights, too. We're just saying we all have rights, and we all need privacy, particularly when ... you know."

"Yes. Well be that as it may, since then, you've gone off on a tangent with this, this 'right to contraception' theory," Marshall stuttered in contempt. "And we're deeply troubled by that."

Nick's last major acting gig had been as the "Little Blue Engine That Could," back in first grade. Since then, he'd been relegated to bit parts. Which may have been a shame, because the act he put on now was worthy of an award.

"But I thought you *supported* employee religious rights in health care plans?" His mouth formed a circle of astonishment. "The *March for Life* case.[23] Wasn't that yours?"

Employees of March for Life, a national anti-abortion lobbying group, had sued for the right to be offered a health care plan excluding contraceptives. Their employer, the erstwhile "defendant," had colluded in the suit. The main opposition came from the government, in support of its general rule that all employers other than religious organizations had to offer healthcare plans that covered contraception. The anti-contraception employees won.

"Yes," growled McCarthy. "But that was different. That was *against* an evil. This is for one."

"But it's the principle that matters, isn't it? The principle of individual religious freedom. Not one particular doctrine or another. We'll never agree on those, especially if they involve contraception. But the principle that people can't be made to violate their beliefs—surely that's what you're all about?"

"The point is ..." Marshall started.

Nick raised his voice to talk over him. Marshall wasn't accustomed to that.

"Now take Santeria. Sacrificing all those animals. Who's for that? Rabbi, I know you Jews used to be, big time, but you got over it. But when the right of these Santeria witches, or whatever they call themselves, to

---

23. *March for Life v. Burwell, supra.*

sacrifice animals by the hundreds goes to the Supreme Court,[24] you all were right there, sticking up for them. I haven't slaughtered anything! Or tortured any animals, either. All respect, Rabbi, but some of us think the way you and your Muslim friends refuse to anesthetize animals before bleeding them to death, like everybody else has to do by law, is really torturing them. But it's all the same thing: religious liberty."

"Animals killed in the biblical manner feel no pain!" exclaimed Rabbi Epstein. "I will not sit here and listen to an anti-Semitic rant!"[25]

"I do apologize," said Nick quickly. "And I'm for you, not against you. Really! The point is, even though the scientists who do brain scans during the kosher meat slaughtering process disagree with you, it doesn't matter.[26] What matters is your freedom. Yours, and all the Jews, and all the Muslims, and all the Santerias, everybody, to be able to ignore rules they don't like. And that includes Jill Matzack. Her conscience matters, too."

Nick paused when he ran out of breath, giving Marshall an opening. "If I may," he began. "As I started to say a moment ago, before we launched into exactly the kind of doctrinal debate our rules are designed to avoid—"

"I didn't start it," muttered Nick, but few heard him because Marshall kept right on talking.

" ... we are up against a powerful secular humanist foe, and we must choose our tactics wisely. We cannot weaken our coalition, which we have so carefully built. We cannot be a Tower of Babel! Now, Mr. Fratelli, you may not be aware of this, but our foundation played a key role in the campaign that led to the *Hobby Lobby* case, establishing the precedent that corporations may act on their religious consciences just as individuals can."

Nick knew to the comma what RFF's role had been in the jockeying

---

24. *Church of Lukumi Babalu Aye, Inc. v. City of Hialeah* 508 U.S. 520, (1993) https://www.law.cornell.edu/supremecourt/text/508/520

25. Martin Hickman, "End 'cruel' religious slaughter, say scientists," *The Independent*, June 21, 2009. http://www.independent.co.uk/news/uk/home-news/end-cruel-religious-slaughter-say-scientists-1712241.html. Adam Dickter, "Fear over European Kosher Bans," *Jewish World Review*, July, 2002. http://www.jewishworldreview.com/0702/euro_kosher.asp

26. Andy Coghlan, "Animals feel the pain of religious slaughter," *New Scientist*, October 13, 2009. https://www.newscientist.com/article/dn17972-animals-feel-the-pain-of-religious-slaughter/.

that led up to *Hobby Lobby*. But he sat quietly, sipping his water, eyeing the donuts. Nick had simple tastes. He liked to eat. Drink. Exercise his genitals, with a woman when possible, which wasn't often. Read. Daydream. Watch sports. He'd like to play them too, if he were better at it. What he didn't like to do was run other people's lives for them—which was the obsession of every other man seated around this table. Notably, there wasn't a single woman present.

"And frankly," Marshall's voice rose, "some folks think you are undermining that achievement."

"I'm not!" Nick blurted out, doing his best to feign offense. "How can pushing for *more* religious freedom undermine religious freedom?" The Secret Plan in a nutshell! He loved tying people in knots—especially assholes who deserved it. He felt at this moment a kinship with the folks who ran the Satanic Temple, an anti-authoritarian religion/activist group that had demanded and won the right to hand out Satanic coloring books in public schools where Christians were permitted to distribute Bibles—at least until the school district had wised up and banned all distribution of religious material on school property.[27] Of course, this is what the Satanic Temple gurus had been after all along.

Marshall gritted his teeth. "You are a guest here. Please let me continue. It's a question of picking our battles, strategically. And not causing internal friction when we don't have to."

Like calling each other damnable frauds, thought Nick. But he knew that in big-money religion, civility was a one-way street.

"The concern," Marshall continued, "and it's one that I share, is that all the work we did in *Hobby Lobby*, allowing it to live in accordance with its corporate conscience by declining to fund the baby-killing of its employees, will be brought to naught. If you give every employee the right to demand those kinds of payments anyway, then Hobby Lobby and other employers will have to do exactly what we fought to prevent them from having to do."

The room fell still.

"Well?" Marshall demanded. "Do you see the problem?"

"Sorry," said Nick, smirking as he cleaned his glasses on his tie. "I

---

27.   Julie Gargotta and Joel Schipper, "Orange School Board votes 7-1 to ban religious materials," February 10, 2015, *MyNews13.com* http://www.mynews13.com/content/news/cfnews13/news/article.html/content/news/articles/cfn/2015/2/10/orange_schools_consi.html?cid=rss.

didn't want to interrupt again. I guess there's a conflict between one person's freedom and another's. Or, between a human's freedom, like I want, and a corporation's freedom, like you do. But those conflicts exist all the time. I have freedom to play my stereo, but not so loud that it blasts away my neighbors. So governments make rules, and people follow them."

"And exceptions to those rules, to accommodate the free exercise of religion." This came from McCarthy. It was hard to keep a lawyer quiet for any length of time.

"And exceptions to the exceptions. Which keep you guys in fat city, much more than if everybody just lived by the same rules. You should be grateful."

"If I may," Marshall testily resumed. "I follow you, Mr. Fratelli. Truly, I do. My own denomination does not have the same objection to ordinary contraception, which I understand is what Miss Matzack is seeking, as our Catholic brethren do. But, you see, that's the point. Cooperation. Collaboration. Compromise. My denomination, and this organization, devoted enormous resources on behalf of Hobby Lobby, even though what they sought was not our direct concern, because we must all hang together. It was George Washington, I believe, who said that we must all hang together, or we will all hang separately."

"Franklin!" Nick chirped. "It was Ben Franklin. Sorry for interrupting again." Nick made a mental note to remember how the guy who spent his time lecturing about how America was founded as a Christian nation didn't know the difference between Ben Franklin and George Washington.

"No matter. You get the point. There are so many important things we could be working on, where we can agree. To pick the one issue that just so happens to undermine a victory we've already won is shooting ourselves in the foot. Do you understand, now?"

"I understand your position, yes."

"So will you drop the case?" McCarthy again, trying to close the deal.

It could be so hard to keep a straight face. "I'll have to reflect on that. I will have to seek inspiration. I can tell you, though, Reverend Marshall, that your words today have made a deep impression on my heart, and I will keep them in mind as we proceed." He placed his hand over his heart, to reassure Marshall that he knew where it was.

"Thank you, my friend. That is all we can ask. We are a voluntary organization. We cannot force our will on anyone. But in unity there is strength. Please keep that in mind."

Marshall turned from Nick to address the group. "Gentlemen. Before I excuse Mr. Fratelli so that we can proceed to our other business, I want to tell you all one thing, and I want to do so in his presence. We have no secrets here. We are all painfully aware that religious belief is declining in America, that we are losing ground to the atheists, the secular humanists, and the so-called 'nones.' This is especially true of the members of Mr. Fratelli's generation. So when I learned of a young man taking a novel approach to these critical issues of religious liberty, I was intrigued. Now I will admit," he said, wagging a fatherly finger at Nick, "that my first impression of what you were doing was similar to that of my friend Adonius. But instead of a knee-jerk negative reaction, I thought it would be better to seek this dialogue, to show some flexibility in dealing with the members of your generation. That's all I'm trying to do here, Adonius. Not to sacrifice our principles, which we will never do, but at least to make the good faith attempt to adapt our methods of living by those principles to this modern age. Do you understand, Adonius?"

Richardson was silent, but his eyes still simmered.

"So thank you for coming, Mr. Fratelli. If you'll excuse us, we'll continue the executive session portion of our meeting now."

As Nick rose from his chair, Marshall added "Just talk to us, ok? It's not a lot to ask." Nick slapped his hand to his mouth and coughed, to keep himself from laughing.

March 7: Natalie's Office

Nick paused outside the G&H lobby, puffed up his cheeks, and entered. "Tonetta!" he sang out cheerily to the receptionist. "You're looking marvelous today. Could you ask Natalie to step out for a moment?"

As Tonetta dialed Natalie's office, he slowly unzipped his coat and removed it. When Tonetta looked up, she started in surprise.

"What are you laughing at, Tonetta?"

"I'm not laughing, sir. I have too much self-discipline for that. But, ah, *what* are you wearing?"

"This," said Nick, spreading his arms and surveying himself, "is my new look."

"Mm-hmm. It's new, all right."

Natalie pushed through the security door and into the lobby. Her jaw began sawing back and forth. "What is that?" she demanded.

"It's my new look," Nick replied. "Like it?"

He twirled slowly, like a Project Runway star.

Nick wore a garment akin to an over-long dashiki. It hung down to his calves in a single piece, with a rough rope cinch around the waist. The embroidered collar lay comfortably far from the neck, plunging several inches at the top of the breast into a square revealing a scraggly patch of sparse chest hair. The entire piece was a brilliant electric violet.

It didn't go at all with the sneakers he was wearing.

"The logo goes right here," said Nick, pointing to the spot above his navel. "It'll be embroidered in gold. It's simple but elegant—like a crucifix, or a Star of David. I'll show it to you. I'm having ten of them made."

Natalie's face had turned a darker shade Nick didn't recognize. "Come back to my office," she snapped. "There may be clients coming through here."

Nick glanced back at Tonetta as Natalie swiped her security card, and discovered that her vaunted self-discipline had its limits. He gave her an exaggerated wink.

"You've got trademark guys here, don't you?" asked Nick as Natalie steamed down the hallway ahead of him. "I need to get the logo and the vestment design registered asap."

"Are you trying to mock this law firm?" Natalie fumed as she reached her desk. "Close the door behind you."

"Nope. I'm trying to win you more business. Like I've been doing, for almost six months now."

Nick had only been inside Natalie's office once before. He'd stolen a peek at the pictures on her desk, and was relieved to find only her parents, not a boyfriend. Natalie was the image of her mother, with just a hint of her father's steely eyes and jutting chin. He could see only the backs of the frames now, but there were still only two.

Her inbox had two interoffice envelopes sitting in it, and her outbox was empty. Other than a laptop and a lipstick-smeared coffee cup, her desk was empty. Nick's own desk downstairs, by contrast, was so littered with detritus that a casual onlooker would not have known whether it was constructed of wood or plastic. Her walls sported a framed diploma and a Nerf basketball hoop. She had played some ball in high school, and claimed to be the star of her team. She was certainly tall enough for it.

"Look," he continued. "This has to be a genuine religion. If the courts start to see it is just a legal ploy, we'll start losing. Real religions have costumes, don't they? Buddhists have saffron robes. Sikhs have turbans. Jews have yarmulkes. So I figure, I gotta have something, and it's gotta be distinctive. It may as well be comfortable, right?"

Natalie moved not a muscle.

"So, the logo. Let me show you. You got a legal pad or something?"

"Does it have to be so ... purple?" Natalie spoke, reluctantly, as she handed him a pad and a pen from her drawer. "You look like a Martian." "Martians are green, silly," Nick replied indulgently. "Everyone knows that. And besides, this isn't just a random choice." He set down the pad to focus full attention on Natalie's eyes as he spoke the next sentences. "I worked with an artist on this. An art student, anyway. A girl I met in Puerto Rico last week. Prissy. Short for Priscilla, I guess."

There! Nick told himself. She *had* flinched. Not a lot, but her eyes had darted ever so slightly—jealousy, without a doubt. Yes!

Nick kept on without missing a beat. "It's important for branding to stand out from the crowd. That's what Prissy says. You don't see this color a lot—we ran searches on it. And when you offset it with the gold that will be in the logo, it's like surreal. That's the word Prissy used—surreal."

Nick took up the pen and the pad. "So, the logo—it's important for it to be simple. Like a crucifix, which is just two lines, right? Or a Muslim crescent, which is just two curves. Neither one of which makes any sense, when you think about it. I mean, a crucifix is an instrument of torture, right? Who'd want a religion symbolized by an instrument of torture? Prissy kept coming up with these complicated drawings on the bar napkins, and I kept saying, nah, you gotta simplify. And finally, we did: just three strokes. Two straights and a curve. First, a long horizontal line like this. Then, right in the middle, a short vertical. Then, on top of that, a shallow upward pointing curve. Voilà! Can you tell what it is?"

He turned the pad so Natalie could see it right side up.

"See? It's an antenna! For receiving inspiration from the Divine Spirit! Prissy and I went to see the giant telescope at Arecibo, and that's where we got the idea. I got the idea, but she drew it. Just like that!"

Natalie looked up from the pad. "Nick, that's a wine glass."

"No, it isn't," Nick protested. "It's an antenna. Haven't you seen like a Direct TV antenna? Lots of people have them."

Natalie leaned back and started to laugh. "Nick, that's a wine glass. Or a margarita glass. Your friend 'Prissy' has drawn you a margarita glass. Is there something the two of you were looking at while you were so hard at work that may have helped this divine inspiration along?"

Nick took back the pad and stared at it in consternation. "It's not. It's an antenna. Don't you see?"

Natalie covered her mouth with both hands. She was beginning to lose control.

"Well, maybe it's both," Nick admitted, grinding his teeth. "But I guess if someone's first impression is ... Look, just laughing at me isn't helping. I've ordered the tailor down there to make ten of these. They're not all that cheap. I even ordered one for you—you're about the same size as Prissy, so we just used her measurements."

"Oh, did you now?" said Natalie, dabbing her eyes with a tissue. "I'll keep that in mind for Halloween."

Nick slumped back in his chair. His shoulders drooped.

Natalie picked up the pad, tore off the top page, chewed on the end of her pen for a moment, then drew her own three strokes. She turned the pad to Nick. Her drawing was the same as Nick's, except the curve at the top was tilted forty-five degrees to the right. Unlike Nick's, it wouldn't hold any liquid. But it still resembled an antenna.

"That's perfect!" bubbled Nick. "You're a genius! I bet the tailor hasn't even started the embroidery yet. They don't work so fast down there. If I call him now, we can get this fixed in no time."

"Just do me one favor, ok?" asked Natalie. "Give mine to your friend Prissy. I'm sure the two of you need all the clothing you can get."

"Well, then she'll get two," Nick muttered.

Natalie's phone buzzed. "I'll be right there," she said after listening for a moment. "Trabicor's in," she announced. "Bring your wand, Merlin."

*****

"Another big win for the home team?" Nick asked as they entered Peter's office. "Is our streak still alive?"

Peter eyed Nick warily up and down, but said nothing about the outfit. He seemed to have grown immune to surprise. "No. It isn't." He shoved a copy of a document across his desk.

Nick's jaw sagged.

"What happened?" said Natalie. "We all thought this was the easy one."

"That's why we need to be meticulous. Cautious. Think everything through." The last three words were aimed in Nick's direction. "It's not a total loss. The opinion is fairly lengthy—twenty-four pages. The good news is, they accepted that CIS is a valid religion, and that Trabicor has a right to act on its CIS religious beliefs even though it's a corporation. But they got hung up on the 'least intrusive means' leg, so they wouldn't grant summary judgment."

Natalie asked, "So we have to go to trial?"

As Nick tore through the pages, Peter flashed Natalie a quick wink. "Some of us might say, 'get' to go to trial. It'll be expensive. Depositions of lots of employees, expert witnesses, maybe discovery on the rule-making process itself. It's a major undertaking."

A second copy for Natalie now emerged from Peter's printer, and he handed it over.

"Well, we're not dead," said Nick, adjusting his glasses. Admitting defeat was never good form. "Not by any means. Big picture, it's almost a win."

"Do you want to be the one to tell Bruce Nielson that?" asked Peter. "'It'll only be another million or so' is not a sentence most clients like to hear. Especially when they had become accustomed to hearing words like 'win without a fight.'"

Nick didn't look up from his pages. "If I'm the one getting the million, sure. What's his number?"

They read on silently for a few moments, with Nick busily underlining, scribbling notes, and making faces. When Natalie finally looked up, Peter said, "The preliminaries are over. It's now time for the main event. With Matteson Enterprises."

"Uh," said Nick quickly. "We need to win this one first. That was the plan."

"We did win," Spillman shot back. "Not for Trabicor, but for Earl. You needed to establish that a corporation could achieve RFRA protection for its CIS religious views, and the court held exactly that on page twelve. Did it not?"

"Yeah, but ... we'd be better off with a total win."

"We'd be better off," Peter retorted, "if everyone held hands and sang Kumbaya, but that's not going to happen. Do you really think Earl Matteson is going to keep paying your salary for you to jet off to God knows where and do God knows what for the next three years while the Trabicor trial plays out? If who gets the money determines who makes the call, I'd like to hear you make that one."

Natalie reached her hand toward Nick's sunburnt nose and made a sharp grabbing and twisting motion.

Peter filled the silence that followed. "Here is a memo Natalie wrote outlining the procedural steps. The environmental folks in our Wichita office think it's sound. Please take a look, Nick, and let me know if this meets with your approval."

The memo was only two pages long. Natalie never wasted words. "Are you sure about this judge?" asked Nick. He asked Natalie, but Peter responded.

"Of course not. We're never sure. But you can see his record. Appointed by W., a career representing energy firms before that, and a solid RLUIPA opinion in the only decided religious liberty case he's had."

Nick knew the case. The Supreme Court had ruled in *Holt v. Hobbs*[28] about a Muslim prisoner, serving forty years for, among other things, conspiring to murder a federal judge. Gregory Holt was allowed to thumb his nose at prison rules barring beards—despite the evidence presented by the prison of how prisoners could conceal contraband like razor blades or SIM cards in their beards, or in their cheeks hidden by their beards. The court had ruled 9-0 in Holt's favor, with one justice cracking jokes from the bench about prisoners hiding guns in their beards. So when a Sikh prisoner who'd murdered his wife demanded unlimited hair length and the right to wear a turban in prison, Judge Thorvaldson had issued a terse opinion upholding his right. "Religious

---

28. *Holt v. Hobbs*, 135 S.Ct. 853 (2015). https://www.supremecourt.gov/opinions/14pdf/13-6827_5h26.pdf

prisoners have rights," he'd written. "Their guards do not."[29]

"That was an easy case, though," Nick murmured. "This one's tougher."

Peter blew out a breath. "We live in this place called the real world, Nick. Perhaps you've read about it? Now maybe on the planet Halo, or wherever it is you spend your time, you can find us a judge who's ruled favorably on exactly this issue. And whose jurisdiction includes a field where Matteson Energy operates. A judge better than the one Natalie found after—what was it?—thirty-four billable hours of research."

After several seconds, Nick replied. "I'm just saying, it would be better—"

"You're being a coward, Nick." This from Natalie, her first words since entering the office.

More seconds passed. Nick turned back to the first of her two pages and fiddled with his glasses. But the words she'd written hadn't changed.

"I guess it's ok," he finally offered.

"You GUESS?" she hissed. "You turn the whole world on its ear, and now you 'guess?'"

Nick steadied himself. He'd tried and failed to come up with a good wiggle out of being blamed for any failure, so now was the time to suck it up and try to limit any damage.

"It's ok," was the best he could manage. He realized right away it still wasn't the best choice of words.

"IT'S OK?"

In normal times, Natalie was about an inch shorter than Nick. Right now, she was at least a foot taller. Sitting down.

"It's good," Nick recovered. "It's really good. I think this should win. Course, you never know. We all thought we'd do better on Trabicor. You never know, right? But you can only prepare so much. Yes, I think we're as ready as we can be. Let's do it!"

"I'll want that in writing." This from Spillman, softly.

"In writing? What for? Don't you trust me?"

Two pairs of granite eyes answered his question.

"No waffling," said Natalie. "Short and sweet. 'I agree with the plan in Natalie Parks's memo of March 2.' That should do it."

"Ok."

As Nick reached the door, Peter called after him. "Oh, and Nick, be sure to wear that nightie you have on to Kansas. Earl will get a kick out of it."

---

29. This case is fictional.

March 23: Kansas

Nick sat with a pair of beefy security goons in the rear seat of one of two vans parked on a desolate western Kansas plain. He'd brought a tablet, but got no wireless signal. He switched restlessly back and forth between a Grisham novel and a database of fantasy baseball statistics. Draft day was coming up next week, and he had tons of work to do to get ready. But it was so hopeless. Sawamura had been traded to the White Sox over a month ago, and Nick had just found out about it. Hopeless.

Natalie and Peter occupied the middle row. Natalie was pecking away on her laptop, as always. Peter was chatting up Earl, who sat in the front passenger seat. Nick knew the game. The more Peter could learn about Earl's business, the more ways he could find for Guilder & Hersh to be "helpful."

Nick wished he hadn't had so much coffee. Asking if he could climb over Natalie to go outside into the frigid wind to pee was a theoretical possibility, but not one he relished. But here in the middle of nowhere, aka Kansas, there weren't any other plausible reasons for him to want to step outside. "I have a deep interest in the ruts on the dirt road we bumped over for fifteen minutes getting here. Mind moving over so I could wander around and take a look?"

He wished that the Incredible Hulk sitting next to him had some sort of hobby other than cracking his knuckles. And that he had thought to shower after this morning's five hundred bench presses, or whatever else he'd done to work up that odor.

He wished that infernal "Ka-chunk … Ka-chunk … Ka-chunk" of the compressor pumping oil out of the ground would stop. Earl had reluctantly agreed it could halt during the actual event, but hated even a few minutes of lost production.

Most of all, he wished he'd never laid eyes on that Prissy bitch. The one who'd talked him into this ridiculous violet ball gown he was wearing. What had he been thinking? Getting laid, that's what he'd been thinking … but he didn't have to go ahead and make wearing her creation a point of honor. In Puerto Rico, it had been comfortable. Here in late-winter Kansas, it was a farce. He'd tried putting thermal wear on underneath, but that looked too absurd even by Nick's low standards. So he'd have to tough it out. And when his bladder hit that cold air ... "Holy man pees down leg during EPA confrontation." That would make a nice headline for Jay, who was sitting over in the other van with Shawnay and her crew.

Aha!

"Hey, Natalie. Could you scoot over and let me out so I could go talk to Jay for a minute?"

"You don't need to do that. You'll freeze out there. Here, use my phone."

Helpful, helpful, helpful.

"Uhh ... I gotta show him something ... on here. Just move, ok?"

After successfully completing his mission, Nick clambered back into the rear of the van. A few moments later, Hulk glanced at him quizzically. Nick ignored him, but quietly shifted his ankle so he could steal a peek at the bottom of his sandal. Damn! There were no dogs out here, so it had to be from a cow, or a buffalo, or something. How long would it take before *that* smell reached Natalie and Peter in the middle seat?

The Divine Spirit intervened on Nick's behalf. A radio squawked in the front seat. "They just turned onto the road, boss."

"Ok!" yelled Nick, with surprising enthusiasm. "Everybody out! Let's get ready for these dudes!"

"We've still got a few minutes," said Peter. "It's a long road in."

"I want to double check on Jay and Shawnay's setup," said Nick, clambering over Natalie again. Good old Jay.

Nick was able to get his sandal scraped off satisfactorily, at the cost of becoming chilled to the bone. He knew once his teeth started to chatter, he wouldn't be able to stop them. "In th-th-the n-n-name of the D-D-Divine Spirit, I c-c-command you to ..." That would make great television. Moses, Jesus and Muhammad had the sense to start their religions in warm weather locations.

The compressor eased to a halt. Thank you again, Divine Spirit.

At least he wouldn't have much to do. If there was any heavy legal lifting to be done, Peter and Natalie were primed and ready, backed up by Hulk and his compadres from the other van. There shouldn't be any problems, though. If you wanted ultra-thorough legal preparation for something, Natalie Parks was the woman to have on your team. Spillman wouldn't add much, other than taking credit with Earl. A tough assignment, but somebody had to do it.

If it had been up to Spillman, Nick knew, none of them would be here, and he wouldn't be freezing his buns off. Spillman wanted it all done quietly, antiseptically, with a civilized exchange of faxes and pdfs.

But Earl got his way, as always. He wanted to humiliate these people. Strut like the cock on the walk. Let them know who was boss. Make them want to pick an easier target next time.

Nick could see the merit to both sides. Earl's option would do a lot more for CIS's visibility, though. And it would help him with his hidden agenda, especially if Jay held up his end.

*****

After what felt like an hour of pacing about and hopping up and down to keep warm, Nick finally spotted a cloud of dust signaling the arrival of the prey. A dusty green Ford Taurus rolled up. The driver looked at the little knot of people waiting for him, assumed they were there for some other reason, and drove around to park on the back side of the rig. Two of the Beef Brothers who had jammed next to Nick in the back of the van trotted after them.

The driver emerged from the car. He was maybe forty, thin and wiry, wearing a leather flight jacket. "I'm sorry," he began. "We don't want to interrupt whatever you're filming. We're from the Kansas Department of Health & Environment, just here for a routine inspection. We have an appointment with Mr. Prentice."

"Don't think so, bro," Hulk said. "Please step over here."

Though he had used the word "please," the rest of his demeanor encouraged the bewildered inspector and his partner to do exactly as he said. So did the second goon, who stepped to the driver's other side.

Shawnay had marked the spot to escort them to with a little red flag stuck in the ground. There stood Nick, purple robe billowing in the stiff wind, between the inspectors and the rig. The Little Blue Engine That Could knew his lines well. When they arrived, brows furrowed with puzzlement, the goons melted away and Nick held up his palm like a traffic cop. Adrenaline kicked in to calm his shivering. Even the wind cooperated, though that wasn't completely necessary. Shawnay had told him she could redub the words later if they were drowned out in the live action.

"In the name of the Divine Spirit, I command you to halt," proclaimed Nick. "You tread on sacred ground. You have no lawful business here. You—"

"Sir," the inspector interrupted. Nick spotted a name badge: R.

Krueg. "I think there's some confusion. We're from the environmental division, and we have an appointment with Mr. Prentice. We don't mean to get in the way of whatever you're doing. Is this some sort of movie shoot?"

One of the guards started to move toward Nick. From behind one of the cameras, Shawnay desperately waved to shoo him back. The drama would be far greater if Nick could prevail purely on his own bravado.

"Mr. Krueg, you despoil sacred ground. The Divine Spirit deposited precious material here, material for its people to use. To heat their homes. To light their lamps. To safeguard their children." The cornier the better, Nick had assured himself. He lifted his hands. "Praise be to the Divine Spirit! For in its glorious wisdom, it has shown this company, this devout corporate member of the Church of Inspired Spirituality, *where* this precious material is deposited, and *how* it may best be extracted for use by the Divine Spirit's people. You shall not interfere. You shall not inspect. You shall not desecrate. You shall depart! I command you to depart, now!" Nick pointed majestically at the Taurus.

Krueg inserted his thumbs in his belt and stuck out his jaw. "I'll ask you one more time to step aside, sir. Otherwise, we'll have the marshals in here. That's a problem you don't want to have."

From behind camera one, Shawnay shook her head violently at the security guards again and waved her hands in front of her face.

Nick withdrew the document from his left sleeve, where he'd been concealing it, and held it six inches in front of Krueg's nose. "If the command of the Divine Spirit means nothing to the unbelievers, perhaps this will. THIS is a temporary restraining order, signed last night by judge Hammond Thorvaldson of the western district. You are ordered to cease and desist your intolerable interference in the religious exercise occurring here, until such time as the government"— Nick snarled the word in best Tea Party style—"can demonstrate that burdening our worship is the least intrusive means of achieving its purpose. Which it can never do. So I command unto you, depart! Or *we* will call the marshals, and have *you* fined for contempt. Not your agency, but you, personally, Mr. Krueg.[30] Begone!"

Krueg studied the order. He bit his lip and handed it to his partner.

---

30. Patrick Gregory, "Muslim Inmate's 'I Love Bacon' RFRA Suit Proceeds," *United States Law Week*, October 13, 2016. http://www.bna.com/muslim-inmates-love-n57982078576/

Nick loomed over them. Some sort of headgear to go with the robe might be good, he thought, to help with the height thing. You couldn't copy a bishop's mitre exactly, but there must be something to enhance the effect. He'd be damned if he asked that Prissy to work on it, though.

"Could you just back off a minute and let us consult?" asked Krueg. Camera two had scooted behind to line up Nick, the inspectors, and their car in his frame. "Depart!" Nick bellowed. They did, at least to their car. Where they consulted for five minutes, then drove off.

Just like that!

Shawnay was thrilled. She could cut the five minute wait easily, making it appear that the government had scrambled in fear from mighty Nick. Of course it was the court order that flummoxed them, not Nick's antics, but that's not how it would look on-screen.

Score one takedown for the Secret Plan. "Religious freedom" used by evil frackers to foul the environment? *That* would set the liberals in a tizzy, even bigger than the one the religious right was in over the Jill Fund and the sabotage of *Hobby Lobby*. How long would it take for Washington tongues to start wagging about the abuse of "so-called religious freedom"? Probably still a while yet, given how rich and entrenched the God lobby was. Which was why Nick knew he had to keep stepping up the pressure. Which was why the next few minutes were absolutely critical.

Spillman, as Nick expected, remained glued to Earl, who was emitting war whoops that would have made Geronimo proud. As he circled his quarry, Nick tried to sneak a peek at Natalie. The pattern in the past had been that he would stare absently at her high cheekbones, exquisite nose, strong chin, and satin skin. She'd catch him in the act, and he'd quickly turn away. But now at his first furtive glance he saw Natalie gazing fixedly at him. And not turning away when Nick caught her.

A magic moment all too brief, because Nick had one more hill to capture. He quickly abandoned the hope that Earl might escape from Spillman's grip voluntarily, and made his way over to Jay, who was helping Shawnay's crew pack up. Nick tapped him on the shoulder and mouthed "Now."

Jay wrinkled his mouth in skepticism, but obediently set down the carton he was carrying, pulled a pad from his pocket, and marched off toward Peter and Earl. Nick sauntered aimlessly, a few paces behind, pretending to admire the prairie. Jay clamped his hand on Spillman's shoulder and pulled him back. "Mr. Spillman," he said forcefully, "I'm sorry to bother you, but I have a deadline. It won't take a minute, but

I really can't wait. I need a little background on you, and your firm, and the other big cases you're working on. What you've done here is so impressive!"

Peter's annoyance melted instantly, as Nick had predicted it would. "But I don't want to crap up my story with all that," Jay had protested earlier. "Who gives a shit?"

"Not my problem," Nick had replied. "Just do it. Say your editor cut it. If you want to be in on the ground floor of more stories, I need him occupied for a minute."

Nick reached Earl three seconds later. Earl flung out his arms and squeezed Nick in a bear hug, punctuated with another whoop. "Well done, son! Those boys won't be back soon."

"Actually," Nick replied a bit ruefully, "they will. Or someone will. They won't just let this drop. But we can keep them tied up for a few years, anyway. And we have a strong case, one that will work in other states too. There's plenty of less intrusive ways the government can get folks clean drinking water, no matter what chemicals you've pumped into it. Like spending a little dough to clean it up again before it hits people's taps, for starters."

"Whatever you say. I only half believed you before, till I saw those boys slink away with their tails 'tween their legs. Hallelujah, brother! Praise the Lord!"

"We use Divine Spirit, not Lord. But look, I've got something else for you. Something even bigger than this. I'm sure it'll work—even surer than I was here."

"Yeeeehaa!" Earl bellowed. "Taxes! You can get me outta taxes!"

Nick blushed a little, "Nah, not taxes. Judges know where their salaries come from—that's a tough one. Maybe someday, but we aren't there yet."[31]

"So whatcha got?"

"It's a little complicated. And I've gotta tell you in advance, Peter doesn't like it. Thinks it's too aggressive. Not as aggressive as taxes, but hey. I think it's even easier than this, because it's already being done, by the Christians. We just have to copy 'em. And it's huge money. Trump huge!" He threw his hands over his head.

---

31. *Tyms-Bey v. Indiana*, No. 49A05-1603-CR-439, 2017 BL 10320 (Ind. Ct. App. Jan. 13, 2017) http://www.in.gov/judiciary/opinions/pdf/01131704jgb.pdf. (Note the dissenting opinion.)

"Pete's scared'a his shadow. That don't mean nothin'. What is it?"

Let him stew overnight. That was the plan. "This isn't the place to talk, with all the press around." Nick jerked his thumb in the direction of Shawnay's van. "Just call me tomorrow, ok? We can talk about it then. And tell Peter not to shoot me, ok? He really doesn't like it, and I've told you that up front, so I'm not sneaking behind his back or anything. I just want you to have all the facts so you can make your own decisions." Nick could be a little dense sometimes, but he was proving fairly adept at the tricks of the Washington flattery game.

But he actually was operating behind Peter's back, quite literally. And Jay couldn't hold him forever. As Nick headed toward the warmth of the van, where Natalie had the sense to have retired several moments ago, he could see Earl wagging a stubby forefinger six inches in front of Peter Spillman's eyes.

*****

Richard Henry Marshall sat alone that evening in his home office. He'd been working on Sunday's sermon, trying to come up with something a little less political. He knew he'd been overdoing the politics, and wanted to get back to something simple. He hadn't done a "Suffer little children, and forbid them not to come unto me" in several years; if he could just find in his files that one he'd done in Memphis, he could rework it a bit and it would play just fine here at home. That was easier said than done, though. After a half hour of frustration, he'd given up and decided to start one from scratch.

One paragraph in, the phone had rung. It was Todd Bickerstaff, telling him he should look at the video news clip he'd just sent over. "You're not going to like it."

Marshall had now watched it. Twice. He caught himself grinding his teeth, as the dentist had told him over and over to stop doing. He tried turning back to the sermon, but that was useless.

To the kitchen for another cup of lemonade. Then back to the screen. It got no better on the third viewing. Neither did the tension in his jaw.

Marshall had met Earl Matteson once, in the VIP tent at a Bertram rally in North Dakota. Nothing about him stood out in Marshall's recollection. Just one more heavy hitter, more aligned with the party's business wing than its social issues wing. Nothing that would suggest going off the deep end like this.

The kid in the clown suit was what galled him the most, though. So much for the promise to keep in touch. Then again, had Nick Fratelli actually made such a promise? Marshall couldn't remember his exact words. And whether or not he'd made such a promise, any fool could see that what he was doing out in Kansas was counter-productive, and would do far more harm than good.

Marshall had supported the great Southern Baptist switch from denial to acceptance of climate change science back in 2008.[32] "We don't need to fight the environmentalists along with everyone else," he'd urged. "We need to pick our battles." The same thing he'd told the little snot on the screen. But there was something going on here that was different than the battles of 2008. Something he couldn't put his finger on. Something evil?

Another head clearing stroll, this time to the patio. It was almost warm enough to start spending more time out here. Judy's daffodils were in full thrall. Christine's new swing set was positioned close enough for Richard to watch her, but not so close that he couldn't get any work done.

"Todd," he said, after getting Bickerstaff on the line, back inside. "What was the name of Harry's opposition research maven? Pearlman? Something like that?"

"Purling. Zack Purling."

"That's right, Purling. Sharp guy. He's got his own decent-sized PI outfit, doesn't he? Industrial counter-espionage, that sort of thing?"

"Yeah. Except it's not all *counter*-espionage, if you know what I mean. At least, that was the rumor."

Marshall remained silent. Todd was used to long pauses in their conversations.

"Was he involved in the South Carolina business? The Klan pictures? You remember that?"

Todd remembered it well, as did Marshall, because it was such a pivotal moment in the primary campaign. A complicated piece of intrigue, involving crudely faked pictures of a younger Bertram in Klan regalia. They were ostensibly distributed by Bertram's opponent, who denied any involvement, but wound up being badly tarnished for "dirty tricks" anyway.

---

32. Neela Banerjee, "Southern Baptists Back a Shift on Climate Change," *The New York Times*, March 10, 2008. http://www.nytimes.com/2008/03/10/us/10baptist.html.

"I don't know," said Todd. "He denied it, but I wouldn't bet against it. It was a slick deal, whoever it was."

Another silence.

"The Lord does not approve of gambling, Todd. Have Purling call me. Tomorrow."

April 7: Metroliner

"The God business," thought Nick wearily, "isn't all it's cracked up to be."

He'd spent another interminable morning meeting with the Project Bandaid team in New York. He'd just barely caught the three o'clock Acela back to Washington. To top it off, he wouldn't be able to go straight home once he arrived. Somehow he'd lost his damn phone last night, and needed to swing by the office to check his messages and pick up another one. If he spent too many consecutive hours off the grid, the entire universe might implode.

What had gone wrong these past two days? What hadn't?

For starters, there was the fact that he had to wait until at least Newark before the bar in the club car opened up and he could buy something to drink. And some food to wash it down with. He'd been planning to pick something up at Penn Station, but the meeting had dragged on too long for that.

Of course, the five-hour meeting itself hadn't provided any sustenance other than coffee. Lawyers' meetings, Nick knew, were generally well stocked with bagels, Danishes, and healthier-looking fare Nick distrusted, all paid for by generous clients. But Laura Boess would have none of that. She'd been given a hefty chunk of the equity to put this health care play together, and was not about to watch Nick gobble up the profits before they were even earned. Nick had thought "Lunch is for wimps" was just a line from an old movie, but he was learning new things every day.

Laura Boess—Boss Boess as he called her. Now there was a piece of work! A great-great-something granddaughter of Simon Legree, without a doubt. Nick had presented his ideas for a new initiative to Earl the day after the Miracle of Kansas, as he liked to call it. Peter had been involved in the video call as well, but had failed to shoot Nick's scheme down. Earl's final verdict: "Go ahead. I'll front the dough. One condition: you ain't running it. You don't know shit about runnin' a business, and you ain't learnin' on my nickel. Pete, you know somebody who can pull this together?"

Thinking back, Nick tried to reconstruct whether he'd seen Peter Spillman yield a thin-lipped smile at that point. He most certainly hadn't done so in the forty preceding minutes. Yoking Nick to Laura Boess's chain gang was Spillman's revenge for going over his head.

Today's meeting—the fourth in the two weeks since Earl had given the go-ahead—was par for the course. Nick hadn't contributed six words all day, but had to sit through a stream of reports from insurance lawyers, marketing gurus, HR consultants, and actuaries. The actuaries were the worst—which was saying something, in a crowd like that. "If they want those Guantanamo prisoners to talk," thought Nick, "forget the waterboarding. Just make them listen to actuaries for a couple of days. There must be some Geneva convention against that, though."

"The club car is now open," said a voice over the loudspeaker. Relief was imminent. So Nick thought, until he found himself at the end of a line stretching the entire length of a rail car.

Nick apologized for bumping into the shoulder of a gray-haired seated rider, getting only a scowl of disgust in return. Maybe that's Mr. Boess, Nick wondered. The thought made him shudder. At a mid-morning break, Nick had tried to explain to Laura Boess that he didn't need to sit through all this. She reacted as though he'd just suggested she perform a public sex act, then sputtered "Of course you do." And that was that.

From what Nick had been able to piece together on the internet and around G&H, Laura Boess was an investment banker who'd made money along with everyone else in the dotcoms, lost most of it along with everyone else with the subprimes, gotten less than her fair share of the inversion racket, and was overdue for a hit. She spent her life with the bases loaded in the bottom of the ninth. Nick had thought about Project Bandaid—a term she despised, and forbade him to use—as a "someday" dream to toy with at leisure. Boess wanted it up and running by June. This June.

The café car line moved quickly. By the time Nick was back in his chair, with two small bottles of red, chips, and something purporting to be a roast beef sandwich wrapped in cellophane, he turned back to downer number two: his latest legal setback.

*****

Belknap Supply, a Sacramento electrical distributor, had recurring problems administering its employee pension plans. The root of the problem lay with Hank Belknap, its seventy-eight-year-old founder, who cut corners everywhere he could. He kept his prices low and demanded the rest of the world do the same. Without much success, especially when it came to complex matters like complying with the ever-changing legal rules governing pension plans. Hank was outraged by the cost per employee charged by outside administrative firms, so he ordered his in-house accounting department to do the work itself. Work they hopelessly bungled, since the department was staffed by the lowest-paid bookkeepers Hank could find. The day the IRS auditor arrived and began examining the records, she wagged her head in disbelief.

Hank knew somebody who knew somebody who had a cousin who insisted that churches never had to worry about IRS pension auditors, because they were exempt. Hank's local attorney knew nothing about pensions, but he did know that Guilder & Hersh had won some legal press headlines with its religious exemption cases. So he placed a call, and Tonetta sent him to Nick, who off-the-cuff replied, "Sure, you can do that. Biggest scam going. There's billions and billions of dollars in these church pension plans, and they don't have to comply with any rules at all, if they don't feel like it. Retirees are getting ripped off right and left. You're too old to work, you think you've got a pension, and then poof, you don't. You don't even have to be technically a church to get around the rules—you can just be affiliated with a church. Like a hospital. There's tons of hospitals doing this. So sure, you can do that."[33]

So Hank had his el cheapo Sacramento lawyer "affiliate" Belknap Supply with CIS, then told the IRS auditor to get the hell out of his hair. To put it mildly, this didn't work. Now Belknap Supply was looking at penalties far higher than they would have faced had they meekly said "Gee, we'll try to clean this up" back on day one. Before Nick had lost his phone yesterday, he'd listened to an extended rant from a G&H employee benefits partner, who was irate not because Nick was wrong on the law—he wasn't—but because he'd pissed away a major billing opportunity for the firm.

It was all fixable, of course. Maybe not for Belknap, but for a business willing to let a top-drawer outfit like G&H set up its "church plan" exemption in the proper way. In fact, the more Nick thought about it, the more exciting it seemed. The pension world, like health care, involved dollar figures with lots of zeroes on the end. Laura Boess wasn't the only one who found such numbers alluring. It fit the Secret Plan to a tee. But it all involved a lot more work, and right at this moment

---

33. *Pension Rights Center*, "The Facts About Church Pension Plans." http://www.pensionrights.org/publications/fact-sheet/facts-about-church-pension-plans

that added up to two and a half strikes against it.

Nick unscrewed the cap of the second wine bottle. A product its makers actually *wanted* you to consume, unlike the hunk of stale bread with only the rumor of a mystery meat slice within labeled as a "sandwich." He tried again to remember when he had last seen his phone, and when he'd first become aware it was missing. He'd used it on the train; that's when he'd learned about the Belknap problem. Then he'd checked in at the Plaza, and killed time at the bar, where things got a little fuzzy. At dinner with the guys from Zubitril, he'd tried to whip it out of his pocket to show them something on the CIS website. But the phone wasn't where it belonged. So it must be back in the hotel room. After a search there, he'd tried the bar again, without any luck. A pickpocket? Nick scratched his ear, trying to think when that might have happened, and came up empty. Again.

*****

Zubitril. Downer number three. "You're getting picky in your old age," Nick muttered to himself. Six months ago, he'd have given his right arm to be in bed with Zubitril. But six months ago, they wouldn't have given him the time of day. It wasn't until Nick won the DC marijuana case that the bright boys at Zubitril had said to themselves "Hmm. Illegal drugs get sold under a religious exemption. We make illegal drugs. More precisely, not-yet-legal drugs. We need an exemption too!"

Nick was well aware of the unanimous Supreme Court opinion allowing for the importation of otherwise illegal (and highly dangerous) hallucinogenic drugs for "religious" use.[34] But his aunt had damaged her heart valve taking fen-phen for weight loss back in the nineties, and gotten only a small settlement in the ensuing class actions. Nick had heard the story rehashed at family gatherings so often he was sick of it. So he was leery of Big Pharma, and of anything that smacked of a shortcut to the normal drug approval process. Which is exactly what Slick and Slack wanted. For free.

---

34. "Court Upholds Use of Hallucinogenic Tea," *Associated Press*, February 21, 2006. http://www.nbcnews.com/id/11188277/ns/politics/t/court-upholds-church-use-hallucinogenic-tea/#.WHAgY1MrKHs. *Gonzales v. O Centro Espirita Beneficentse Uniao do Vegetal*, 546 U.S. 418 (2006) https://www.supremecourt.gov/opinions/05pdf/04-1084.pdf.

Those weren't their real names. Slick was Jason Lamb, the tall blonde-haired salesman who did most of the talking. Slack was ... Nick couldn't remember his name. But he had his card somewhere.

And they weren't asking for "free." Just awfully close to that. For starters, they'd paid for his room at the Plaza, and for a dinner that Nick had to admit was over the top. A steak the size of home plate, asparagus so well-prepared that even Nick liked it, an endless river of magnificent wine—Nick was learning to distinguish the good from the bad—and a slab of chocolate cake that kept him buzzing like a quart of coffee. A dinner grand enough to carry Nick through such a late lunch without collapsing in a heap. They'd even hinted broadly at some after dinner special entertainment, but Nick was too wary to accept such an offer.

Their product, also called Zubitril, was "the next Prozac." But without the side effects—"especially the impotence!" Slack had found that line hilarious, both times he'd said it. "It's being used in thirty-four countries," Slick had stressed. "Without any problems. Starting with Brazil, where the home office is located. We're all over Latin America, Asia. But here? We've got years and years to go. The big players—the Lillys, the Pfizers—they've got the system rigged against us. If we sold out to them, we'd get approved in a heartbeat. But try to go through the approval process on our own? Forget it. Years and years, millions and millions. So the big bullies win, and the new kids on the block lose, like always."

Nick did not dispute Earl's conviction that he had no head for business. Especially when a hovering waiter refilled his over-sized wine glass every time he took a sip. But Nick had his doubts about whether Zubitril was really "the next Prozac," and whether it had issues these guys weren't telling him about. The kind of issues that could shift this into the "trouble I don't need" category—Secret Plan or no Secret Plan. But if they were telling the truth, the whole truth, and nothing but the truth, then the Church of Inspired Spirituality's assistance in speeding up entry to the US market would be worth a hell of a lot of money. Like, another thousand or so of these thousand dollar dinners.

As deftly as he could—which wasn't very, he admitted to himself— Nick tried to steer the conversation in this direction. He quickly learned how well-prepared they were for such a tack. "Oh, certainly!" Slick had said. "Zubitril USA is already a fully paid member of your church. We have been since January. We love it! In fact," he went on, playing his ace, "we believe Zubitril is *such* a natural fit for a message like yours. As you yourself pointed out in the heroic work you did on the 'pee in peace' matter, and again with the Jill Fund, relief from stress is *critical* to free communication with the Divine Spirit. And of course, let's not forget your cannabis sales case that got the whole ball rolling. Zubitril *annihilates* stress! It's *tailor-made* for your message! Much more than a random weed like cannabis. Your membership will soar once it's your members, and only your members, who have the legal right to purchase Zubitril. It will be a bonanza for you!"

This is when the "Slick" nickname had popped into Nick's head. "Slack" just seemed to tag along with it. Nick tried, a little less subtly, to raise the notion of an up-front advance. Slick understood what he was saying all right, but kept wiggling away like an eel on the end of a fishing line. The best Nick could extract was a vague reference to "eight thousand, maybe ten, sure, but I'd have to clear it with Rio. And they're going to have a hard time understanding why you're not paying *us* for the privilege of earning so much revenue off our product. Maybe that's something we should talk about?"

Nick stopped trying to negotiate at that point. He knew he wasn't any good at it. And he knew that Earl Matteson, as sharp as they came, relied more on his judgment of a potential partner's character than on hyped projections in a business plan. A test Nick wasn't sure these slimeballs would pass.

Plus, he couldn't stand Slack's nose hair.

Maybe the thing to do was to sic Boss Boess on these guys. She'd squeeze them dry. But she was so single-minded on the Bandaid launch, and so demanding that the rest of the universe should be of the same mind, that Nick would be frightened to ask her.

Nick had finished his second bottle and allowed the rhythm of the train to lull him to sleep well before Wilmington. When he finally pulled into Union Station, he splurged on a cab ride to the office rather than his usual Metro, intending to add the fare to his Zubitril expense reimbursement. A new smartphone was on his desk when he arrived. On his office voicemail, there was only one message, the rest having already been dealt with by Tonetta.

"Mr. Fratelli." The voice was male, low, and so quiet that it was a bit hard to make out the words. "This is Zoltan Fiola. We need to talk. I want to give you eighty million dollars."

April 8: Politraffic

Zoltan Fiola did not wish to speak on the phone. He asked Nick to make a reservation in his own name at The Palm, Washington's power restaurant. It used to be, anyway, before the tourists discovered that it was Washington's power restaurant. Or so Nick had overheard at G&H events. Still, he mused, the Plaza and the Palm in the space of forty hours—beats the hell out of Subway and Mickey Ds.

Nick arrived a few minutes early, and waited outside the door for a single male diner. By ten after noon, he went inside to see if perhaps the mystery guest had arrived early. He had, and had left a sealed envelope with the maître d'. "Meet me at the park at Eighteenth and M," was all it said. It was typed on plain white paper, and signed with a huge "Z."

There wasn't much else to do other than stroll over to Eighteenth and M. As he began to cross Eighteenth, Nick spotted a short, spare man with slicked back dark hair rise from a bench to greet him. He was holding a half eaten hot dog. Nick wanted to study the eighty-million-dollar man longer, but the "Walk" light was insistent.

"How do you do?" He clicked his heels, bowed his head gravely, and offered his right hand—the one not holding the hot dog.

"Mr. Fiola?" asked Nick.

"Zoltan, please. It is such a beautiful day!" He leaned in, to speak quietly into Nick's ear, even though there were no other pedestrians within earshot. "And at the Palm, the walls have ears."

Nick thought it was actually pretty chilly. And overcast. Even before achieving affluence, he'd been dubious about street vendor hot dogs. He doubted any ever got thrown away, no matter how long they'd lived at the bottom of the pot.

"Please excuse my starting without you. A thousand pardons. Please—" he pointed at the food truck. "Then we can begin."

Nick settled on a bag of chips and a Diet Coke. He'd eat later. They settled onto a bench still glistening from a morning shower, a sea of mud at their feet.

"We will prefer wire transfers, of course," said Zoltan. "Far more efficient than checks."

"Whoa—whoa—whoa," replied Nick. "For what? What is this about?" Most meetings Nick had attended had begun with some perfunctory small talk.

"Your eighty million dollars. I thought I explained that."

Zoltan was wearing a shabby black suit, a skinny tie, and a collar frayed at the top by rubbing against a poorly shaven neck. At least he assumed that's what had happened to it, since it's what happened to Nick's old shirts. Nick wasn't certain what eighty million dollars was supposed to look like, but Zoltan wasn't it.

"So I'm sure you're about to tell me," said Nick, arching his eyebrows skeptically, "that all I have to do is make some small deposit in your account first to facilitate the transfer, and suddenly I'll have eighty million bucks? Do I look like I was born yesterday?"

Zoltan drew himself up sternly. "Please, do not insult me. I do legitimate business. Strictly legitimate. If you have no interest in eighty million dollars, please say so."

"Could you just back up a little? Who are you? What is this about?"

Zoltan fumed for a moment. "Perhaps I overestimated you. I am Zoltan Fiola. I am a political consultant, well known in this town. Well known, at least, in *influential* circles." To which Nick, evidently, did not belong. "I specialize in political finance. The lubrication of the American engine."

"I'm not running for office."

"No, you're not. But a number of fine men and women are. Men and women who believe in religious liberty. Men and women in sympathy with the important principles of your fine religion, even if they may not officially belong to it."

"Therefore?"

"I connect. I connect those who wish to make their voices heard with those who lack the resources to achieve their noble aims."

A long pause, while Nick pondered whether he was just stupid or Zoltan was being opaque. So he tried to out-opaque him. "What would be the overarching chronology of our involvement?" When all else fails, add syllables. He'd learned that in law school.

It worked. "I represent two disparate groups. Let's call them A and B. They have a concern. Confidentiality. If you contribute directly to a candidate, your privacy is in tatters. You can be subjected to abuse! Each group has an affinity for a separate collection of candidates. If they give directly to the candidate, the thugs at the Federal Election Commission will flush their privacy down the toilet. But if they contribute to your church, the FEC is not involved."

A pair of absurdly high pink heels clicked by, attached to a long pair of legs, only the upper third of which was covered by a tight skirt.

Nick suspected that this young woman would have a profound interest in eighty million dollars. As would many others.

"We don't give money to candidates. We're a church."

"No, but you can communicate with your congregation on candidates' behalf. That's all we seek. Your primary method of communication is the internet, is it not? You will freely choose to promote your religious beliefs by encouraging your followers, and others who may happen to view the advertisements. All of the advertisements will, of course, carry a religious message as well. Here is an example."

He produced a binder from a briefcase Nick hadn't noticed. The first sample read "Roger Lampert: Champion of Freedom." A small CIS logo appeared at the bottom, with "Paid for by the Church of Inspired Spirituality—promoter of Religious Freedom" in fine print. Other tabs listed the candidates on Zoltan's A list and B list, few of whom Nick recognized.

"There's a lot more Lampert here than there is CIS," Nick grumbled.

"Buy your own ads," Zoltan shrugged.

"So we're not really getting eighty million dollars," Nick said, trying to conceal his disappointment. "It's just passing through our hands. You just want to use us, to launder your money."

"Please, do not insult me. We launder nothing. This is *entirely* legitimate money. And we do place a value on the confidentiality you provide. The contributions you receive will total eighty million dollars. The advertising buys will total seventy-nine million dollars. The remainder we trust you will use for your extraordinary work on behalf of religious freedom. So that you will become a far stronger organization for the next election cycle."

That was the quickest seventy-nine million bucks Nick had ever lost. Or the quickest one million he'd ever gained, depending on how you wanted to look at it.

"What's to prevent us from just keeping the whole eighty million and not spending it on these candidates?"

"Your good conscience. And the fact that you only get a small piece at a time, and if you disappoint your contributors, the gravy train will end. And ... if you earn a reputation for double-dealing in this town, you'll wish you hadn't. It isn't worth it."

Nick hated to ask the next question, but figured he'd better. "Is this illegal?"

"I wouldn't need you for that. Illegal I could do on my own. What I need *you* for is to make things legal."

An endless procession of cars snaked up Eighteenth Street. A woman in a blue Fiat leaned on her horn when the car in front responded a millisecond too slowly to a green light. A taxicab aggressively cut off a Toyota Corolla; an Uber logo affixed to its side explained why.

Nick truly did not understand what was going on. But a flat "No" to a possible effortless million bucks seemed like a bad idea, even to a poor schmuck with no head for business. "Ok, I'm interested. But I'll have to talk to some folks first. When would it start?"

*****

An hour later, after finishing a real lunch on his own at McDonald's, Nick plopped onto a chair in front of Natalie's desk. Since the Kansas victory, she'd become available a lot more readily for his chats than she had been before.

"I've just met with none other than Zoltan Fiola," Nick grandly announced, waiting for an appropriately awed response.

"Gwerbl atchit bik mulx," he may as well have said.

"Don't you know who he is?" Nick asked.

"It's a he?"

Nick rehashed the proposal, with special emphasis on the free million dollars aspect. When it became clear that Natalie was as clueless about the political money world as Nick had been, she punched a few buttons on her phone and put a government relations partner on speaker. He'd never heard Zoltan Fiola's name either. "Tell you what, though. It's a big world. There's an outfit we work with on the Hill. Politraffic. They have incredible databases, AI, the works. If there's an answer, they can find it. But they're not free. Is this billable?"

Natalie sprang to attention. This was her favorite question.

Without hesitating, Nick gave him the CIS billing number. "Can you get me in there this afternoon?"

*****

Another hour later, Nick arrived at the Pennsylvania Avenue office of Politraffic—conveniently located near Washington's Barracks Row bars, which cried out for his attention after what was becoming a thirst-building day. The office occupied the space above a Chinese restaurant. The smell of hot garlic and ginger drove Nick crazy—he'd gain two hundred pounds if he worked in a place like this.

Somehow, it didn't have that effect on Marco Boyers, the only staffer on duty that afternoon. He was maybe thirty-five, lean and athletic, with close-cropped hair just beginning to gray. He wore the jeans, sneakers, and frayed t-shirt that Nick found eminently civilized. Zoltan Fiola, he reported after a brief search, was a bit player. Probably not the main guy behind an eighty-million-dollar placement. "What I can do more with," he said, "is the list of donees. We have some sick software that will take a group of candidates, run through their record votes and other issue positions, and find a common denominator. It will even work with opponents—see if a donor is trying to bump somebody off rather than keep somebody in. We don't have much use for it, but it's awesome when we find something."

Nick handed him the A list from Zoltan's binder. Sixteen names, all followed by an R-something: R-IL, R-MD, R-TX, etc. Boyer glanced at the list, ready to type the names into the program, then handed it back with a blink of disappointment. "That's just the DNC hit list. The most vulnerable Republicans up for reelection this year. Anyone who wants to maintain Republican control of Congress will want to contribute to the guys on that list. What else you got?"

"Is anonymity really that important?" Nick asked, as he handed over the B list. "To pay a … a lot of money for?"

"Anonymity? That's what he told you? Gimme a break." Boyer pursed his lips in contempt. "You're a tax-exempt church, right? So some top-bracket dude who gives you a million bucks gets a $390,000 income tax deduction, and then you spend the million to support his favorite candidate. Plus state deductions too, depending. Now if the same guy gives the same million straight to the candidate, he gets no deduction. So which would you do?"[35]

I'd keep the million, Nick thought. But he kicked himself for not figuring out the tax deduction angle before. "So why doesn't everybody do this?" he asked. "Why not contribute through the Catholics, rather than through CIS?"

"Maybe they will, if this play works," Boyer answered. "Catholics don't directly endorse. But plenty of Evangelicals do. Jews, others, I don't

---

35.   Michael Stone, "House Votes To Repeal Johnson Amendment, Making Churches Super PACs." *Patheos*, July 19, 2018. http://www.patheos.com/blogs/progressive secularhumanist/2018/07/house-votes-to-repeal-johnson-amendment-making-churches-super-pacs/

know. The thing is, churches are supposed to lose their tax exemption if they promote candidates. That's a big deal when you live on donations. But ever since the first days of Obama, they stopped enforcing that law.[36] The pastors made public protests about Big Brother censoring their sermons, or some-such, so they just let it go. Guess they figured Obama never would've beat Clinton without all the work from the black churches, so why punish your friends?"

Nick still didn't get it. "Eighty million bucks is a little bigger than just a preacher saying 'Go vote for Joe Smith.'"

"Yeah, but that's how the world progresses. First a toe in the water, then next thing you know you've got the Seventh Fleet. So you think churches ought to be censored?"

Nick chewed on that one for a minute. "What about the B list?" he finally said, sliding it across the table.

Boyers glanced at it. It was bipartisan, with a few more Ds than Rs. Several names had no titles, suggesting they were not incumbents. "Well, this looks a little more challenging. Let's fire this baby up."

He typed in the names, circled his index finger over the "Enter" button, stopped in mid-jab and said "You know, the manual says it works better if you first sacrifice a goat."

"Hurry up," said Nick. "It's almost happy hour."

Boyers stared intently at the screen. "Well no shit," he murmured, as he leaned back in his chair. "Damn! You're good!" He was speaking not to Nick, but to the screen.

"Whatcha got?"

"Hold on." A few more bangs on the keyboard, and paper began erupt from a machine to Nick's left. "My friend," Boyers announced, "you are in bed with the Mumbai Mafia."

Color vanished from Nick's face. "The Mafia?" he gurgled.

"Not *that* Mafia. It's a collection of congressmen and senators who routinely favor India, or oppose Pakistan, any chance they get. F-16 sales, trade deals, satellite sharing, lots of stuff. And these five

36. Stephanie Strom, "The Political Pulpit." *The New York Times*, September 30, 2011. https://www.nytimes.com/2011/10/01/business/flouting-the-law-pastors-will-take-on-politics.html; Nanette Byrnes, "As churches get political, IRS stays quiet," *Reuters*, June 21, 2012. https://www.reuters.com/article/us-usa-tax-churches-irs/as-churches-get-political-irs-stays-quiet-idUSBRE85K1EP20120621

challengers are all running against pro-Pakistanis. Sweet! And here's the clincher—an aggregation of contributors from outside the home states of each member on the list who make contributions to a majority of names on the list, but not to others. There's an overall correlation of point-seven-two ..." Boyers prattled on excitedly for a while. Nick couldn't follow all the logic, but he could follow Boyers's tone of certainty that Zoltan represented a pro-India crowd. With a bunch of red circles he excitedly splashed on the printouts to prove it.

Nick nodded occasionally as Boyers walked him through the analysis, to pretend he was following it. The torrent of words eventually slowed, as Boyers thumbed through the pages and queried the program a few more times. "You said eighty million, right? Is that split fifty-fifty?"

"I guess," Nick replied, trying to remember whether Zoltan had said that. "Why?"

"These contributors have never ponied up more than twelve million bucks before. Total. Weird."

May 22: DVH Back Office

Laura Boess, to no one's surprise, met her deadline for getting Project Bandaid—now officially called "Inspiration Health Sharing," or IHS, up and running. Corporations were formed, payment schedules were coded, accounts both domestic and foreign were initialized, trademarks were registered, ad buys were scheduled. Nick had thought there would be a press conference for the kickoff. But when he mentioned that at one of the last all-hands meetings in New York, Laura had reacted with horror. "You? Answering unscripted questions from the press? Get a grip."

Somewhere, in the Nick to Natalie to Peter to Laura grapevine, Laura had gotten wind of the proposal from Zubitril to use a CIS religious exemption to bypass the normal FDA approval process for their "next Prozac" drug. She quickly finagled her way into control over the negotiations. The net result was no upfront payment to CIS, but a commission on sales of the drug through the CIS website. All of which would be remitted to Boess Enterprises, LLC, as a management fee. "But CIS will get the benefit of all the membership growth," she assured Nick.

Nick thought that was the same deal he'd had for CIS back at the Plaza, when he was wasted, minus the ten grand up front. But he had no head for business.

Shawnay's firm had been hired to produce some of the advertising for the IHS rollout. She could reliably keep her mouth shut, and was cheap compared to production firms in New York. She'd been given a script for this performance several days earlier, along with graphics to help demonstrate the product.

The recording was uneventful. Nick had grown comfortable in front of the camera, after accepting Shawnay's suggestion that he spend time watching other preachers. He even critiqued some of their performances. But since no one else he knew had seen them, he had to keep his advice to himself.

"So, my friends," he wrapped up, "we conclude another broadcast. Please think about this week's message, and about your own healthcare. Are you just part of the herd? Or are you listening to the Divine Spirit's voice? You can't truly say that until you've at least explored Inspiration Health Sharing. Remember, you won't find us with all the others on the benefits exchange. They won't let us on, because our Inspiration program and prices are so much better than any secular insurance plan—and more efficient than the Christian health sharing plans like Bartimaeus that aren't on the exchanges either. You can find us only at www. inspirationhealthsharing.com. That's www.inspirationhealthsharing. com."

"Until next week, may the Divine Spirit continue to inspire us all. This is Niccolò Fratelli, for the Church of Inspired Spirituality."

Nick froze his best smile for a moment, then unclipped his microphone, stood from his armchair and stretched.

"Whadja think?" he asked. "Good enough, or do we need another take?"

"Your call," said Shawnay, "The ending was a little peppier than the first take, but the beginning was weaker. Maybe I can cut and paste."

Shawnay cut the stage lights, flipped off the camera, and headed for the editing console. Nick stopped in the kitchen for some coffee, then joined her there.

"Same intro and close as usual?" she asked, without looking up.

"Yeah. Unless you want your name a little bigger in the credits. 'Produced, directed, and edited by Shawnay Jefferson. Who also makes the coffee.' Maybe with a drum roll?"

"I'm not sure I want my name on this at all," she murmured.

"What's the matter? You're not religious?"

"This isn't religion. I don't know what it is. It's like those late night infomercials that just lie to people and try to rip them off."

"I think you just described most religion," Nick volunteered.

"Maybe. I haven't been to church since my wedding, and that was eleven years ago. But I don't get this 'Inspiration Health Sharing' at all."

Nick frowned. If it didn't make sense to Shawnay, who paid closer attention to his words than anyone else on the planet, maybe he wasn't doing a good job of explaining it. Then again, if people understood it too well ... He needed to hit that happy medium.

"It's just a voluntary cost sharing program. We all have medical bills sometime or other, right? But you can't ever predict what they're going to be. So everybody chips into a pool, and then that pool—after we've covered overhead expenses—is available to reimburse the members as they incur medical expenses. So you don't need that expensive, government-mandated healthcare anymore."

"Reggie says you can't possibly be insuring people for $75 a month. He says even the cheapest insurance costs way more than that."

Nick tried to avoid a condescending tone, but was not completely successful. "I'm sure your husband is a fine nurse. If I ever get sick, tell 911 to take me straight to his hospital. But he's not an actuary. We've hired actuaries, and worked this all out. The numbers add up."

"What do they add up to, other than that limo you pulled up in?"

"That's not mine. It's just the firm's car service. The numbers add up to probable coverage for one hundred percent of all requests for reimbursement that fit the profile conditions."

"*Probable*? What do you mean, probable?"

"I mean probable. Like you're *probably* going to get this video edited and posted for Sunday, right? Unless you get hit by a meteor or something. But unlike secular insurance, we have a safety valve. We can just cut back each reimbursement a little bit, if we have to. That's what makes us nimble." "Nimble" was a word that impressed Laura Boess.

"Cut back by how much? Half?"

"Nah. It'll never come to that, that I can see. Because we've got the profile conditions, and those are gonna knock out a bunch of invalid claims."

"Knock out?"

"Like people who don't follow our requirements. This *is* a religious program, you know. If you don't follow the religion, we don't reimburse you. We don't ask for much—mainly that you log into the weekly sermons. That's why what we're doing here is so important."

Shawnay had three windows open on her computer screen at once, while she was engrossed in trying to splice the two segments together seamlessly. After a moment, she asked: "You mean, if somebody misses your podcast for a week, and gets cancer, you won't pay the hospital?"

"Oh, we don't cover cancer anyway. That's an exclusion."

She whirled on him incredulously. "Oh my God! I can't believe you're doing this. If you don't cover cancer, what's the point?"

"Most people don't get cancer. There are plenty of things we do cover, ok? The glass is way more than half full. But cancer makes the actuaries crazy."

Shawnay looked profoundly skeptical.

Nick didn't like the cancer exclusion, either. He'd had the temerity to question it during one of the endless meetings with Laura's team in New York. The entire room had glared at him like he'd just suggested free Riviera vacations for welfare mothers. So he bit his tongue. Secret Plan, Secret Plan, Secret Plan. Make people understand religious exemptions enough to hate them, whatever it takes. Fuck up that fishing reel beyond repair.

"Look," Nick went on, "a lot of people don't want to pay *anything* for health insurance, right? They'd rather just take their chances. That used to be easy, until Obamacare came along. Even then, they didn't really enforce the penalties for a few years, so people got away with ignoring the laws. Now the screws are getting tighter in some ways, in some states, and looser in others. This is like a middle ground. Simple. A whole lot better than nothing, but set up so people—our people, anyway—can afford it. Is that so terrible?"

"It is if you get cancer!"

Nick tried to conceal his exasperation. It was so difficult to explain sophisticated concepts to a non-lawyer. "But most people don't. So for all those people, it's a good deal. Am I right? And if somebody does get cancer, they can just switch over to one of the programs on the government exchanges. Presto! Those suckers have to take everybody, even if they have preexisting conditions—like cancer. The Christian health sharing schemes don't have to cover preexisting conditions, including cancer, because Congress wants to promote religion. So why should we?"

"Besides," he continued defensively, "I didn't invent this myself. The Christians came up with it, decades ago. There are four Christian health cost sharing companies, they've all got their own limitations and exclusions just like we've got, and it's all perfectly legal. Like that Bartimaeus deal you've probably heard about, with Richard Marshall and LaPelletiere promoting it. All I did was say hey, if Christian churches can do it, then my non-Christian church should get equal treatment, too. So is it fair that Christians can do it, but I can't?"

"I'm not sure it's fair for anyone," Shawnay replied. "Reggie says the whole point of Obamacare was to make everyone get insurance, so everyone can pay a little less than if only sickly people get it and healthy people don't, 'cause even healthy people get sick when they least expect it. Wasn't that the point?"

Of course it was the point. And it was the point of the Secret Plan to ram home to anyone willing to pay attention, maybe even to some who weren't, just how off-the-point Bartimaeus and the other Christian "cost-sharing" scams were, by carrying their logic to an absurd extreme—although the Boess bean counters didn't find it so absurd. Shawnay was being not only unfair, but downright annoying in making Nick look like the bad guy when it was actually everyone else who was the bad guy, and Nick the hero. Which he couldn't tell anyone. Especially Shawnay, who thought only in straight ahead three-yards-and-a-cloud-of-dust terms.

So he raised his palms and shrugged. "It's a big law. Thousands of pages. On one of those pages, it said if you join one of these four religious programs, you don't have to get secular insurance. So now, instead of just four, there's five. One of them for our guys. I don't get your problem with this."[37]

"What about you? Do you have this Inspiration whatever, or real insurance?"

"I pay my $75 a month for Inspiration Health Sharing just like everyone else. My ID number is 000001. Gimme a break. You think I would sell this program to my members if I didn't use it myself?"

Ah, the truth, Nick thought, as he donned his best pose of indignation. Such a flexible, multifaceted construct. Indeed, he did pay his $75 a month, as anyone examining Inspiration Health Sharing's books could verify. What those books didn't reveal, though, was that Nick also had a gold-plated insurance policy with full dental and drug coverage, no deductibles, and premiums paid indirectly from the "overhead" charged by Inspiration Health Sharing. But behind the indignation, he felt like a worm. It will be so great when this is over, he thought, and health insurance can go back to being health insurance—for everybody.

Shawnay edited quietly for a little longer. Then she looked at Nick and said, "Well, you're right about the cost. It's crazy. We're skipping vacation this year, because we just can't do everything. So should I get this Inspiration deal for Reggie and me and the twins?"

Nick had met Ashante and Tyrell at the studio on a day when their soccer practice had been rained out. Devils, both of them. But Secret Plan or not, he couldn't bear to think about someone he actually knew, as opposed to an abstract statistic, being sick or injured and then getting cut off from coverage by one of the fine print loopholes that let him push the monthly contribution rate down to $75. "It might be better to wait," he said, anxious to end the conversation. "We're working on

---

37.   Sandra G. Boodman, "Seeking Divine Protection," *Washington Post*, October 22, 2005. http://www.washingtonpost.com/wp-dyn/content/article/2005/10/22/AR2005102200046.html. There are actually only three such firms, not four. The fourth firm described here, Bartimaeus, is fictional.

some big improvements for next year, that I can't tell you about now, but it might be better not to jump the gun."

*****

Marshall exploded. "May God DAMN his soul to hell!" He hurled his empty coffee cup across his home office. He at least had the presence of mind to aim it toward a couch. It bounced harmlessly onto the carpet.

"Is this deliberate? Is he trying to destroy us? This not only competes with the good work we're doing, but it places us in the *worst* possible light." He was standing, shouting into the phone, his empty hand clenching and unclenching in rage.

Todd Bickerton had heard Marshall angry before. The night Bertram had lost the Wisconsin primary, despite their pollster's assurance they were ahead, had been rough. Especially for the fired pollster. But he hadn't heard any violation of the third commandment before. Maybe the complete sentence cursing of someone's soul somehow cured that.

"A man will sooner forgive you for murdering his father than for tampering with his patrimony," Machiavelli wrote. There might be something to that, Bickerton thought. Marshall's seventeen percent commission on Bartimaeus revenues that he'd worked out with Raymond LaPelletiere, coupled with the cachet of his connection to the new president, was minting money. Bartimaeus sales had tripled in the past six months, and were forecast to double again by the end of the year. Unless there was a sudden renewal of regulatory scrutiny, or unpleasant press attention as had so badly damaged the reputation of Bartimaeus' competitor Christian Brotherhood back in 2000—reputation damage they ultimately solved by the simple expedient of changing their name.[38] Under the radar was the place this business needed to stay. And the place it had stayed—until now.

"It gets worse, sir."

"Worse?" Marshall slumped back into his chair. "How can it get worse? Hold on."

Marshall's door cracked open, and Christine's worried face appeared.

---

38. Abby Goodnough, "Christians Flock to Groups That Help Members Pay Medical Bills," *New York Times*, March 10, 2016. https://www.nytimes.com/2016/03/11/us/christians-flock-to-groups-that-help-members-pay-medical-bills.html.

"Daddy? Are you all right?"

"Daddy's fine, darling. You just run along. Please close the door behind you. I'll be there to read your story soon."

"Worse?" he repeated.

"He's going to sue for subsidies."

"SUBSIDIES!" Marshall struggled to regain control. It took a few seconds, but his voice still wobbled. "He cannot do that. The law is crystal clear. That would just ... "

Todd mentally completed the thought for him. Subsidies would trigger congressional scrutiny of the finances and practices of all four existing Christian health cost sharing ventures. While they were beneath the radar, they could largely do what they wanted, so long as they took care to avoid the "insurance" magic word. Once they started receiving tax money, a swarm of regulators would descend.

"There's that word 'cannot,' sir. Technically, he 'cannot' enter this business at all. There are only four companies grandfathered in by statute, and he's not one of them. But he's going to make an equal protection argument—that it's unconstitutional to make this benefit only available to Christians, and not to other religions. Candidly, I think he has a good case."

"But subsidies? We don't get subsidies. We'd rather not have them than have them! We want the bureaucrats out of our way, not second-guessing every time we move a muscle."

"I know it," said Todd. He was all too aware of the mountain of muck hidden behind the Christian health sharing wall of secrecy. Phlegmatic bureaucrats tracking whose pockets taxpayer subsidies wound up in was the last thing American Christianity needed.

Todd was used to Marshall's long telephone silences, while he pondered. He resented being interrupted with "Are you still there?" Once Todd had sat on a dead line for five minutes before the recorded operator finally started squawking that he should hang up the phone.

"How do we know about the subsidies?" Marshall finally asked. "The podcast didn't mention subsidies. Is it from Purling?"

"Let's just say, we know. He's going to make a combined RFRA and equal protection claim. Since people who use secular health insurance can get subsidies to pay for health insurance, then religious people should be able to get the same thing. I don't think it's quite as strong an argument, but it's not bad."

"Mmm."

Another, even longer silence. Todd summoned the courage to break it. "Maybe we should talk to him again, sir?"

"Talking didn't work too well the first time. I hate to look like I'm groveling in front of a twit like him. Let's sleep on it." In a final burst of exasperation, he added: "Will no one rid me of this troublesome pest?"

June 5: Bettina's House

Nick and his parents pulled up in front of Bettina's snug little house at 11:30 Sunday morning, half an hour before the show began. Nick had spent the previous night in his old room at home a few blocks away in Rockville, which Mama had preserved as a shrine to her baby boy. One wall was filled with birthday portraits, ages one to eighteen, all from the same three-quarters left angle so the viewer could track his development. Another was filled with framed diplomas and certificates, from kindergarten through debate team through bar admission. An Ikea display case was filled with eleven sports "participation" trophies little Nicky had earned by sitting on a variety of benches. On his old desk was a pile of recent newspaper clippings she hadn't yet gotten around to pasting into his scrapbook, in part because they were pouring in too fast.

Nick had already downed an enormous breakfast and was not disappointed at the spread Bettina Gimenez had laid out for a post-show lunch. After the obligatory hugs and cackling, they all began to settle in front of the television. Half a dozen neighbors had taken all the available chairs, so Nick obligingly sprawled on the carpet, carefully balancing a plate of Fritos and cheese dip on his lap. He and Jay had spent a lot of hours on that carpet. First with cartoons, then the Xbox, then MTV.

Another news show was wrapping up. Bettina muted the TV so it wouldn't interfere with the gossip.

"Hey, Pop," Nick said. "Your Father's Day present should be arriving next week. It's a beast! I got a flat-screen just like it a month ago. Seventy-four inches, 8K organic LED, auto DVR, sound you can hear down the block if you want to crank it up."

"Yeah, that's what you said," his father grunted. "Where the hell am I supposed to put it?"

"I was measuring last night. You'll have to move some furniture, but it'll fit. We got Mama's fridge to fit, didn't we?"

Another grunt.

"You using all those features yet, Mama? Like I showed you, you can get a picture on your phone anytime of what's inside, like when you're at the store, and don't remember whether you need milk or not. It'll play music, and you can order groceries right from the screen on the door."

Mama dropped her head sheepishly. "Nah. You gotta come home more and show me again. It keeps the food real cold, though." Another syllable of disdain from Pop.

Nick spied traces of a grape juice stain he'd made, under the couch, a decade and a half ago. Now that the money was rolling in, maybe he could spring for a new carpet for Bettina. He knew that if it had been humanly possible to get that stain out, meticulous housekeeper Bettina Gimenez would have done so long ago.

Bettina squawked and reached for the remote: the TV screen showed "Coming up next: Federal Focus, with Deborah Pugh."

"Quiet, everybody!" she commanded. A bit prematurely, it turned out, as there were several commercials to endure before Deborah Pugh's hawkish face finally filled the screen. "Good afternoon, and welcome to Federal Focus. This week, our special guest is journalist Jaime Gimenez—"

The room erupted in cheers. Only Nick, sitting closest to the television, heard the disappointing part: "But first, we turn to Crocker David, for a report on the new nuclear cooperation treaty between Pakistan and Iran. Crocker?"

Nick studied Deborah Pugh, wondering how Jay would fare with her. Where did she get those heavy black glasses, anyway? Had her mouth been surgically altered to prevent any joy from leaking out? He was glad it was Jay being interviewed, and not himself. So was Jay.

The doorbell rang. Bettina looked around, puzzled. "Everyone's already here. Are you expecting anyone, Nick?"

Nick sat bolt upright, his mouth agape. "Uh, maybe." He sprang to his feet as nimbly as he had at age eight, trailing Fritos in his wake. "I'll get it."

He yanked open the front door. "I hope I'm not late," said Natalie. "You're here!"

"You're so observant. May I come in?"

"I didn't think you were coming."

"I told you I would if I could. Has the show started yet? I brought this for Mrs. Gimenez."

Bettina was right behind Nick. "Who is this?" she asked.

"Oh! Mrs. G, this is Natalie Parks. She's my, well, she's my lawyer, actually." My lawyer, he might have added, whose attitude seemed to have warmed dramatically since a windswept morning on a Kansas prairie.

Bettina surprised Natalie with a bear hug. Natalie responded a bit awkwardly, intent on keeping the box she was carrying level. Nick helped her by taking the box.

"This is an opera cake," Natalie explained. "Is there some place I can put it?"

"Opera? Well, I'm sure it will be just fine," said Bettina. "You go on in. Jay should be on soon."

After a quick scramble, a lawn chair was produced from outside. Mrs. DeAngelo moved into a hallway to sit in it, letting Natalie occupy the armchair above Nick's spot on the floor. His face was six inches from her knee. Nick could see Mama fidgeting with a million questions for Natalie, but Bettina had the sound turned up loud enough to make conversation in the living room impossible.

Finally, after two more Subaru commercials, the screen turned to Deborah Pugh on the left and Jaime Gimenez on the right. The room erupted again. "Quiet!" Bettina barked.

Nick wasn't sure he had ever seen Jay wearing a suit and tie before. Maybe at a dance? Anyway, he looked professional. And calm—much calmer than Nick would have been. All of Nick's shows were pre-recorded, with no potentially hostile interrogator to deal with, and with opportunities for second and third takes if anything went wrong. Jay was facing down the lion in real time.

"Since last fall," Pugh began, "we've witnessed the growth of a new religion, the Church of Inspired Spirituality. Some say this is the beginning of a reversal in the demographic trend of young people abandoning religion. With its aggressive exploitation of new media, CIS has attracted tens of thousands of new adherents, many under the age of thirty."

Make that hundreds of thousands, Nick said to himself. We broke into six figures last month. Zubitril had its benefits.

"Others, however, are concerned about the often litigious nature of CIS, saying it spends most of its energy bringing one lawsuit after another in defense of its peculiar definition of religious liberty. With us today is Jaime Gimenez, the independent reporter who first broke the CIS story last September and who has special access to the inner hierarchy of CIS."

A pronounceable acronym might have been better, Nick thought. CIS could only be pronounced like "sis" or "kiss," neither of which sounded appealing. The silver lining, though, was that some commentators simply called it "the church," which is exactly how Nick preferred it.

" ... does resonate with young adults," Jay was saying. Damn, he sounded authoritative. "For some time now, we've seen so many people calling themselves 'spiritual, but not religious.' This is a religion for them. A religion for *this* century. A post-modern religion where the rules are not top-down, but bottom-up. The Divine Spirit will speak to you, if you will but prepare yourself to listen. That's powerful stuff, for many in my generation."

If Nick barfed now, he really would need to get Bettina a new carpet.

Deborah Pugh was leaning forward earnestly, hands clasped on her lap, pretending to hang on Jay's every word. She turned toward the camera. "And yet, some are troubled. Just a week ago, officials at the Department of Health and Human Services expressed concern over a new lawsuit the church has brought about Alzheimer's coverage in healthcare plans. Can you bring us up to date?"

"The theory of the lawsuit isn't new, Deborah. The Eighth Circuit has ruled that an individual policy holder has the right to purchase a healthcare plan that doesn't violate his religious beliefs, just like Hobby Lobby does."[39]

"You're talking about contraception," Pugh interrupted, in a condescending tone. "That's been the teaching of the Catholic Church for a century or more. This case has nothing to do with contraception. There is no religion that teaches that Alzheimer's disease is a spiritual experience."

"CIS doesn't teach that, either. They just say it's part of the Divine Spirit's plan. No one ever 'recovers' from Alzheimer's, right? All the expensive new treatments do is slow down some of the symptoms—at terrific cost—but they don't cure anything. Nick—I mean CIS—says that's because Alzheimer's is an intermediate step between this life and the next. So it's not a disease to be cured. That's why it's so offensive for CIS believers to pay, even indirectly, for chemical drugs that they believe thwart the Divine Spirit's plan."

Nick snuck a peek over at his father and caught him gazing intently at Natalie, rather than at the screen. Just as Nick had done, all through

---

39. Kurt Erickson, "After lawsuit, Missouri senator enrolls family in contraception-free health insurance plan," *St. Louis Post-Dispatch*, November 2, 2016. http://www.stltoday.com/news/local/govt-and-politics/after-lawsuit-missouri-senator-enrolls-family-in-contraception-free-health/article_a06d85a3-347f-5a82-b84f-b577086c6d02.html

law school.

Pugh peered over her thick glasses at Jay, disapprovingly. She raised her voice an octave. "But thousands of health insurance purchasers, especially those under forty, are now demanding policies that exclude Alzheimer's. The whole point of health insurance is to spread costs among the entire population. If younger people, who are less likely to need Alzheimer's care, purchase insurance that excludes Alzheimer's, that could raise costs dramatically for older people."

About fucking time those old geezers paid their fair share, thought Nick.

Jay shrugged. "When churches and church hospitals don't cover contraception in their plans, Uncle Sam picks up the tab.[40] He can do it here as well."

"That's irresponsible," Pugh sniffed.

Bitch, Nick mouthed, almost loud enough to be heard. But no match for Jaime Gimenez.

"Some people think what the Catholics are doing on contraception is irresponsible, too. Like telling people in third world countries condoms won't prevent AIDS, when everyone knows they will.[41] Anyway, either you have religious liberty, or you don't. That's what CIS would say."

You da man, Jay! Nick rejoiced silently.

"So let's review the bidding," Pugh continued. "We have marijuana sales. We have a case against the Department of Labor rules against pressuring employees into wellness plans. We have a religious objection to laws protecting our environment, when nearly every major religion *supports* protecting the environment. We have employee demands for exceptions to Catholic doctrine against contraception. We have powerful drugs escaping FDA scrutiny. We have a demand for, of all things, a religious right to wear shorts at work. A religious right to wear shorts! My goodness! At least they lost that one."

Nick began to visualize various disgusting things this woman could

---

40. 45 CFR §156.50. http://www.ecfr.gov/cgi-bin/
retrieveECFR?gp=1&SID=142b66b63a215e903291ae0df9f902b1&ty=
HTML&h=L&mc=true&r=PART&n=pt45.1.156#se45.1.156_150
41. Rod McCullom, "An African Pope Won't Change the Vatican's Views on Condoms and AIDS," *The Atlantic,* February 26, 2013. https://www.theatlantic.com/sexes/archive/2013/02/an-african-pope-wont-change-the-vaticans-views-on-condoms-and-aids/273535/

do to herself—even though, if it weren't for the Secret Plan, he would have agreed with her. And what she didn't know was that he'd made enough off the Jill Fund to pay G&H to handle the shorts case appeal. A case even Natalie thought they'd win. Why are shorts so different from hijabs? The Supreme Court, no less, had allowed employees to wear hijabs at work, by a vote of 8-1, and the military had scrapped the whole idea of a "uniform" in favor of a "roll-your-own" appearance code permitting hijabs, turbans, beards, and dreadlocks—so long as you said you were religious.[42] A North Carolina high school student had won the right to wear an otherwise-forbidden nose stud because of her membership in the "Church of Body Modification." Some states even allowed so-called "Pastafarians," who tongue-in-cheek claimed to believe the world was created by a Flying Spaghetti Monster who lived behind the moon, to wear colanders on their heads for their driver's license photos.[43] Shorts made a lot more sense than nose studs or colanders.

Even more to the pants-length point was the Pentecostal bus driver who had won the right to wear skirts rather than slacks, because the Bible told her so. Plus $47,000 for her anguish.[44]

And once they won, the demand for dollar-a-week memberships to let church members wear shorts to work would skyrocket. He made a mental note to talk to Laura Boess about selling their own brand of religious shorts on the CIS website. Designed by anyone on the planet other than Prissy.

"And now a so-called health cost sharing company," Pugh was

---

42.   *EEOC v. Abercrombie & Fitch*, 575 U.S. ___ (2015), https://www.supremecourt. gov/opinions/14pdf/14-86_p86b.pdf. "U.S. Army eases rules on beards, turbans for Muslim, Sikh troops," *Reuters*, January 5, 2017. http://www.reuters.com/ article/us-usa-defense-religion-idUSKBN14P2AD.

43.   Susan Bird, "A Federal Judge Just Told You if Your Religion Is 'Real' or Not," *CARE2.com*, April 25, 2016. http://www.care2.com/causes/a-federal-judge-just-told-you-if-your-religion-is-real-or-not.html "Pastafarian gets to wear strainer on head in license photo," *Associated Press*, November 13, 2015 http:// bigstory.ap.org/4191999673474f2fa25674d5888297f4. "Oregon man wins right to wear 'silly fox hat' in ID photo," *United Press International*, March 15, 2016 http://www.upi.com/Odd_News/2016/03/14/Oregon-man-wins-right-to-wear-silly-fox-hat-in-ID-photo/1161457974560/

44.   Karin Hamilton, "Pentecostal woman wins fight to not wear pants uniform," *Religion News Service*, September 2, 2009. http://usatoday30.usatoday.com/ news/religion/2009-02-05-pentecostal-pants_N.htm.

saying, "offering coverage that experts regard as a bad joke, that could undermine the national health insurance program even further. So is there anything else on the horizon?"

Jay leaned back and paused for just the right length of time. "Yes."

Pugh leaned in. "Well?"

"Assault weapons."

Pugh jerked her head back as though she'd been slapped. "Assault weapons! You can't be serious."

Assault weapons had been banned back in Bill Clinton times, at the urging of urban police departments. George W. Bush had allowed the ban to expire. Quite a few states, though, had created their own bans, which the Supreme Court had let stand—one of the only few legislative victories liberals had won in years. If ever there were an article of faith among the Beltway intelligentsia, it was that the assault weapons ban was an achievement to protect at all costs.[45]

"Believers who live in dangerous neighborhoods," Jay explained condescendingly, "legitimately fear for their safety. You can't deny that. Fear impedes the serenity that CIS believers yearn for to permit unfettered communication with their Divine Spirit. Reducing crime is fine, but there are plenty of ways to do that without trampling people's religious beliefs. Aren't there?"

Deborah Pugh, for once, was flummoxed. She wrapped up the interview two minutes early, then devoted an extra two minutes to touting next week's guest, an expert on America's "crumbling infrastructure." At least that was a public policy the maniacs at CIS couldn't undermine. Yet.

*****

The unanimous opinion at the Gimenez buffet table after the show was that Jay had done marvelously well. "Such a handsome boy, when

---

45. I am not aware of religious exemptions to gun laws, but there are cases of religious exemptions to rules against carrying knives on school property. "Religious dagger OK at Auburn elementary school," *Seattle Times*, October 23, 2014. http://www.seattletimes.com/seattle-news/religious-dagger-ok-at-auburn-elementary-school/. See also John Beauge, "Amish man challenges photo ID requirement to buy firearm as violation of his religious beliefs,'" *PennLive*, October 10, 2015. http://www.pennlive.com/midstate/index.ssf/2015/10/amish_man_says_photo_id_requir.html.

he's all dolled up!" one neighbor exclaimed. Mama cornered Natalie, and peppered her with questions. Where are you from? What do your parents do? Where do you live? Is Nicky taking care of himself? Do you have any nieces or nephews? We love children!

Nick was busy with the opera cake. He told himself he didn't want Natalie's feelings to be hurt if no one touched it. And it beat the hell out of the Jello mold Mrs. Kapinski had brought.

"You sure you know what you're doing?" It was Pop, trying to prevent an overly ambitious helping of baked beans from sliding off his paper plate.

"Sure. Things are clicking right along," Nick replied. "We have some ideas in the pipeline Jay doesn't even know about yet. Diversification—that's the key."

Pop's brows were knitted in worry, about more than just the beans. "You're running in some pretty fast company, is all."

"We have a good team. It's not just Natalie, even though she's a helluva lawyer. There's all these other guys, too. I've got—"

"I don't mean that. I mean the guns. We had a driver shot three years ago, you know."

"Aw, it's not like that. I've never even seen an assault weapon, and I never plan to. It's all just papers and court filings." Nick glanced around anxiously to see if anyone was listening. No one was, but he lowered his voice anyway. "But it's like I was telling you last summer. You saw how worked up that Pugh bitch was, didn't you? She's pissed at us right now—hard to blame her, actually. But eventually, if we keep winning—which we will—then she and all the rest of the 'chattering class,' as they call 'em—will finally wake up and start chattering about the real problem. The high and mighty God experts, who think they can get away with anything, just by being sanctimonious and saying 'Oh, it's our religious liberty.' Fuck that!"

He'd let his voice rise a bit too much. Mrs. Kapinski was looking at him quizzically.

Pop spotted her too, but ignored her. "You just watch yourself, ok? Your mother gets all worked up sometimes. I know you've got your Secret Plan, but just be careful, ok?"

Nick promised he would, then drifted over to rescue Natalie. She was holding her own, chatting away with Mama about her last visit to her cousins back in Seoul. "I guess we need to get on down the road," Nick interrupted. "Lotta stuff we need to get ready for tomorrow. Natalie, can you give me a lift?"

"Don't you want to stop by the house for coffee?" Mama asked. "I can show you Nicky's room."

"No!" Nick said immediately, flushing. "I mean, there's not time today. We've got some big projects cooking."

"I'd love to, Mrs. Fratelli," said Natalie, "but I really do need to go into the office." She thanked her hostess warmly, insisted she keep what was left of the cake, and they were off. Before they reached the highway, Nick suggested that maybe they could go visit the park at Sugarloaf Mountain. "It's got an amazing view," he offered.

"Sorry. I wanted to come because I knew this was important for you and Jay, but I've got two memos due tomorrow. I'm going to be working till midnight as it is."

"Yeah. Whatever. Can you just drop me at the Metro? I've got some basketball that needs watching."

"I liked your mom," Natalie said, with a sly grin.

"She's pretty subtle, huh? Pop, too."

This elicited a laugh. "Must run in the family!"

"Inscrutable, we're not. That's for folks from the mysterious East."

*****

Nick had eaten enough opera cake to hold him until dinner, and he had some leftover lasagna in the fridge, so there was no need to stop at the 7-Eleven between the Metro and his apartment. The basketball playoff game he planned to watch had tipped off at three, but with the new DVR in his marvelous new TV he never started watching any show on time any more. He knew if he flicked on the set when he reached his apartment around four, skipping through commercials, halftime, timeouts, and free-throws, he would reach the final buzzer just about the time it actually sounded. He had it all down to a science.

The asphalt was so hot, Nick felt it through the soles of his sneakers. At least his apartment had good A/C. For the past few years he'd set the thermostat at seventy-five in the summer to save a few bucks, but now he could afford to keep it so cold he sometimes had to wear a sweater. He was dripping with sweat after the eight-block walk from the Metro, planning to change into a dry shirt when he arrived to avoid catching a chill.

Through the lobby, up two flights, around the corner. Nick reached into his pocket for his keys, inserted them into the deadbolt, and froze.

It wasn't locked.

If there were such a thing as a neighborhood where it was ok to leave your door unlocked, east Silver Spring wasn't it. It was no ghetto, but locking the bolt when he left the apartment was as automatic for Nick as breathing. There was no way he had left it unlocked before leaving for Rockville last night. Then again, sometimes he could be lost in thought, especially now that he was responsible for the world's fastest-growing religion. So maybe he'd made a mistake. It wouldn't be the first time.

He previewed what a call to the cops would sound like. "Hi. My deadbolt is unlocked, and I don't think it should be. Could you send someone over to hold my hand while I walk in? I'm scared." None of that sounded good.

"Hello? Anybody there?" He nudged the door open and stuck his head in. It was too dark to see much, but the little that he could see didn't reveal anything amiss. "We're home now ... anybody there?"

He ventured three steps further in.

What happened next was a jumble Nick never did fully sort out. First were the gloved hands that slammed down around Nick's throat and smashed his head against the wall. The wall, of course, on which was mounted Nick's prize seventy-four inch 8K organic LED television. It shattered, leaving two shards in his forehead the ER doctors missed. They had to be removed a week later.

"There had to be at least two," Nick managed to croak to the police officer an hour later, propped up in bed in the emergency room at Holy Cross Hospital. His ribs and groin hurt so badly it was difficult to speak. "One of them had me in a headlock. The other one kicked me. Over and over."

"Did you get a look at them?"

Nick shook his head, triggering more pain from the muscles in his neck. "Too dark. There was a mask, like a pullover ski mask. When they were leaving, I saw one guy with that on. Only clothes I saw were black. I think."

"Did they take anything?"

What an idiot. How was he supposed to know if they'd taken anything? He was practically dead.

"Did they say anything?"

Nick knew this one was coming. To the extent he could concentrate at all, most of his frontal cortex had been weighing the pluses and minuses of how what they had said would play on CNN. It would generate plenty of attention, but not attention that was entirely positive. He was pretty sure Laura Boess would grumble about any message that wasn't tightly controlled. Of all people, Peter Spillman was the one whose opinion he wanted most right now. A greedhead, maybe, but a smart one. Someone who could weigh pros and cons coolly, rationally, on a true scale.

But Peter wasn't there, and it didn't seem right for a crime victim to be asking the cops for a lawyer before cooperating in their investigation.

"Sir: did they say anything?"

He finally hit upon a solution. "I don't think so … It's kind of a blur. If I think of anything, I'll let you know."

They had said the same thing, over and over, once with every kick.

"Leave! God! Alone!"

June 12: Crisfield

By nine p.m., X-rays, blood and urine tests had determined that Nick had no serious ruptures or other internal injuries, so there was no need to keep him hospitalized overnight. He had four cracked ribs, a badly cut forehead, a wrenched shoulder and a smorgasbord of bumps and bruises, but there was nothing to be done about those other than pain medication and rest. Nick placed his second call to Natalie, to tell her he could be discharged, once again pleading with her not to call his parents.

"Don't they have a right to know?" she demanded, just like she had two hours ago. "You'd want to know if your son had been attacked."

"Not now, ok? I can't deal with it now. I just want to get out of here and sleep."

"Where? You said your apartment is a wreck. You have no place to stay."

A terrific question. There was one place he did have in mind. That would be just his luck, wouldn't it? To finally score a sleepover at Natalie's, and not be able to do anything about it once he got there. Fabulous.

"Anywhere. Just get me out of here."

An hour later, a scowling nurse's aide told Nick that someone had arrived to pick him up, then wheeled him out to the lobby.

"Here I am," chirped Peter Spillman. "No, she isn't coming. Now your day is complete."

In other circumstances, Nick might have enjoyed a ride in Peter's pimped-out Mustang. Especially if Peter weren't in it. And if every road-hugging clatter didn't send shock waves coursing through his ribs.

The pain medicine left him woozy, but he was able to tell Peter what his attackers had said. Peter said he'd handled the matter well, not telling the police right away. "We can always do that later. Let's try some other things first."

"Other things?"

Peter touched his index finger to his lips. Nick had no clue what "other things" he was talking about. He dozed off again, waking when the car rolled to a stop. They were at the toll booth for the Chesapeake Bay Bridge.

"Where we going, anyway? I thought you were taking me to a hotel."

"We're going to my place at Crisfield. It's quiet there. We'll get you fixed up."

A nearly full moon peeked through the clouds, down onto the bay. A barge was heading north toward the bridge, and the lights of half a dozen pleasure boats twinkled below. Nick had driven past the sign for Crisfield on his way to the ocean before, but had never ventured in. He finally asked the question: "What 'other things' do you mean? Like a private eye or something?"

"I don't know. Haven't started working on it yet. But I'll tell you what." Nick could see Spillman working his jaw. "There are rules to the game, for a reason. That's what makes us different from little punk third-world hellholes. Sometimes you win, sometimes you lose, but you follow the rules. This"—he pointed at the stitches on Nick's forehead—"is not following the rules. Do you get what I mean?"

He did not.

Peter drove on a few more miles in silence, past a Sheetz convenience store that reminded Nick he'd never gotten any dinner. "Let me put it this way," Peter finally offered. "You don't fuck with Guilder & Hersh. Period. That's all you need to know right now."

Nick dozed off again, awaking only when they reached Peter's house. He couldn't see much, but he heard waves lapping against a bulkhead.

"I'll be heading back to town early," said Peter, "when you're still asleep. My housekeeper, Louise, will take care of you. She'll bring you food and fresh clothes. Anything you need, just ask. But one more thing: I want you to stay off the internet."

"What?"

"Not forever. Just until we sort some things out. And don't use the phone. When we want to reach you, Louise will let you know."

"Oh, come on," Nick complained. "I'm not a baby. I need to know what's going on."

"If I may be so bold," Peter replied, walking Nick back to the guest room. "The one problem everyone has working with you is that we never know what's coming next, until after you've done it. Now I'll grant you, things have worked out well so far. But this is different. You don't know everything we can bring to bear here, and frankly you don't want to know. So, for once, you just have to trust us. And that, my friend, means staying off the phone, and off the internet. Will you promise me that?"

Nick was too drained to resist, so he mumbled an "ok." As Peter headed toward his own room, Nick called after him: "Hey, Peter? If I gotta stay off the internet—did the Wizards win?"

"No, sorry. By the way, the firm has a whole suite at Verizon Center. We can get you in for plenty of games. Hockey, too."

*****

On Monday, new muscle aches emerged all over Nick's body. He never made it out of the bedroom. Tuesday was a little better, but he wouldn't have had the energy to go online even if he hadn't made his promise. Wednesday was better, except for his ribs, which reminded him of the beating with every breath.

Thursday, around noon, Louise stepped out onto the porch where Nick had begun to hang out to enjoy the sun. She was carrying a cell phone. "Do you feel up to talking?" she asked. He snatched the phone, hoping for Natalie, fearing it might be Pop.

"Hey, son!" the voice boomed. He moved the phone an inch away from his ear. "It's Earl. Didja get in any good licks?"

"No, I don't think so. It all happened pretty fast."

"Yep, I guess it did. So how you feelin'? When you comin' back? Life's pretty dull when you wake up in the morning and don't get to wonder what ol' Nick did yesterday."

"Gee, Earl, I don't know. Hurts like hell, I gotta tell you. If I didn't have to breathe every minute or so, it might not be so bad."

"I got crushed by a steer once. Took me a month, easy, to get back to work. But it don't last forever."

"Seems like a month already."

"You just rest up. Now, the reason I called ... actually the reason I waited to call, 'cause I wanted to call right away, but I waited so you could have a chance to set a spell and think before you answer my question. So here it is, straight up: Are you mad? Or are you scared? You have a right to be either one, but I want to know what you're thinking."

Nick didn't answer.

"You there, son?"

"Yeah, I'm here. I guess I'm both. I'll admit I'm scared. I'm not going back to that apartment again. But I'd sure like to kick the shit out of somebody. If it didn't hurt just to turn my head, that is."

"That's fair. Mm-hmm, that's fair. Ok, you take care now. Anything you need?"

"No, I'm doing fine. Louise is amazing," he added, winking at her. "Says she's got a daughter, but she's already married. Other than that, I'll be out of here soon. Thanks for calling."

"We'll be in touch."

*****

By Sunday afternoon, Nick was starting to fidget. The ribs still hurt, but he'd grown used to them. He could keep up with news and sports scores on TV, but he missed all the inanity on his religious news websites. His new hobby was fine Scotch. That's what Peter preferred, as was evident from the offerings at the bar, so Nick decided to up his game. A tough assignment, but somebody had to do it.

A flight of three different brands were poured and ready for a rigorous taste test as soon as the clock struck two, when his morning pain pill would officially wear off. Just before tipoff, Louise walked in, caught herself at the sight of the three glasses, and said, "You have a visitor. If you feel up for it."

The visitor's face, hair, and especially her upper body Nick recognized at once. The name took him a second longer. It was fortunate she had arrived right at the cusp of his peak lucidity, between the pain pills and the Scotch. He blurted out, "Doris! Did you fly that helicopter all the way here?"

"Sweetie!" she bellowed. She threw out her arms, ready to embrace him. Nick jumped back a foot and screamed "No! My ribs!"

Doris rapped the side of her head with her knuckle, in the universal "I'm an idiot" gesture. Then she laid both her hands on Nick's cheeks, leaned in, and kissed him. A long one, smack on the lips.

For the first time in a week, Nick stopped thinking about his pain. "Wow. I missed you, too," he said. "Why are you here? Are you flying me somewhere?"

"Earl wanted a first-hand report. You're lookin' good to me, lover! You sure about them ribs, now?" She flashed her green goo-goo eyes at him.

"Yeah, I'm sure. I could take a rain check, though."

"I bet you could. Anyway, I'm here to make a delivery. Take a look in this box, would you?" Turning to Louise, Doris said, "I hear you make the most wonderful lemonade on God's green earth. Could you spare a little drop for a thirsty girl before she has to get back on the road?"

"You're leaving right away?" Nick asked, disappointed. "You just got here."

Doris pierced Nick with a glare, jabbed her index finger three times in the direction of the box, then headed off toward the kitchen with her bare arm around Louise's shoulder.

Inside the box was a plastic bag of chocolate chip cookies, resting atop two new laptops with assorted cables, a new tablet, and a new cellphone. Nick followed the tech news nearly as closely as he followed the religion beat, and knew that these were all state of the art, fully loaded models. This would give him plenty to do, just checking these babies out. On the bottom of the box sat an envelope, unaddressed and unsealed. It contained three sheets of printed paper, the first without salutation or signature.

> There were three attackers. Security cameras in the apartment building's lobby captured useable images of two of them. Facial recognition software, run against a database of likely suspects, confirmed these individuals as members of the Christian Apostolic Legion, a paramilitary organization. This information was not shared with Montgomery County police.

> In-operation investigation of the Christian Apostolic Legion revealed that it had previously obtained possession of your cell phone. From it, they had access to all of your files, all of your passwords, and all of your accounts. As a result, many of your files have been infected with spyware viruses. These are being cleaned now. Do not access any of your files until Wednesday. Otherwise, you are free to use your new equipment, which replaces your previous devices. A new set of passwords for this equipment and all of your accounts is enclosed. Attached article may be of interest. Return this document to the messenger.

Nick took a deep, painful breath and unfolded another sheet. It was a printout of a page from the website of the Mitchell, New York, *Bugle*. Its date was yesterday, June 11.

Arson Destroys St. Mercurius Retreat Center

> Fires deliberately set by intruders leveled all six buildings of the St. Mercurius Retreat Center last night.

> An unknown number of assailants overpowered three armed security guards on duty shortly after midnight. None of the guards was seriously injured, though one was admitted to St.

Augustine's Hospital with injured ribs. All three were bound, blindfolded, and tied to trees half a mile from the blaze, where they were later found by firefighters.

Chief Edwin Julian of the Mitchell Fire Department stated that "traces of accelerants in all six buildings make it certain that these fires were deliberately set. Whoever planned this knew what they were doing. The buildings were engulfed before we received the first call."

Police chief Howard Jameson announced that he has requested assistance from the FBI to investigate a possible hate crime. Unnamed police officials speculated that the investigation may target the Catskill Secular Humanist Association, which is well-known for its anti-Christian views.

Jacob Napoli, the guard who was injured, stated after his release from the hospital that a blanket had been thrown over his head while he was at his desk. "I never heard nobody come in. Just boom, it's all black, and I'm on the ground. Then somebody starts kicking me through the blanket, for no reason, and I hear this woman's voice saying 'Leave God alone!' These people are insane!"

Napoli added that he did not think the woman's voice had a foreign accent.

Genevieve Dumont, a spokeswoman for the Catskill Secular Humanist Association, officially denied that the association had any involvement. "Violence is for religion," she said, "not for people like us."

St. Mercurius was the headquarters of a Christian military veterans' organization, the Christian Apostolic Legion. It hosted conferences, retreats, and private religious events. The national Religious Freedom Foundation had been scheduled to hold its annual retreat at the center next month.

Holy shit! Nick slumped into an armchair and ran through the article again, to make sure he hadn't misread anything. He hadn't.
Doris towered over him. The corners of her mouth were turned

up, but her eyes were hard.

"Did you ...? Were you ... ?"

She clasped her hands to her breast in shock. "Me? I been busy bakin' cookies, hon. I do *burn* a few now and then, though. Now my boyfriend," she leaned in conspiratorially, "he can be a real son of a bitch. You done with those papers yet? I need to hit the road."

Nick meekly handed up the papers. She headed toward the door. Before reaching it, she turned back and said, "You need to get back to work, bud. Sittin' here feelin' sorry for yourself sucks. And by the way,"—she nodded in the direction of the bar where the three untouched glasses sat—"if you let a fly pee in that Scotch, he'll ruin it."

July 4: The Potomac

Once Nick got his new equipment set up, he found he could work nearly as efficiently from Crisfield as he could from DC. He used his quiet time productively, re-organizing his clippings and exploring new exemption ideas. He deeply resented the fact that someone had intruded on his files, even booby-trapped them. The files were him—the way he thought and viewed the world, laid bare for anyone who took the time to understand how they worked. The Secret Plan wasn't spelled out in so many words, but it may as well have been. Maybe the Christian Apostolic Legion thugs wouldn't do that, but if RFF were involved—as he suspected more and more—then it was like playing poker with the other guy able to see your cards.

Then again, he thought he was holding four aces, so maybe it didn't matter whether RFF could see them or not.

Then again, how many westerns had he watched where one guy at the poker table pulled a gun on the guy with all the chips and shot him?

Then again, Earl, Doris, maybe Peter, and others he'd never met had gone way, way out on a limb for him. Was Natalie involved, too? He doubted it, but he wasn't sure. It didn't matter, anyway. There were enough others who'd stuck up for him that he just couldn't let them down.

*****

By the end of the month, Nick was itching to leave. Peter was ignoring his emails to that effect, but finally Nick got him on the phone to make his case.

"But where are you going to stay? You can't go back to your place," asked Peter.

"I'll find something. This is starting to feel like a prison. If you're too busy to get me yourself, send somebody else to pick me up. Besides, you're almost out of Scotch."

"What! How can I be almost out? I had half a dozen cases."

"Well, you're almost out of the Bowmore. There's other stuff here, but I decided I like the Bowmore best."

"Did you, now? Did you also know it's over four hundred dollars a bottle?"

He did. They all tasted pretty much the same, so he looked up the prices and decided to hone in on the most expensive brand, when someone else was paying. On his own nickel, Bud Lite still hit the spot.

"Whatever," Nick replied. "Just get me out of here."

"I'll tell you what," Peter said. "I'll pick you up on the morning of the fourth. Be ready to go by, say, ten o'clock. Then we can watch the fireworks that night." "Uhhh ... ok, other than the fireworks part. I've got this special spot I go to. Best view in the city. So thanks for the offer, but I want to go to my spot." With Kyle, and Kyle's latest girlfriend. Who maybe had a roommate, or a sister? Crisfield was a lonely spot.

"You do not have the best view in the city," said Peter. "Where we're going is far better, I can assure you."

"Peter, I've had lunch up on your rooftop, man. It's not that great. Where I go is right underneath the action."

"Be ready at ten on the fourth. It will be a busy day."

*****

Nick was packed and ready by eight. He was sitting in the kitchen, sifting through the previous day's religion news, when Peter walked in.

"I didn't hear you drive up," said Nick.

"Who said anything about driving?" Peter summoned Nick to follow him toward the back of the house. Alongside the pier was an enormous yacht, which Nick later learned was over twenty yards in length. "The traffic is horrific on holidays. This will get us back in no time."

"Ok," said Nick. "I'm officially impressed. Now you're going to tell me this is where we watch the fireworks from?"

Peter beamed. "With a case of Bowmore on board."

They reached the Alexandria wharf around five pm. There was the sight he'd longed for: Natalie, in an oversized floppy yellow hat, looking happy to see him. For once, though, the glow of Natalie's sun did not obscure all objects around her. Especially the object named Laura Boess. And the stocky fellow with the shaved head and no discernible neck standing next to her.

"You're kidding," Nick protested out of the side of his mouth to Peter, while waving gaily at Natalie.

"Ralph Boess. You'll be staying with him and Laura tonight, and maybe longer. He's into a little of everything—construction, real estate, home improvement. He's one of the bigger private clients in our New York office. He'll help you find a new place to live."

"Staying with them tonight? I'll get you for this."

*****

There were a dozen other passengers in total. Nick tried to engage, but he had no more in common with them than he'd had at the firm reception a year ago. One in particular, a doctor who owned a chain of nursing homes, was downright hostile.

"Have you ever seen anyone with Alzheimer's?" he demanded. Without waiting for a response he added, "There's nothing remotely holy about it. I think what you're doing is a disgrace."

"I'm not hurting anyone with Alzheimer's. I'm trying to give them some dignity."

The doctor shook his head in disgust. "You know exactly what you're doing. You're tearing the foundation out of the whole financial structure that allows us to give these patients the treatment they need. Of course younger people want insurance that doesn't cover Alzheimer's. They're not stupid. That just drives up the premiums for older people."

Nick shrugged. "The system says you get religious liberty. If you don't want to pay for a plan with contraception coverage for your daughters because of your religious beliefs, you don't have to. Courts are clear on that.[46] So if you don't want Alzheimer's coverage because of your religious beliefs, you shouldn't have to pay for that, either. What's the diff?"

"There's a huge difference, and you know it. A handful of troglodyte fathers opting out of birth control for their daughters, a cost that's peanuts, versus millions of young people opting out of a cost that's hundreds of billions. It's totally different."

He was right, of course. Except for the "millions" part—interest was nowhere near that level. Yet. But as word spread that young people could save hundreds of dollars a year on their mandatory health

---

46. Kurt Erickson, "After lawsuit, Missouri senator enrolls family in contraception-free health insurance plan," *St. Louis Post-Dispatch*, November 2, 2016. http://www.stltoday.com/news/local/govt-and-politics/after-lawsuit-missouri-senator-enrolls-family-in-contraception-free-health/article_a06d85a3-347f-5a82-b84f-b577086c6d02.html. *Wieland v. Dept. of Health & Human Services*, Case No. 4:13-cv-01577-JCH, E.D. Mo. 2016. http://www.becketfund.org/wp-content/uploads/2016/07/Wieland-Summary-Judgment.pdf.

insurance by demanding a plan that didn't cover Alzheimer's, based on a religious exemption, the numbers were bound to grow. What better way to highlight the absurdity of the loophole for "troglodyte fathers" than widening it enough to drive an Alzheimer's truck through? But this guy would never understand all that. So Nick just shook his head, and said, "Principles are principles. You're saying that some religions get liberty, and others don't?"

"Well then change the whole thing. Make everybody pay for contraception, and everybody pay for Alzheimer's. What's wrong with that?"

Score one convert for the Secret Plan! Another hundred million or so, and victory would be his.

"Because I haven't been elected king yet. Now, if the law gets changed like you just said then, yeah, it would be consistent. Sure."

"You're a dangerous fraud."

Nick polished off his second Bowmore's. If he'd had none at all, he'd have mumbled something and slunk away. If he'd had four, he'd have done the same, maybe after giggling first. Instead, it occurred to him to ask, "You own nursing homes, right?"

"I do."

"Ah," said Nick, shutting his eyes and throwing his head back in a "Eureka!" moment. "Now I understand. Fewer dollars for Alzheimer's means fewer dollars in your pocket!"

"Now see here—"

"Dr. Arrigo!" said Natalie, leaping to the rescue. "I know Rachel has been dying to talk to you." She grabbed his shoulder with one hand and his wrist with the other, forcibly turning him ninety degrees in a move that a tango master would have applauded—giving her extra credit for simultaneously inserting her body between the doctor and Nick and piercing Nick between the eyes with a dagger.

Nick took a step back from the frying pan, directly into the fire—in the person of Laura Boess.

"Do you want to know what I don't understand?" she demanded.

Nick looked about, and saw that the railing on the side of the boat was only two running steps away. He could clear it easily and find himself in the relative safety of the Potomac River. This gave him a confidence sorely lacking when she had him cornered in her forty-fifth floor conference room with the unbreakable glass.

He began attempting to formulate the response that no, he didn't want to know what she didn't understand, because she was so much smarter than he was, as she had pointed out often before, so there was no way he could even begin to understand anything that she couldn't, so why bother trying?

Before he could string all that logic together properly, though, she said, "I don't understand why you're cannibalizing your own business."

"I'm what?"

"You heard me." He had. "You're cannibalizing your own business. Eating it alive."

The mental image of Laura Boess eating someone alive made Nick shudder.

"I'm sorry. I think. How'm I doing that?"

"First you lead us all down the path of Inspiration Health Sharing. Hundreds of people, thousands of man-hours, millions of dollars spent creating real value. Then you wake up one morning, and, just on a lark, you kick the props out from underneath it."

"I did?"

Scorn poured from Laura's eyes like lava from Vesuvius. "Cost differential!" she barked. "We're the most inexpensive alternative to traditional Obamacare. By a huge margin. We're the only game in town that can do that, unless you're a born-again maniac. So what do you haul off and do, consulting no one? You lower the cost of conventional plans, our competitors, by giving them an easy way to cut premiums by skipping the Alzheimer's coverage. Our main selling point for millennials, pissed away. What were you thinking?"

"Oh, quit ragging on him," said a gravelly voice from behind Nick's shoulder.

Nick turned quickly, almost knocking into Ralph Boess's Scotch.

"Shut up," Laura shot at him. "We're having a private conversation. And put out that cigar. It stinks."

Nick agreed with her about the cigar, but was so relieved at the change of subject that he thought about asking Ralph if he had any extras.

"We're outside," Ralph shot back. "Or didn't you notice? And we're on a boat. Having a party. So quit ragging on him."

She didn't actually bite him, but she looked like she was considering it. "We'll deal with this later," she said darkly, then stalked toward the front of the vessel.

Nick had no doubt that they would. Forgetting screw-ups, real or imagined, was not a part of Laura Boess's makeup. He was relieved, though, at the chance to spend some time concocting an explanation, especially one that might be better received than the truth: that he'd never stopped to consider the effect one bright idea of his might have on another. What fun is there in doing *that* all the time?

"So you're the great creative genius?" Ralph asked.

Nick feigned turning around, as though to identify someone else whom Ralph must be addressing. With what he hoped was a winning grin, he replied, "That would be me. My genius seems a little unappreciated this evening, though."

Ralph waved his cigar dismissively. "Don't mind her. I've had thirty years of being a hopeless incompetent—all the way to the bank. Just let it bounce off. Anyway, I understand you're looking for a house."

"No, just an apartment. I can't stay in Silver Spring. Something closer to the office would be nice."

Ralph ticked off a few options. When he mentioned the word "Watergate," Nick snapped to attention. "You mean the Nixon Watergate?"

"Yeah, the Nixon Watergate. It's not all offices, like some people think. It has apartments too. A little pricey, but there are some small units you could afford."

Nick, the self-styled master conspirator, was tickled at the thought of living in Nixon's Watergate. "Awesome! If I can get something there, that's what I want."

"Done. Anything else you need?"

There sure is, thought Nick. Stick close by in case she comes back. With that end squarely in mind, he asked, "What else do you do? I hear you're into development, home improvement, all sorts of things."

Ralph launched into a litany of all the different pots he had his fingers in. Nick steered him toward a discussion of the battles he'd fought with zoning boards. Ralph had a low opinion of the land use regulation process.

"What if," Nick asked, "there was one big project where you could wave a magic wand and poof!—the zoning problem disappears. What would that be?"

Without needing to think hard about it, Ralph mentioned some undeveloped land he owned on Cape Cod. "The red tape is unbelievable. And it's not just red tape—they just won't let you do anything at all, no matter how much bureaucracy you go through. They got theirs, and nobody else gets anything. Have you got a creative genius way around that?"

Nick pursed his lips, squinted, and cocked his head slowly to one side. He tried to make it appear that he was thinking hard about the question. In fact, he believed he had a can't-miss wiggle around any kind of zoning obstacle, and was in search of an obstacle big enough to make the effort worthwhile. But you don't want your customer to think what you're doing for him is too easy.

"We should talk," he finally said. "Explore the possibilities. I may have an idea that could help. But I have another question for you—completely different. With all the different projects you're involved with, do you get caught up in much litigation?"

"Don't you know it," Ralph said bitterly. "I singlehandedly keep your New York office in business."

"Technically, I'm not with G&H. But what kind of litigation?"

"The biggest pain in the ass is the home improvement business. People expect to pay Chevy prices and get Cadillacs. When they don't, they sue. You wouldn't believe all the wacky theories trial lawyers come up with. 'Well the picture on the internet showed a granite counter-top, but all I got was Formica.' Yeah, lady, right. And the contract you signed said Formica, in plain English. Plain Spanish, too—everything's bilingual now."

"Are you in court mostly, or do your contracts send disputes to arbitration?" Nick knew that many contracts nowadays had boilerplate providing that disputes be settled by "arbitration," rather than by resort to the governmental court system. Arbitration was something like a private court. The "judge" was typically a lawyer, not a government appointee, and the process was quicker and less expensive than a court trial. Courts almost always upheld arbitration rulings, because they knew that without the arbitration system, their case backlog would explode.

"Court," Ralph replied. "G&H tells me courts are more predictable than arbitrators. Between you and me and the lamppost, I think it's because they make more money off court cases than arbitrations. You're not telling me you can get me out of litigation, are you?" asked Ralph. His expression reminded Nick of Earl Matteson's face when Nick had first boasted he could do something about the fracking regulators, just over a year ago.

Nick shook his head wistfully. "Not if I get strangled in my sleep by a crazed investment banker who thinks I've somehow pissed away half a point off her rate of return. If it weren't for that, then yeah, I've got some ideas."

"A whole half a point? My God. Better keep your door locked. I've got a baseball bat you can keep by your bedside, just in case."

Darkness was finally rolling in. Nick briefly explained what he had in mind to Ralph, who was duly impressed. He then addressed the urgent problem of his too long empty Scotch glass, taking the long way around the deck so he could figure out where Natalie was.

The good news was that he quickly found Natalie attempting to appear interested in the exploits of a crotchety old fart leaning heavily on a cane, the kind with the little tripod at the bottom to help the user maintain balance. One swift kick and he'd topple like a Jenga tower, leaving Nick alone with her. That might not be necessary, though. Strictly from an actuarial standpoint, there was a decent chance he could die of old age by the time Nick returned from the bar.

Natalie almost, but not quite, appreciated Nick's rescue mission as old fart hobbled off. "What were you doing with Dr. Arrigo?" she hissed. "Don't you know he's a client?"

"He called me a fraud!"

"I don't care what he called you. You need to show more respect."

"Yeah, whatever. You been out here before?"

Peter's yacht had been doing slow laps between the Wilson Bridge and Georgetown. Washington spread in glory before them: the spherical-roofed Jefferson Memorial, the majestic white Capitol dome, and the surrealistically shaped Watergate complex, his new home. More than likely he wouldn't get a river view—this year.

"Not on a boat, no," she said. "I do love the view flying in, though."

"You must be hot, wearing that sweater. Come to think of it, you never took off your suit jacket at the fireworks last year, either—it was even hotter then."

The indirect compliment seemed to catch. "You remember what I was wearing a year ago?"

"Sure. You always look terrific. But seriously—aren't you hot in that thing?"

"A little. But I ... I always wear long sleeves. I'm a little self-conscious about my arm. I burned it in the shop when I was seven, and there's still a scar there. Not as ugly as it used to be, but still ... I wear long sleeves."

Nick thought back, and realized he'd never seen Natalie's bare arms. "Does it hurt?" was all he could think to say.

"No. It just looks gross. It's no big deal."

After another sip, Nick said "Maybe you could get a tattoo, from a top-rate artist, and he could work your scar into the design."

Natalie shut her eyes. "You are just a fountain of ideas. If you keep trying, maybe someday you'll have a good one."

Nick watched Roosevelt Island slide by, an oasis of parkland between the towers of Rosslyn on one side and the behemoth Kennedy Center on the other. He'd be able to walk there easily from his new Watergate apartment, which he was already drooling about.

"I've already had two, right on this boat ride." A slight exaggeration, since he'd had the ideas at Crisfield. "These are going to make you guys so much money, you'll be able to tell that Arrigo asshole where to shove it."

Natalie glanced around quickly.

"Don't worry," said Nick. "Nobody can hear. But listen to this ..." He leaned in and outlined brainstorms number one and number two, using shorthand legal jargon that Natalie had become familiar with.

For once, Natalie simply gave Nick a hopeful look, rather than informing him that he was wrong. Just before they reached the Fourteenth Street bridge, the boat slowed. Nick's new smartwatch vibrated, telling him it was 9:10 pm. Right on cue, the first skyrocket shot into the sky, and a dozen members of Washington's power elite stopped talking about ways to game the system and moved to the railing to watch the show.

An enormous red-white-and-blue burst got things started in earnest. Nick raised a stealthy hand behind Natalie's back, and laid it gently on her opposite shoulder.

One ... two ... three ...

At 3.4 seconds, Natalie picked Nick's hand off her shoulder, and let it fall behind her back. A new record! Woo-hoo!

Halfway through the show, Nick spied Ralph and Laura Boess, standing just to his left. Holding hands, arms intertwined, her head resting on Ralph's shoulder. They looked like two awkward teenagers. Who'd have thunk it?

August 18: George Washington Memorial Parkway

As arranged, Nick met Natalie in the lobby of the Logan Airport Hilton early Thursday morning to catch the shuttle for their flight back home. A trip rather than a videoconference had been necessary, Nick felt, to establish the fact of close church involvement in the design and construction of the "temple" on Ralph Boess's Cape Cod lot. A "temple" consisting mostly of timeshare condos—fifteen stories of them—in flagrant defiance of a century of zoning restrictions. The same smug bastards who'd killed Cape Cod's offshore wind farm project because it might disturb their million-dollar views would be helpless trying to stop a house of God, though. The federal RLUIPA was a Sherman tank, sweeping all local land-use obstacles from religion's path.[47] Nick's favorite case was the "swingers club" in Tennessee that won RLUIPA exemption to operate next to a school once they recharacterized themselves as a "church."[48] A close second was the rodeo, calling itself a "Cowboy Church," that plunked itself in the middle of a posh McMansion community outside Houston.[49] Thanks to RLUIPA, there wasn't a damned thing anybody could do about it.

RLUIPA, the "Religious Land Use and Institutionalized Persons Act," was a federal law that overrode every state and local land use and zoning ordinance. Religious organizations could build whatever they

---

47.   Dave Collins, "Appeals court revives Connecticut synagogue suit," *Associated Press*, September 22, 2014, http://www.sandiegouniontribune.com/sdut-appeals-court-revives-connecticut-synagogue-suit-2014sep22-story.html
48.   "Swinger's church? Denied sex club permit, Tenn. developers get creative," *CBS News*, April 17, 2015. http://www.cbsnews.com/news/tennessee-developers-want-to-open-swingers-club-as-a-church/ Vincent Fumaro, "Nashville Swingers' Sex Club Poses as 'Church' With 'Choir' and 'Handbell' Rooms to Legally Operate Next to Christian School," *Christian Post*, May 4, 2015. http://www.christianpost.com/news/nashville-swingers-sex-club-poses-as-church-with-choir-and-handbell-rooms-to-legally-operate-next-to-christian-school-138395/
49.   Christian McPhate, "Church walls divide area," *Denton Record-Chronicle*, October 15, 2016 http://www.dentonrc.com/local-news/local-news-headlines/20151016-church-walls-divide-area.ece.

wanted, wherever they wanted, unless the local land use authority could prove it had a "compelling interest" in stopping them, and that stopping them was the "least intrusive means" of achieving that interest—which, according to most federal judges, it never was. It might even be possible for the Cape Cod "temple" to ignore building and fire codes, like the Amish did, but there was no point pressing their luck.[50]

Ralph's architects already had plans for a high-rise drawn up. They'd been told to rough out some modifications to make it a better candidate for an RLUIPA exemption. Nick had feared the architects wouldn't make it "churchy" enough, but they had risen to the challenge. Nick was tickled by each unit's "inspiration nook," that by purest coincidence resembled a home theatre. Unit purchasers had to be members in good standing of CIS, and they needed a place to watch his weekly sermons, right? Nick had actually toned down one of the architects' bright ideas: "baptismal fonts" modeled on hot tubs. "We don't really do baptisms," he said ruefully.

Nick had wanted to talk about the drawings with Natalie on the plane, but she shushed him, pointing at the people sitting around them. "Half these people love the Cape just as it is," she whispered. "Fine, fine," he replied, a little annoyed. "But look. Here's what we've gotta work on. The property tax angle on this alone, aside from the zoning scam, is massive. You guys are smart. There's gotta be a way, somehow, for us to buy up property, even properly zoned property, get a religious property tax exemption for it, lease it out to some CIS business member, call it a church, and split the tax saving profit with them. No point just *giving* it away, right?"[51]

---

50. Charlie Butts, "Amish who escaped persecution have new problem in Wisconsin," *OneNewsNow,*, August 25, 2014 http://www.onenewsnow.com/legal-courts/2014/08/25/amish-who-escaped-persecution-have-new-problem-in-wisconsin#.U_yRLPldV8F. "Ruling: Amish must apply for building permits," *Associated Press*, August 20, 2014. http://www.twincities.com/localnews/ci_26375541/ruling-amish-must-apply-building-permits. Chuck Rupnow, "Judge: Building, sanitary permits not burden for Amish," *Leader-Telegram*, August 19, 2014 http://www.leadertelegram.com/news/front_page/article_ad1418ec-2821-11e4-8ae8-0019bb2963f4.html. Valerie Richardson, "Religious exemption sought for Amish after Wisconsin family forced out of home," *The Washington Times*, March 25, 2015 http://www.washingtontimes.com/news/2015/mar/25/religious-exemption-sought-for-amish-after-wiscons/?page=all#pagebreak.
51. Bob Kellogg, "ADF taking on 'clear-cut case of discrimination,'" *Onenewsnow*, May 11, 2015. http://www.onenewsnow.com/legal-courts/2015/05/11/adf-taking-on-clear-cut-case-of-discrimination#.VVDDG_lVhBc.

Natalie shot him an arched eyebrow that said yes, it might be possible, yes, it's a novel idea, and yes, I'm still pissed at you anyway, for reasons so obvious that I'll be even more pissed at you if you dare to ask. So he didn't.

When they finally reached the car she'd left back at the Reagan National parking garage, though, she finally showed her hand.

"I don't get what you were saying this morning about CIS not lasting as long as this building," she said. "Don't you have a long range plan?"

"My long range plan after the demise of CIS," Nick said grandly, "is for you to support me. I'll be the househusband, puttering around, deciding which restaurant to order takeout from every night. Keeping you up to date on all the baseball scores. See, you'll be made a partner in the firm after all your billing credit for this, making more money than you know what to do with. Especially because you never have time to spend it. You work all the time, and you'll never stop doing that. Supporting me will be like a safety valve for your bank account, so it doesn't explode from the pressure."

"That's quite a plan. Just in case that doesn't work out, what's Plan B?"

A hanging curve, over the heart of the plate. "You don't know what Plan B is? You better learn, girl. Plan B is the pill I leave for my women on the dresser in the morning, after all my conquests, just in case. You want one?"

Natalie's knuckles turned white as she squeezed the steering wheel. "Would you be serious for one minute? I thought you were trying to take this church somewhere. Build it into something permanent."

Nick stared out the side window. A shower had slowed, but not ended, and the parkway was filled with puddles. "You really don't get it, do you?" he said quietly. "You don't see what I'm trying to do at all, do you? I would have thought it's obvious."

"If it were obvious, I wouldn't have asked."

If she really didn't get it, then maybe it was time to try the truth. Nothing else was working with her, and there were no women anywhere needing Plan B pills after any encounter with Nick. He didn't think she would appreciate the Secret Plan, but he may as well spit it out.

"What's obvious is that these laws are insane. You know that. And they're getting worse and worse. Everybody who claims to know all about God gets to be a law unto himself anymore, making up his own rules, shitting on the rest of us. I am so sick of it." He ground his fists together.

"But that's exactly what you're doing."

"Bingo! Move to the head of the class. I'm deliberately trying to push it past the limit, don't you see? Like all these millionaires we're gonna piss off on Cape Cod. Don't you think they're going to start bitching about RLUIPA once you whip their ass in court? Sure they are. It can't last. Eventually we'll get back to neutral laws, leaving God out of it. I'm just giving the whole process a shove. 'Worse is better,' like the revolutionaries used to say."[52]

A pained silence, as Natalie waited for traffic to allow her onto the Fourteenth Street Bridge.

"That's crazy, Nick. A lot of people are invested in this. Like me, for starters. You're saying it's all a joke?"

This was worse than talking to Pop. Pop wasn't a lawyer, but Natalie was, so why couldn't she see this? "It's no joke. I'm dead serious. I want to bring it all down. Boom! This is the best way I know to do it. You got a better way?"

"And then what? What do I do? I'm spending all this time on a project you're trying to self-destruct?"

"You're getting paid for your time. You're making more off this than I am, and it was my idea."

Nick knew that Natalie was aware to the penny how much she was making off this. And if all her billing on his brainchild pushed her a year faster up the partnership track, then she was out-earning him by a mile. You'd have to do a time value of money spreadsheet to really test it out.

"Sure as hell," Nick continued, "Earl's getting paid—he's making millions more now. So what if it doesn't last forever? What does? It's all a big fucking game, anyway. Except when I'm done, at least some of the game is gonna be changed. So everybody has to play by the same rules, whether they're preacher wackos or not. If you make a little money along the way, if I make a little money along the way, fine. But what I'm doing"—he was quite loud by now—"makes a real difference. Not many people can say that."

"I don't know how to respond to that," Natalie said at length. "I didn't know you had me mixed up in a giant scam."

"Oh, come on. Most of what you K Street law firms do every day is

52. Albert L. Weeks, "The long shadow of Lenin's 'worse is better,'" *Christian Science Monitor*, April 23, 1980. http://www.csmonitor. com/1980/0423/042334.html.

a giant scam. You know that. The difference is, *this* scam has a chance to change things for the better. It's not just screwing ordinary folks for the benefit of fat cats."

"We're just following the rules."

"So am I," Nick said bitterly. "Rules that suck. By the time I'm done, people will see that. Your rules just keep rolling along, because nobody's got the guts to do what it takes to change them."

*****

Natalie wasn't kidding about not knowing how to respond, so there was no further conversation. Nick was genuinely surprised that she hadn't figured out the Secret Plan by now, because if anything it all seemed dangerously obvious to him. How could any thinking person believe he really meant all the bullshit he spewed out? That he really meant to hurt Alzheimer's victims, or cancer patients, or people shot by automatic rifles, or Zubitril users, or vacationers' enjoyment of nature at Cape Cod? Of course he didn't. It was all just a temporary... what? A temporary collateral damage. Like the prick of a vaccination shot—painful for a few seconds, but necessary long-term. A big thinker like Nick could see that. Natalie, whose idea of "big thinking" was "big dollars," couldn't. Well, too bad for her. Nick's fantasy of intimacy with Natalie wasn't going anywhere anyway, so to hell with her.

Natalie parked in the building's garage, they boarded the elevator together, and she said nothing at all when Nick got off at his office's basement level while she headed up to the eighth floor. He'd sublet the basement space from G&H after the first Jill Fund money started trickling in. The suite was dreary and lonely, but at least a hair more dignified than the secretary's cubicle he'd first been assigned. He didn't have to deal with the firm's security, and could come and go as he wished. But a window would have been nice.

As he turned onto the corridor toward his office, Nick saw a large cardboard box sitting in front of his door. Then he smelled it. "What the hell ...?" The lid wasn't taped shut, and when he pulled it off the stench hit him like a brick.

Inside the box was a little silver curly-haired dog, her stiff legs pointing up. A schnauzer, maybe. Her tongue hung to one side and her lifeless, opaque eyes stared right at him. Taped to the side was a scrawled note, big capital letters on grade-school lined loose-leaf:

"Your frackers posted signs saying 'Boil ground water before drinking.' Rosie couldn't read. You berry her. I can't."

August 20: L'Avignon

After the first block, Nick realized he should have caught a cab, or better yet used the G&H car service. It was too hot to think. The steambath of a Washington August seeped in through the nose and ears, causing too many short circuits in the brain. Hurried drivers leaning on their horns made thinking all the more difficult. So Nick's plan of using the walk over to L'Avignon to work out whether—and more importantly, how—to talk to Father Bob about Rosie was another bust.

Which was unfortunate, because he badly wanted to talk to someone, or take a pill or something, to wipe that little dog's image away. He couldn't trust Jay to keep quiet about it, or Kyle not to laugh, or Mama not to cry, or Pop not to say, "I told you so." He didn't want to risk looking weak in front of Natalie, whether or not she could appreciate the Secret Plan. Peter would care about nothing other than the image of the firm. Earl would tell him how many dogs, snakes, deer and other varmints he'd had to shoot. Shawnay would complain about the boys' dog and how Reggie never walked him. Seeing a shrink would make marvelous press when it leaked out, as it surely would.

Father Bob, though, had always lent a sympathetic ear back in college. Even after Nick had reneged on converting to Catholicism, Chaplain Father Robert McIntyre had always been there for him, through all the loneliness and self-absorbed angst. Father Bob had no magic dust to bring Rosie back to life, but maybe a kind word from him could make the nightmares go away.

Nick had spent the week since receiving the surprise call from Father Bob dithering over where to meet him for lunch. Should he impress him with Angelique's, with its hard-earned reputation as the priciest spot in town? Should he choose a deli, to show he was still just folks? The Palm, where he'd still never been since the bizarre encounter with Zoltan Fiola? One thing you had to admit about Zoltan, though: he was as good as his word on the cash flow. At this rate, they'd rake in quite a bit more than the originally promised $80 million.

Ultimately Nick settled on L'Avignon. A place as other-worldly as this conversation with Father Bob was likely to be.

Nick's shirt was plastered to his back by the time he stepped into the lobby, which was downright frigid. "Well it looks like you're not missing many meals!" boomed Father Bob, loudly enough for several heads to turn.

"Good to see you, too, Father." A roaring start.

A black suited waiter who looked like he'd just arrived from his second job at the funeral home wordlessly navigated them to a table. The restaurant was housed in three adjoining nineteenth-century townhouses, with doorways knocked through the walls, and single steps of varying height up and down where least expected. Management kept the lights down low, which made the risk of tripping on the way to or from the rest room even worse. Each table was separated from its neighbors by heavy red velvet curtains, lending an air of secrecy. If you wanted to plot some intrigue, this was the place to do it.

"It's wonderful to see you," Nick said, after they settled in. "So what's this confer—"

"Would you care to review the wine list, sir?"

Nick glanced hopefully at Father Bob. "Not for me, thanks. But you go right ahead."

With a tinge of regret, Nick handed back the wine list to the waiter. "No, just the menu."

Father Bob did not look six years older, but maybe he would in brighter light. Perhaps he had a touch more gray mixed in with his auburn crew cut, but his shoulders were as powerful as ever. His cheeks, as always, were a bit florid and puffy. Perhaps this resulted from drink, but Nick had never seen him over-indulge.

"Just the usual seeking out how to be a better chaplain spiel," said Bob. "Tips and tricks."

"You should be giving that lecture, not listening to it," said Nick. "You were the best!"

"To tell the truth—which is always a good idea—I couldn't pass up the chance to come to Washington and check in on my most famous student. Or most infamous, to hear some people tell it." There was a little finger wag on "always a good idea."

Aw, shucks. "If I'm the best you can do, you need to work a little harder. Haven't you got any, like, senators? Or serial killers? Or reality show stars? I'm just a little YouTube guy."

"Never bullshit a bullshitter, Nick. You're a lot more than that, and you know it. There's so much same-old same-old that goes on, especially here in Washington. Conservatives say they want to cut taxes. Never happens. Liberals say they want to help the little guy. Definitely never happens. Then along comes my Nick, and suddenly things start to happen. Not necessarily good things, but at least unpredictable things.

At the end of the day, the world is different than it was in the morning. No senator or reality star can do that like you've been doing it."

A blow job from Miss Universe would not have sent Nick soaring any higher.

"I dunno, I just—"

"Are we ready for our orders, gentlemen? Have I told you about our special prix fixe luncheon?"

Once all the gastronomic details were taken care of, Nick turned earnestly to Father Bob. "All I did was to look at how religion really works today, and chart a course that would draw people, especially younger people who have abandoned traditional religion, back into communion with the divine."

"Cut the crap, Nick. This is me, Father Bob. I know exactly what you're doing. You hate religion, in every form, and you're trying to destroy it." He took a long sip of water, without breaking eye contact.

So much for getting any sympathy about Rosie.

Nick fiddled with his glasses. "Well I ... I don't know about that. There's a lot of complexity here, you know? I don't hate ... what someone else wants to do. Really. I don't give a shit. I mean—sorry—I don't care. I just ... I don't see why they're better than me. Religious people. I mean, other religious people, 'cause I'm a religious person now, too. They get to ignore laws, and I gotta follow 'em. Is that right? I don't think so. So now, things are evened up. People who think like I do—and there's a lot of us—we get to pick and choose our laws, too. Isn't that fair?"

"It's mockery, Nick. Just because you disbelieve, what entitles you to mock the deeply held convictions of others? You may not believe in sin, but you used to believe in common decency. Now I'm not so sure."

The booth enveloped inside the red velvet drapery began seeming less "intimate," and more "claustrophobic." Nick squirmed for a way out. He felt like he had the time Mama found the broken crystal he thought he'd carefully concealed at the bottom of the garbage can. A quick sidestep was in order.

"We're not really indecent. Say, speaking of common decency, remember Ahmed? He was a piece of work. Have you heard anything from him?"

Bob shook his head. "Not since graduation. He had an extreme take on Islam, I'll grant you. A bit arrogant for my taste."

"A bit? He thought the rest of us ought to be paying the jizya tax for the privilege of remaining non-Muslim. Do you think he ever went back and joined ISIS? That would have been right up his alley." If he had, thought Nick, and had ever tangled with Doris, Nick would've bet on Doris.

"Could be. He was only here on a student visa, so either he went back to Qatar or he's here illegally. But think about arrogance, Nick. You're not calling the kettle black, are you?"

Here we go again. Was there no way to switch this conversation over to baseball, or movies, or something else safe?

Nick played with his fork. "I don't really see us as arrogant. Maybe we're not perfect, but look—how many other religions out there say it's ok to be in more than one church at the same time? Catholics don't let you be Muslim, or Buddhist, or whatever, at the same time you're Catholic. But we do. That's not arrogant. It's downright humble."[53]

"The arrogance," Father Bob said sternly, "as you well know, lies in your glib mockery of faith traditions that have comforted millions. When you sail in and say, 'Oh, I just got a new email from God,' you are being fundamentally profane."

Oh, for a slug of Scotch. Nick could win this argument, at least in his own mind, if he could just relax a little. "Everything starts somewhere. You could've said the same thing about Moses, or Jesus, or any of those guys. They all flew in the face of the traditions of their day. Now don't get me wrong. I'm not saying I'm Jesus. I don't do miracles, and I've got no magic powers. But if there is a supernatural force out there, who's to say that it doesn't communicate to different people in different ways at different times? Seems to me it probably would. Sort of a mid-course correction deal."

"You just said 'if.' Are you receiving communication from God, or are you not? You're swearing to the world that you are. Are you lying?"

Nick had expected Father Bob to oppose what he was trying to do. He just hadn't expected him to be so good at it. Where the hell was the food? Chewing would give him time to think. Instead, he sipped his water, cleaned his glasses for the second time in five minutes, and took advantage of the fact that he had not yet unfolded his napkin to spread it on his lap.

"It's hard to explain. I'm doing what I think is right. And I think that,

53. For more on the trend of "dual religious belonging," see Harriet Sherwood, "York Minster criticised for allowing Buddhist meditation," *The Guardian*, May 17, 2016. https://www.theguardian.com/world/2016/may/17/york-minster-criticised-zen-buddhist-meditation-grounds

ultimately, people will be better off. I really do. Now did I get the idea for this totally myself, or was there some outside force that spurred me on? Who knows, really? It's a little—sometimes not everything moves in a straight line, ok? But—"

"What you're doing is making money, pretending to sell messages from God. You need to admit that, at least to yourself."

"Oh, yeah?" Nick snapped. "And when I've made, what, like another trillion or so, then I'll catch up to you guys. So you can make money off God, but I can't? Is that the deal? The only way that works is if you have the monopoly on God's truth, and I don't think you do. So if you don't, then you put out your pitch, I'll put out mine, and we live and let live. Ok?"

Now it was Father Bob's turn to pause and regroup. Nick tried again to move the conversation away from the honesty thing, which he knew wasn't his strongest ground.

"I'll tell you a secret," Nick said, leaning in. "Our next big splash. Gonna break it Sunday. This'll be big—as big as anything we've ever done. We're—"

"Gentlemen," announced the waiter, swooping down, "here we have your Delmonico cut, medium rare with balsamic onion sauce, and ..." on and on he went.

After a first bite, Bob said, "Ok, I'm still on the edge of my seat. You've already told me you don't do miracles, so it's not that. Is it a vision?"

Nick smirked. "You could say that. It's a vision, all right, of a world where paying social security taxes is optional. Not mandatory, like it is now."

"And what do you call this vision? Our Lady of No Social Security?"

Nick had thought that Father Bob would register a bit more surprise. But maybe nothing Nick did surprised people any more. "No, we call it being fair. See, there's case law that says government can't favor one religion over another.[54] Lots of it. And the Amish, well they don't have to pay social security if they're self-employed, which a lot of them are. Special rule, just for them.[55] The kind of special rule you're

---

54.   *Larson v. Valente*, 456 U.S. 228 (1982)   https://supreme.justia.com/cases/federal/us/456/228/case.html.

55.   According to the US Social Security Administration, "Members of certain religious groups (including the Amish and Mennonites) may be exempt from paying Social Security taxes." https://faq.ssa.gov/link/portal/34011/34019/Article/3821/Are-members-of-religious-groups-exempt-from-paying-Social-Security-taxes

not supposed to have for just one religion, under the Constitution. So if our theology is the same as theirs on this—which it is—then we shouldn't have to pay social security, either. We've got plaintiffs lined up who are going to demand a refund of what they've paid since they joined CIS, and when they don't get it we're gonna sue, and we're gonna win. It's a big deal, like I said."

Father Bob grimaced in disgust. "Now there you go. An outstanding example. You're picking on the Amish, of all people? What a beautiful, simple folk they are! They have their ways, they keep to themselves, they demand nothing. All they ask is to be left alone."

Nick was relieved to be back on terra firma again. "I don't know about beautiful and simple. People who won't educate their children, to make sure they'll never leave the farm? People who get totally ostracized from the only community they're familiar with if they question the authority of one of the self-appointed elders? And anyway, we *are* leaving them alone. We're just saying, if they get an exemption, we get the same exemption too. What's wrong with that?"

"Don't lie to yourself, Nick." There was the honesty thing again. How did he keep getting back to that? "You know as well as I do that no one has ever converted to Amish in order to avoid paying social security tax. And that there are only a handful of Amish anyway, so the impact on the overall social security system is negligible. But if all of a sudden any self-employed person can say 'I'm a CIS Catholic' or 'I'm a CIS Methodist' and stop paying social security taxes, then Congress is liable to throw out the baby with the bathwater and repeal the whole exemption for everyone. *That's* how you're hurting the Amish. And you know it."

Nick considered and rejected the idea of raising the ante by mentioning that Father Bob himself didn't pay Social Security taxes either, thanks to a special tax loophole Congress had enacted just for ministers. Nor did he have to pay tax on his church-provided housing, thanks to yet another loophole.[56] But he stuck to the high ground rather than ad hominem attacks against someone he truly admired.

"Hurting? By putting them in the same position I've always been

---

56. Lisa A. Runquist, "Special Tax and Other Considerations for Employees of Religious Organizations," *American Bar Association*, December 2012. http:// www.americanbar.org/publications/gpsolo_ereport/2012/december_2012/ tax_considerations_ministers_employees_religious_organizations.html.

in? Sorry, Father, I don't buy it. I don't think they're better than I am, or deserve more rights than I do. They can believe whatever they want, and so can you, but we should all follow the same laws. If I've been inspired to accomplish anything, it's exactly that."

"A world of stifling uniformity, with no role for the individual conscience? That's what you've been inspired to accomplish? Not by any kind of God I believe in."

"Who said anything about that?" Nick felt more and more in command now. "Not me. There can be exceptions from laws, sometimes, for conscience. When it makes sense for society as a whole. Like if we ever have a draft again, it's pretty clear there are some people, even some atheists, who'd say, 'I'm not gonna shoot people. Jail me if you want, but I'm not gonna do it.' Is it better to put those guys in jail, or better to let them roll bandages, or do something else useful but not force them to shoot people? I think that's smarter, even if you're going all out to win a war. What you can't have is one group showing up saying, 'My religion says I can shoot people, but only on Tuesdays,' or, 'My religion says I can't shoot people, but I can stab 'em, so gimme a knife.'"

Father Bob's face was a bit redder than usual. "Which is exactly what your so-called religion is doing, on everything from drug laws to healthcare laws to dress codes to what you're now telling me is an attack on social security."

For a fleeting instant, Nick was glad he hadn't had the Scotch. He jabbed his fork toward Father Bob. "According to you—not me, but according to you—what I'm doing is trying to crash that whole system of religious privilege, by making it obvious even to the dimwits in Congress what happens when you get away from the simple idea of one law for everybody."

"Crash the whole system," Father Bob sneered, "by driving it to an extreme. Interesting. Sounds like Lenin, radicalizing the proletariat. That turned out well, didn't it?"

"Better than having a czar, yeah. You add up all the evil things the czars did and compare them to the evil things the commies did. The czars win—by a mile. And the communists, misguided as they were, at least were trying to do something they believed was ultimately good for people, even if there were problems along the way. Change is hard."

"So you're saying the end justifies the means?"

Nick wagged his fork playfully back and forth. "I don't think I invented that one, Father. Remember that paper I did on the Jesuits? Hold on a second." He pulled his cell phone from his pocket, and started punching buttons. "I keep all my juicy stuff where I can get at it easily … hold on … Here it is: 'Actions intrinsically evil, and directly contrary to the divine laws, may be innocently performed by those who have so much power over their own minds as to join, even ideally, a good end to the wicked action contemplated.'[57] That's your guys talking—Jesuits—not me. And Ignatius Loyola, the great founder of the Jesuits, he said it even better. 'We must see black as white, if the church says so.'"[58]

"I'm not a Jesuit, Nick. You know that."

"I'm not either. But sometimes, you know, you gotta break an egg to make an omelet."

Father Bob chewed in silence for a while, then tried another tack. "Are you happy, Nick? Are you at peace?"

"I pee in peace."

"Touché. But most people, religious or otherwise, believe that real peace can only come when you are true to yourself. Not when you're living a lie."

Nick took a big bite of medium rare, to let himself chew for a while. He sought inspiration from the oil painting that hung over the table, but found none. It would be far more pleasant to sit along the bank of the river it showed, gazing off at the purple mountains in the distance, than to fend off this sharp interrogation from someone who knew him way too well. The painting held no answers. But he'd already spent enough time on K Street to learn that the best defense was usually a good offense.

"But you don't believe everything your church teaches. At least, you've said you didn't. Like the existence of me. You told me once you didn't agree with the church on in vitro fertilization, without which I wouldn't be here. But you're still a priest. So aren't you living a lie, like you say I am? Which, for the record, I do not admit."

"I think I said I had doubts, not that I definitely disagreed. It's a tough question."

"No it isn't!" Nick stammered. "You're saying it's a tough question whether I should exist or not?"

"You know what I mean. All the human embryos who are destroyed in the IVF process. Millions of them, across the country. Do you just

---

57. Alexander Duff, *The Jesuits.* Edinburgh, Johnstone & Hunter 1852, p.11.
58. Edmond Paris, *The Secret History of the Jesuits.* Chick Publications, 1975, p.33.

ignore them?"

It felt so good being self-righteous. "You know what? I do. I really do ignore all those little eight-cell or whatever things you can barely see with a microscope, so I could exist, and Mama could have the baby she wanted. I think Mama and I are more important than they are. I don't worry much about the ants I used to step on in the back yard, either."

An unfortunate analogy. Dead animals of any kind brought back the image of Rosie, staring up at him out of the box, which he was striving mightily to forget.

"I'll take your non-answer as a no," said Father Bob. "Seriously, Nick, we all have our points of view. I respect yours, and I hope you respect mine. But there are honest ways to disagree, and not-so-honest ways. Are you sure you haven't strayed across the line?"

"What do you want me to do, write a blog post saying, 'Nick thinks everybody ought to follow the same laws?' How much impact would that have? Then you guys keep winning, and my side keeps losing. Good plan." Nick chafed at the underlying notion that he could only be a good sport if he lost. Playing to win was unseemly.

"It wouldn't be lying. That's something."

Again they were interrupted by the waiter, wanting to know if there was any other way he could possibly be of service. Nick refrained from suggesting that the best service he could offer would be to shrivel and die, and asked for the check.

"It's something all right. You guys lie your way to the top, then try to make me feel bad for catching up. That's something, too."

Both boxers were arm-weary now, so no more hard punches would be thrown. Nick finally succeeded in moving the conversation back to the safe ground of his classmates and what they were probably doing now, how much money the college was wasting on sports, and whether the latest Netflix series was worth watching.

As they reached the door, Father Bob snuck in one last shot at the bell. "You're a bright young man, Nick. But I'm not certain you always act wisely. You've moved mountains, and I can understand your pride in what you've done. But you still have to look at yourself in the mirror every day, and you're going to have more and more trouble doing that. I didn't come here expecting that we'd have a pleasant chat and you'd suddenly smack your forehead and exclaim 'Now I see how wrong I've been!' But I'm asking you, Nick, as good old Father Bob who was always there when you needed him—I'm begging you—to think more carefully about what you are doing. You are hurting a great many people. And yourself, too. Deep down, you know that. I know you're smart enough to figure out a way to change course, keeping your dignity. Promise me just to think about it, ok?" He bear-hugged Nick even more intensely than he had when they met.

"I will, Father. I promise. It really was great to see you again."

Nick kept his promise to think more carefully about his course. All the way down the block. Then he finished thinking about it. Fuck McIntyre, he thought. I'm winning, for once in my life, and I'm not going to piss it away.

September 10: The Mayflower

"All rise."

Tonetta James, taking a break from the G&H reception desk, called to order the first-ever spiritual conciliation conducted by the Church of Inspired Spirituality.

Nick strode into the hotel conference room, violet robe flapping behind him, feeling vaguely like Groucho Marx in a picture whose title he couldn't recall.

Location had been an issue. It would have been easier to conduct the conciliation in a Guilder & Hersh conference room, but since G&H represented the "defendant," the optics of that would have been bad. So Nick settled on the Mayflower Hotel, picking a date when he could get the same conference room where he'd first met the RFF board. That room was far too expensive, though, so he had to settle for a much smaller room upstairs.

"Thank you all for coming," Nick began. That didn't sound judge-like, did it? "Please, be seated."

He opened his file folder. "So. We're here today to discuss a problem that has arisen between members of our church. The first party is Harold and Margaret Petrone, and the second is Speed-Is-King Home Improvement, Inc. Mr. and Mrs. Petrone, are you here?"

The only audience member wearing a suit and tie rose, buttoning his jacket as he did so. "Vincent Casciano, Reverend Fratelli, of Edmonds & Casciano in Trenton, representing the plaintiffs Harold and Margaret Petrone."

Vincent Casciano would not have passed for a G&H partner. The bags under his eyes looked like leather pouches, and the hair sticking out over his ears should have been trimmed at least a week ago. That could so easily have been me, thirty years from now, thought Nick. Whew!

"Mr. Casciano," Nick asked, "are you an attorney?"

"Yes, your honor. Reverend. I am currently admitted to practice in New Jersey and Pennsylvania. We can add local counsel from DC if necessary, but given the nature of the proceedings we expect that will not be necessary."

"No, it will not. In fact, Mr. Casciano, your presence isn't necessary either. Lawyers are not permitted in these proceedings. So, please leave." Nick motioned toward the door.

Casciano's jaw dropped. "Come again?"

"Am I not speaking loudly enough for you?" Nick raised his voice and formed his syllables with exaggerated clarity. "Lawyers are not permitted in these proceedings. So leave. Now."

"Seriously?"

"Seriously, or casually, so long as you wind up on the other side of that door." Nick stole a quick glance at Tonetta, who was doing a poor job of concealing her delight at a lawyer being dealt with in this fashion. She was sitting between Jay Gimenez and Natalie, who seemed far less amused.

Casciano's puffy face flushed. "I must enter my strong objection, on the record. My clients are being denied the benefit of counsel."

Nick folded his arms and leaned back. "See, this is the problem. There is no record. You see a court reporter here, to keep a record? No, you don't. We don't have a record, we don't have objections, we don't have any of that stuff. We have two members—three members, I guess—of this church, with a little disagreement, and we're gonna work it out. Lawyers just get in the way. And as for being denied the 'benefits' of counsel!" Nick faced the couple he didn't recognize. "Mr. and Mrs. Petrone—I assume that's who you are?—don't pay this guy anything. He's doing nothing, other than trying to tick me off, which doesn't seem like a good idea. But that's okay, I'll ignore it. Now, as soon as he departs," Nick said, extending his arm dramatically toward the door, violet sleeve drooping down, "we can get started."

Casciano looked down at the Petrones, who looked back at him helplessly. "This will not stand," he muttered, as he snapped his briefcase shut and left.

Oh yes, it will, thought Nick. It's stood for religious arbitrations a lot more outrageous than this one is going to be, and it will stand here too.

The click of door as the lawyer left was Nick's sweetest moment since Kansas. Feel the power! he silently rejoiced. Nick turned back to the Petrones. "Sorry for that unpleasantness. Now, what seems to be the problem?"

"Why can't we have our lawyer?" asked Margaret Petrone. She spoke in a whiny voice with a thick Noo Joisey accent. "We can't do this by ourselves."

"Sure you can," said Nick indulgently, like he was telling a six-year-old she could make pancakes. "I've read the letter you sent me, and the contract, and Mr. Costa's reply, so I know what's going on. I just want to get all of you together to work this out. So to get us started, please explain again, in your own words, what the problem is."

Both Petrones started to speak at once. Harold looked about sixty, but his shortage of hair may have added a few artificial years. His plaid shirt was missing a button. Margaret had a DIY dye job of flaming red, and cheeks that made her look like she was storing walnuts for the winter.

"These jerks promised us that ... / We signed a contract with a deadline ..."

Nick couldn't make out who was saying what. "Whoa—whoa—whoa! This won't work. "Mr.—no, Mrs. Petrone. You start, and then Mr. Petrone can fill in anything he'd like to add."

Harold mumbled something Nick couldn't hear, but Nick was pretty sure it wasn't positive.

"As I was saying," Margaret continued, with a sideways glare at her husband, "he signed a contract to fix up our garage so his mother could move in, with this so-called Speed-Is-King company. Hah! What a joke!"

Harold Petrone growled in assent. At least they agreed on something.

"A joke how?" Nick asked.

"The speed!" Margaret exclaimed. "They've done nothing. Not a Goddamned thing. And Sheila—Mrs. Petrone, his mother—she won't go into a home. Oh, no, not her. She's too special to go into a home."

"Peg ..." Harold Petrone's fist was clenched so tightly his knuckles went white.

"Well? My mother went into a home. Yours won't."

"Your mother wasn't the one who gave us the down payment for the house, was she? Your mother was the one who didn't even leave enough to cover the cost of the bronze casket you said we had to have, much less the plot and the funeral."

"Don't you start in again on my mother!" Margaret flared. "She—"

Nick had considered bringing a gavel, but didn't think that was the right image. Live and learn. All he could do now was shout.

"Hey! Not here! I don't want to hear any of that. Just tell me what were they supposed to do, and when were they supposed to do it."

Margaret won a quick stare-down. Nick suspected that happened a lot.

"They were supposed to put in a full bathroom, wallboard everything, tile the floor, and do whatever so she'd have electricity and a kitchenette. By the end of this month, so she could move in. And make my life hell."

Harold didn't respond to the last dig. Nick guessed that was because he hadn't heard it. He was too busy undressing Natalie with his eyes.

"And they haven't started yet?"

"No! And there's no way they can finish on time now. We want our money back—every penny."

"Ok," said Nick. "I get it. Now, someone is here for Speed-Is-King?"

A curly-haired Hispanic man sitting to the left of the Petrones raised his right index finger, without straightening from his slouch.

"And you are ...?"

"Braulio Costa. Trenton district manager. Sir. Your reverence."

"We can all skip the reverence part. Just tell me what happened. Why haven't you started work yet?"

"ICE. We got raided. Took our best guys. Fucked everything up. 'Scuse me, but they did."

"Ice? In August?"

"Not that ice. Immigration. Immigration and Customs Enforcement. Guys couldn't find their papers in time. You know how it is."

"Wetbacks?" Margaret shrieked. "Oh my God!"

"Hey!" Nick shouted again. "He let you talk. You let him talk. Besides, we're all in the same church together. We can work this out."

"We ain't in any church," she whined. "We're Catholic. I don't know why we're here. I just told Vince we should sue the bastards and get our money back. He took our retainer and then said we had to drive down here. I don't get it."

Nick shuffled through his papers and found the original contract. "Oh, you're in the church all right. See, both of you signed right here, and even paid fifty-two dollars in advance for a year's membership. But it's ok. You can still be Catholic too, if you want."

"That's what the fifty-two bucks was for?" she asked. "He said it was so we could get a five percent discount. Hah! Some discount. A discount for nuthin'."

Nick wasn't sure whether the contempt she dripped from the word "he" referred to Mr. Costa or her husband. Didn't matter. "You signed it," he repeated. "And you agreed that all disputes would be arbitrated through the church's conciliation process rather than in court, which is why you're here. It's the coming thing. Lots of churches are doing it now."

"It's just another ripoff, if you ask me," she sniffed.

"Now, where were we?" Nick continued. "Mr. Costa, you were explaining that the delay was caused by circumstances beyond your control. Is that correct?"

"Definitely. Way beyond."

"Yet your estimator signed this contract, with a five percent discount, promising completion by September 30."

"Yeah. Everybody gets a discount. Sizzling Summer discount, Autumn Leaves discount, whatever. This was a church discount. It don't matter."

Not a data point Nick would have preferred spill out, but it was too late now. "So will you be able to complete the work by September 30, as it says here?"

"Nah, not by then. But we'd already be started, if it weren't for all this."

"Aha!" Margaret shouted in triumph. "They broke the contract! Case closed!"

"Mrs. Petrone," said Nick, as calmly as he could muster. "I told you to stop interrupting. Now there are two ways we can do this. With you here, or with you gone. So are you going to cooperate, or not?"

"Cooperate? What's to cooperate? He just admitted everything."

Nick pointed at the door, the right sleeve of his gown drooping onto the table. "Ok. Leave. Without another word. If you don't leave immediately, I'll find for the company, in full. Now scoot!"

"Harold!" She turned on her husband menacingly. "What are you going to do?"

Harold had wiped off his smirk just in time. "I'll handle this guy. You go find Vince."

After a few more comments that Nick chose to ignore, she finally exited, face contorted with rage, slamming the door on her way out.

"Let's just cut to the chase," Nick resumed. "I've got another meeting to get to. Mr. Costa, can you get this work done by the end of October?"

"We got full crews now. Sure."

"Documented crews?"

"Uh, yeah, sure."

Nick caught Harold ogling Natalie again. He tried to send her a telepathic message to undo one more button at the top of her blouse, which would ramp up Harold's cooperative spirit considerably. Either she didn't get the message, or she chose to ignore it.

"Mr. Petrone," Nick continued. "Sitting here, right now, do you have anyone else lined up who can finish the job before the end of October?"

"No. But the contract said September."

"So I've heard. Does your mother have a place to stay until the end of October to keep her off the street? Is there a room in your home?"

"There's a guest room, yeah, but she drives Peg batty. That's why we're fixing the garage, to keep those two apart."

Serendipity! Maybe he should give the company another year rather than another month.

Nick shuffled his papers, turned back to Harold and said, "One more thing. I assume your mom has to move in from somewhere, and she's got a lifetime worth of stuff. Do you have anybody lined up to help with that move?"

"No, 'cause we don't even know when it's happening."

"October thirty-first. That's when it's happening. So now you can write that down. And you," he said, aiming his pen at Costa and deciding firmly that next time he'd have a gavel, "are gonna supply some big guys—big, documented guys—and a truck, and you're gonna move Mama Petrone in on October 31. And if she needs anything stored before then, you're gonna do that too, someplace dry and safe. Right?"

"Uh, I'd have to check with regional. We don't usually do that kinda work."

Nick leaned back, supremely satisfied with himself. "No. You don't have to check. Because guess what? If you don't move this lady into a unit that's perfect—I mean perfect, everything works to the last detail on October thirty-one—then you're paying this guy back every penny. Double!"

"Yes, sir."

"That's Halloween. You all can have a party to celebrate." Nick restrained himself from suggesting that one of the celebrants might not need a mask.

"And Mr. Costa, you might want to get some of your employees who have trouble 'finding' their papers to join the church and call Ms. Parks here if they get in trouble. No guarantees, but she might be able to help. There are religious exemption angles to immigration laws, too. Now, Mr. Petrone. I know this isn't what you originally planned. And I sympathize with you, for lots of reasons. But you're walking out of here a lot better off than when you walked in. Now: if you fuck this up by getting that ambulance chaser involved again, then the whole deal's off. No more work, no refund, no free move, no free storage. And you'll lose if you go to court. No doubt about it. Before you let greedhead talk you into going to court—which I know is exactly what he's doing with your wife, as we speak—you get him to explain to you, in plain English, why your case is any different from the Garcia Scientology case, or the Teen Challenge case.[59] Ms. Parks here can write those down for you. Go spend some time talking to her before you leave. Religious arbitration was upheld in those cases—not even a close question—and it'll be upheld here too."[60]

Nick caught Tonetta's eye, and she gave another solemn "All rise." He flapped out the back door, praying to the Divine Spirit that he could find a men's room to hide in before encountering Margaret Petrone and the lawyer again. Luck was with him. From the safety of a stall, he removed his robe and sent a text to Natalie and Jay.

Not a bad start, he mused from "chambers" as he waited for an "All clear" reply. The result was fairer than the two sides would have gotten in court. By the letter of the law, the Petrones should have gotten their money back. That would just have hurt the company without doing the Petrones any good. They'd have wound up spending more than their refund for a finished product at least a month, if not more, later than they would get it now—not to mention the free help with storing and moving the old lady's stuff.

Not every case would be this easy. He knew that. And when the caseload picked up, as it surely would once Jay's story broke, there were bound to be times when the fair thing to do would be to rule against the CIS member company who had buried a religious arbitration clause in the boilerplate of its standard form contract. Did he have the guts to do that, if the company was a major player in the church? Could he rule against Earl Matteson? Even if Nick himself could always be fair, which was doubtful, he'd have to farm out a lot of the caseload to other arbitrators he would hire somehow. Or let Laura Boess hire, Divine Spirit help us. What kind of rulings would they come up with? How could he keep it all under control?

The answer lay in his favorite line from *Gone With the Wind*: "I'll

59. Scientology case: Tony Ortega, "Garcia Fraud Case Ended as Judge Grants Scientology Arbitration Motion," *The Underground Bunker*, March 13, 2015. http://tonyortega.org/2015/03/13/garcia-fraud-case-ended-as-judge-grants-scientology-arbitration-motion/. Teen Challenge: Michael Corkery and Jessica Silver-Greenberg, "In Religious Arbitration, Scripture Is the Rule of Law," *New York Times*, November 3, 2015. http://mobile.nytimes.com/2015/11/03/business/dealbook/in-religious-arbitration-scripture-is-the-rule-of-law.html.
60. David Tereschuk, "Arbitration by Faith," *Religion & Ethics News Weekly,* May 6, 2016. http://www.pbs.org/wnet/religionandethics/2016/05/06/arbitration-by-faith/30328

think about it tomorrow." He wouldn't think too hard, though. Of course there would be absurd results, mostly in the direction of the party with more money. That was the point: to demonstrate how off-the-chart mindless it was for courts to honor religious arbitration in the first place. Worse is better, worse is better, worse is better.

Fifteen minutes went by, which is a long time to spend on a toilet. At least the Mayflower kept the place clean, though the ammonia smell was starting to get to him. He tried another text, but still no response. I bet that lawyer came back in and is re-trying the case to make himself look useful, Nick thought. Or maybe Harold is making his pass at Natalie. He hoped she wasn't too annoyed because he really wanted her there at the next meeting, which was only a few minutes away. What's taking so long? he wondered. This next meeting could be rough, and Nick needed Natalie there to vouch for how he handled it.

So many pots on the stove now. Shorts litigation was popping up everywhere. A whole hospital workers local had joined the church en masse, seeking to invoke a religious garb clause in their contract, originally designed for Muslims, to justify the wearing of shorts at work. Inspiration Healthcare enrollments were surging, as were sales of Zubitril. There were unconfirmed reports that a combination of Zubitril and ginseng produced an Ecstasy-like high. That could be good or bad, if it were true.

The biggest drag on Nick's time, though, continued to be all the fracking litigation. It astonished him to learn how many different layers and branches of government had their fingers in the fracking pie, how many thousands of bureaucrats justified their existence by this, that, or the other piece of paper regulating some tiny aspect of the process. RFRA, in states where it had been adopted, let a believing company like Matteson Enterprises—and the half-dozen other energy companies who had joined the church's ranks—crunch through the rules like a bulldozer through barbed wire. Not by itself though; only with the able assistance of the Guilder & Hersh law firm and its rapidly expanding Washington office, which currently had twenty-six different cases at early stages of the litigation process. All of which kept Nick flitting to and fro like a fly dodging a flyswatter, trying not to blow any critical deadlines. He had dreamt up a defense theory he was rather proud of that tied a number of regulators in knots. A federal court in New York had used some sweeping language in an opinion preventing the police department from conducting surveillance of mosques and other Muslim venues, despite the rather obvious need to identify where the bad apples might be.[61] You can't profile people who belong to a particular religion any more than you can profile people of a particular race, the court said. Wasn't that exactly what all the state agencies honing in on poor little religious Matteson Enterprises were trying to do? Maybe yes, maybe no. But there was no "maybe" about the extra year or more of litigation this could add to any state agency trying to enforce environmental rules against Earl. Except for all the agencies unwilling to endure that extra expense. For the ones that did, that extra year let Earl earn more money than the GDP of some African nations, with a side helping of some excellent bonuses for the toiling masses of Guilder & Hersh.

A couple of cases seemed headed toward a jury trial, the mere prospect of which gave the G&H litigators a collective orgasm. There was already a case where armed protesters had been acquitted of occupying a federal wildlife refuge after making the flimsiest imaginable religious liberty argument.[62] There really wasn't any law at all in the Wild West any more, Nick mused. Where was Wyatt Earp when you needed him?

Nick was worn down keeping track of it all. These precious minutes in the can were a welcome break that contributed to the serenity and tranquility on which CIS had been so wisely founded. Everybody deserved breaks like this, he thought. Muslims got prayer breaks five times a day, didn't they? Though they seemed to involve chanting more than serene reflection. But wasn't there some EEOC case law backing them up?[63] This could be great! Tranquility breaks for everybody every couple of hours, to tune in to what the Divine Spirit wanted them to do. Sweet! thought Nick, that should give the membership rolls a boost.

---

61.   *Hassan v. City of New York*, 804 F.3d 277 (3rd Cir., 2015). http://www2.ca3. uscourts.gov/opinarch/141688p.pdf

62.   Scott Brantford, "Armed occupation leader cites religious faith in justifying Oregon refuge takeover," *Reuters*, October 6, 2016. http://www.reuters.com/ article/us-oregon-militia-idUSKCN127051. Andrew Selsky, "Acquittal raises fears that militant groups could get bolder," *Associated Press*, October 28, 2016. http://bigstory.ap.org/0365969ff0fd4020b4afe3ae6bf46349

63.   EEOC, "EEOC Pattern or Practice Claims Against JBS to Proceed to Trial, Federal Judge Orders," July 24, 2015. https://www.eeoc.gov/eeoc/newsroom/ release/7-24-15.cfm Lucy Schouten, "Are employers required to grant prayer breaks to Muslim employees?", *Christian Science Monitor*, May 25, 2016. http:// www.csmonitor.com/USA/Society/2016/0525/Are-employers-required-to- grant-prayer-breaks-to-Muslim-employees

And members were worth way more than the paltry buck a week they paid (which needed to be raised, anyway). Membership list rentals alone brought in far more than that.

Nick grew so excited projecting the possibilities that he almost missed Natalie's text telling him it was safe to return. His shoulders drooped. Dreaming of the next big play was far more fun than cleaning up the messy details of the last one.

As expected, Natalie was in a sour mood when he arrived. "I can't believe you just snuck away and left me here with that woman."

Nick feigned surprise. "But you're my lawyer! You're supposed to handle disagreeable people for me."

Natalie dropped her chin to her chest.

"I think," said Jay earnestly, "it may have been a tactical error when Natalie mentioned that religious arbitration was the basis for Muslim sharia law in the court system, and that if the Muslims could do it then CIS could, too.[64] Mrs. Petrone seemed to miss some of the nuance there. 'Aaak!'" he squealed in falsetto. "'Muslims! Terrorists! Harold, what have you gotten us into!'"

"Mmm," said Nick, eyes dancing. "I can see that. Might have been better to leave the sharia law out of it. Anyway—Mr. Gimenez. On pain of purgatory, you need to keep your embargo promise. You're a free journalist, you can write whatever you want, but you can't do it until the matter is fully resolved. In other words, November first. Not a word until then."

"So I can write about denying the right to a lawyer, the foul language from the bench, the seat of the pants nature of the whole proceeding?"

"Absolutely. Whatever you want. So long as you wait until it all plays out, and verify—as you'll be able to do on November first—that this is the best possible outcome from a bad situation, and how much real good can be done when you rely on the Divine Spirit for guidance, rather than lawyers."

"We might not keep the lawyer ban," Natalie offered. "I'm not so sure that's a great idea, Nick."

"*We*?" Nick inquired. "There's a first. Why, because it means less work for lawyers? Gee whiz. I got it. We'll put in a rule that says the

---

64. "Islamic Tribunal benefits: People get access to religion, US laws not violated," *RT.com* February 12, 2015 http://rt.com/op-edge/231703-islamic-tribunal-texas-us/ See also http://www.islamictribunal.org/.

parties can have lawyers, but only gorgeous ones. So you'll get all the work you can handle, and I won't have to sit here all day with guys like Casciano in my face."

Perceiving that this fell a bit short of melting her heart, Nick added, "Hey—it's my religion. I can do what I want." Which didn't help, either.

September 10: The Edgar

"Don't drink too much here. This could be important."

Mother Superior Parks, Nick thought, as Natalie hurried him down the hall toward the rendezvous in the Mayflower bar, for which they were already late. He tried to picture her in a nun get-up. Talk about depressing! Sure, her flawless face divorced from her shining hair and noble figure was still head-turning, but what a waste. Nick mused about the "women's rights" debate in France over the law banning the wearing of full-body covering Muslim burkas.[65] What about men's rights, to enjoy the view of these marvelous individuals the Divine Spirit had created? What about that, huh?

" ... rollup, then an IPO. Those are huge."

"Rollup?" Nick had daydreamed through the first part of whatever Natalie had said.

"Pay attention, would you?" she snapped. "Christ, what I have to put up with."

"Divine Spirit. We don't do Christ. See, he was just someone moved by —"

"Zip it. We're late. McManus is a partner in Laura Boess's firm. The plan is to buy up a few dozen mom-and-pop childcare operations, paying with stock in the combined company instead of cash. Start with ones in the sixteen states that already have religious exemptions from state daycare licensing rules, and migrate them all to CIS. Then—and this is the key—move into a few states that don't have such exemptions, but do have RFRAs. There's twelve of those, including some big ones. Is Texas big enough for you?" Natalie was clearly annoyed with him. "File a couple of lawsuits saying a RFRA state has to exempt religious daycare, and bang! You've got sizzle. Wall Street will sniff the upside — which is massive. Then you spring the IPO. You sell stock in an initial public offering, at ridiculous prices, through a bunch of street-savvy underwriters, even before you've started winning the cases. Because everybody wants to be in on the ground floor. It's a gold mine. It's

---

65. "French 'burqa ban' violates human rights, rules UN committee." *DW.com*, October 23, 2018. https://www.dw.com/en/french-burqa-ban-violates-human-rights-rules-un-committee/a-46007469

better than a gold mine, because you don't have to actually find any gold. You just have to make people think you're going to."

These were the most words Nick had ever heard Natalie string together at one time. Too bad she was way off base.

"Uh, that's great, but I don't see how you could use RFRA for that. I mean, we push the envelope as it is, but safety rules for kids? I don't see us doing that."

"Gene says you can."

"Gene?"

"Gene Tucker. In corporate. You know him, don't you?"

Gene Tucker?! Golden Boy? Peter Spillman, fifteen years younger, but even more so. The first lawyer in the eighty-year history of the firm to make partner two years ahead of schedule. Unmarried, as far as Nick knew.

Shit. Double shit. Triple shit.

"Well, all respect," Nick stammered, "but he doesn't know what the fuck he's talking about. You can't just, just waltz in not knowing anything about it and start making theology."

"Gene says he's read the cases, and it's not that hard."

"Gene Tucker can take a flying fuck! What are you talking to him for, anyway? You—this is bullshit!"

"Uuugghhh!" Natalie groaned. "You're impossible! Just hear McManus out, ok?"

*****

The Mayflower bar was named "The Edgar," after J. Edgar Hoover, its most famous patron back when it used to be called the Rib Room. Paul McManus was already there when Nick and Natalie arrived. He looked like a TV grandfather, with half a head of white hair, a bushy mustache, and a perpetual friendly grin. A long white beard would make him Santa Claus.

McManus ordered a ginger ale, and Natalie a coffee. Nick, still steaming, asked for a Bowmore's and got a blank look. "Just some sort of Scotch, then. But not Johnny Walker."

McManus launched into a lengthier riff on what Natalie had already outlined. He could have been offering free donuts for life, and Nick still wouldn't have cared. He was damned if he was going to let Gene Tucker start running his religion. Even aside from that, there was Sammy Boone. Back in preschool, Sammy Boone had stuck his hand in the wrong spot on a playground carousel, and lost two fingers. All the screaming and the blood had made Nick vomit. It might again, if he thought about it hard enough.

"I get the general picture," said Nick, interrupting a monologue on underwriting fees in the Shanghai market. "But if there's no regulation, what about the kids? Who looks out for them?"

McManus cocked his head indulgently. "The children come first. Absolutely. We're all about the children. Here—let me show you something." He pulled out his wallet and began guiding Nick through the photographic history of the McManus dynasty, which sported far more than its fair share of freckles. Nick couldn't have remembered any of that information thirty seconds later if his life depended on it, except that son number two's wife was really hot. At least before she had those four kids.

"I could never hurt a child, Nick. Never. Inspiration Daycare won't, either." No violins played in the background, but they may as well have.

"I envy you," Nick murmured, sneaking a peek at Natalie. Mixing his own dumpiness with her perfection would be poor eugenics, for sure. "And if you personally were running the daycare in Beverly Hills, or wherever those beautiful grandchildren are, you'd take care of them. But if you got some minimum wage dude in what, Queens, and he's got no random inspections to be on his toes about, what happens then? I mean, I assume you pay minimum wage, unless Gene thinks he can get you out of that, too, which he can't."

McManus ignored the glare at Natalie. "Management controls," he said firmly. "Dead children are bad business. We're very big on that."

The Edgar's theme was brightly lit crystal. Its namesake would have preferred more wood, subdued lighting, and quiet efficiency. As it was, the clatter of glasses and the ricocheting laughter from other parties helped cover up a rather long pause in the conversation, ultimately broken by Natalie. "What we need—and it's not just Gene, I've looked at it too—is another sermon. Or podcast, whatever you call it. Something to make it crystal clear that CIS demands self-regulation of daycare without government regulation. Like the Christians have now.[66] There's a little bit to justify that in what you've done already,

---

66. Wendy Gittleson, "So You Want To Run A Daycare Center But You Have A Sketchy Past? Just Say You're Religious," *Addicting Info*, February 9, 2015. http://www.addictinginfo.org/2015/02/09/so-you-want-to-run-a-daycare-

but it's a stretch. We need something more direct. I can shoot you an email with talking points."

"So that's what you need, huh?" said Nick bitterly. "What do I need? How do I get around the little problem of telling the world I believe in something if I don't really believe it?" Secret Plan or no, there was a limit to how much collateral damage he could accept. He was winning anyway—why overdo it? Especially with kids. Grown-ups picking a lame health care plan or an untested pharmaceutical had only themselves to blame. Unlike Rosie. Unlike kids. What would the first injury in an unregulated CIS daycare look like? As bad as Sammy Boone's finger stumps? Worse?

McManus, oblivious to Nick's real concern, settled back on familiar turf. "If you're talking about some sort of, uh, stipend, or offering, I don't think that should be a problem. How much did Matteson Enterprises pay? Of course, we'll never have their revenues, but I think we could reach something fair."

"That's not what I meant at all!" Nick sputtered. "I'm not for sale! I do all this 'cause I believe in it, and … 'cause I think it's the right thing to do. In the long run. Earl Matteson helped at the start, yeah, but that's just to get it going. And I think *he* thinks I'm right, too. He's an amazing guy—he's a lot more thoughtful than most people realize. I'm uncomfortable about doing anything to put kids at risk, I gotta tell you. Not a definite no—I'll think about it, and read your stuff, and I really will try to listen to the Divine Spirit. But kids? I don't think so."

He pursed his lips, shook his head vigorously, and drained the rest of his Scotch. He was upset not only about the daycare scam, but about what he knew would come next, the second shoe that was bound to drop: using a religious exemption to get private schools out of complying with regulations to protect disabled kids. Disabled kids![67] Even the Secret Plan had lines not to cross, and kids were Nick's line. Uh-uh. No way.

McManus turned to Natalie, who said quietly, "You should know, Nick, that your friend Earl Matteson owns forty percent of Inspiration Daycare. Make sure you pass that on while you're communing with the Divine Spirit."

center-but-you-have-a-sketchy-past-just-say-youre-religious/
67.   "Federal judge: Religious school exempt from disability laws," *Associated Press*, April 6, 2016. http://bigstory.ap.org/6a423a4775f14847941fc6f2c3936990.

September 19: The Firehouse

"Shut that off. I wanna watch *Family Guy.*"

"You've seen it already. They're all re-runs. This is a new *Liberty Hour,* and I want to see it."

Ethan Beekins yawned and sauntered over to the refrigerator to refill his cup with iced tea. There was little point in arguing with Sophia. He'd just lose, and he'd lose because she was probably right. He'd seen every *Family Guy* episode more than once. And to tell Sophia she shouldn't watch the *Liberty Hour* was being disrespectful to her religion. Not a smart idea in an engine company where team cohesion at a fire site could easily affect life or death. Besides, it had been over an hour since the last run—for a false alarm—and by the law of averages they should be getting another call soon, making the television choice irrelevant. Let it go.

"And now," the host was saying, as Ethan sunk back down onto the musty, coffee-stained couch, "I'm delighted to welcome back to the *Liberty Hour* Dr. Richard Henry Marshall, who has just returned from Washington, DC. How goes the battle, doctor?"

"Thank you, Wesley," said Marshall. "The Lord has given us strength, given us strength. The progress we've made these past two years has been remarkable. Home schooling is now safe from the bureaucrats, abortion mills are being shut down left and right. We're starting to win our fair share of funding for Christian education and abstinence, we're driving atheism out of the military, we're putting God back into health care, and we've stopped the homosexual lobby in its tracks. All we need is one more vacancy on the Supreme Court, and President Bertram will be able to complete his mission of restoring Christianity to its rightful place in the public square."

Ethan stuck his finger into his throat in a gagging motion. Sophia shot him a dirty look.

"What he's sayin' is, he's got his hand on my wallet, and he ain't lettin' go," said Ethan. "These people make me sick."

"Shush up," replied Sophia. "I saw you praying when we pulled Dave out of the house on Nineteenth Street."

"I wasn't praying, I was scared. So were you. And it's a good thing McNeece was busy doing CPR rather than praying, or we'd have lost Dave."

"Shush up."

"Clouds on the horizon?" Marshall was asking, when they turned attention back to the set. "Yes, there are. We must always be vigilant. One of our greatest concerns now is this contemptible class of people who are deliberately perverting our religious freedom laws, making a mockery of all we have achieved."

"I assume you mean the so-called 'Church of Inspired Spirituality,'" said Wesley, frowning dutifully.

"Yes, that's what they call themselves. But we know who's really behind it. It is the Evil One. It is Satan himself, sowing confusion and discord as he so cleverly does."

"Is he talking about that Frenelli kid? He's a hoot!" said Ethan.

"Shush," said Sophia, but she couldn't stop herself from smiling. "He's a crazy ass, I'll give you that."

"Crazy like a fox," said Ethan, anxious for conversation about something, anything, to avoid listening to these pious pricks. "He's really stuck it to these bastards, hasn't he? Look at 'em squirm!"

Sophia giggled. "They don't like him, that's for sure. I think he's funny. I just wish they could all stop arguing so much, and just talk about Jesus, and helping people. That's the kind of religion I like. Not all this arguing."

"Yes, Wesley," Marshall was saying, growing more and more agitated, "I think you may be right. These may well be the days of the Antichrist, and he may walk among us. He must be destroyed."

"Just don't use arson," Ethan pleaded. "Shoot him or something, but no more fires."

Marshall was leaning forward on the edge of his seat, stabbing his index finger into the camera. "Our problem, as always, has been our over-generosity. This is a Judeo-Christian nation, after all. It is not a Muslim nation, or a yoga nation, or a Satanist nation, or a CIS, whatever that is, nation. When we enacted laws like RFRA to protect our Judeo-Christian heritage, we unwisely left open loopholes for these fraudulent religions as well.[68] Or, really, anti-religions, which is what Satanism and this CIS really are. You know, Wesley, it's supposed to be

---

68. For calls to exclude Islam from the benefit of religious liberty laws, see David Gibson, "Georgia Baptist official says religious freedom is not for Muslims," *Religion News Service*, June 9, 2016. http://religionnews.com/2016/06/09/georgia-baptist-official-says-religious-freedom-is-not-for-muslims/; Rev. Austin Miles, "Islam Is Not a Religion," *NewsWithViews*, January 1, 2017 http://www.newswithviews.com/Miles/austin106.htm.

the religious freedom law, not the antireligious freedom law."

"Reverend Marshall," said Wesley, oozing sincerity, "in these perilous end times, there are many things Christians must do. But one thing we must all do is to pray. Will you join with me to ask our father in heaven to deliver us from this evil?"

"I will, Wesley."

Both men knelt on thick cushions that had previously been positioned in front of their chairs. It took Marshall a little longer to get down there than it took his younger host. Wesley stretched out his clasped hands toward the camera. "Christians, won't you join us? Won't you lift your heart to the Lord and beseech his aid in our hour of need? Kneel. Right where you are, in your own homes. Kneel with us, open your heart, and pray for deliverance."

As both men bowed their heads, closed their eyes, and appeared to be murmuring something with their lips, a disembodied yet urgent voice explained to viewers exactly how they could go about making their financial contributions to the cause of authentic religious liberty, right then, using Paypal, Apple Pay, Google Wallet, or any major credit card.

Ethan shot Sophia a desperate look. "Are there any *Judge Judy* reruns on?"

"I think so," she sighed, picking up the remote.

October 6: CIS Office

Nick's weekly sermons were becoming a grind. Most of his life, no one had listened to him at all. Now, thousands hung on his every word.

Well, maybe. There were thousands—over eighty-three thousand last week—who paid their dollar and had Nick's video run for its allotted three to five minutes on their computer screens. How many were actually paying attention, though, he couldn't confirm. Especially for some of the corporate members, Nick knew that a secretary was given the assignment of "watching" the video, which satisfied the attendance obligation for the entire firm. Senior executives paid no attention at all. Some weeks there were distressingly few comments posted on the sermon website. Was anyone listening?

I could test it by screwing up, Nick mused, as he walked from the Watergate to work on a rain-pelted Monday morning. He could accuse the pope of sex with sheep. Or say the Divine Spirit changed its mind about marriage, and all men now needed six wives. See if anybody notices, Nick laughed to himself.

He tried to force his attention back to the issue at hand. Studio day was Wednesday, and he needed four scripts completed by tomorrow night, even if that meant staying late. So far he had one idea he liked, one idea he didn't, and two clueless blanks. Bummer.

He'd already held his nose and done the daycare piece for Natalie, who had softened after McManus left and allowed that she too was troubled by the child safety aspect of his plan. Even so, a public company was likely to be a lot better managed than most of the mom-and-pop Christian outfits that took advantage of the existing religious exemption. Right? Moreover, McManus had even more ideas that didn't involve children at all—like a CIS investment vehicle, similar to a mutual fund, but with a religious exemption from all those nasty federal investor protections that just got in the way of making real money for the depositors.[69] Nick had spent some time in the shower

---

69. Rob West, "New Research Highlights Major Flaw in Many Christians' Thinking," *Christian Post*, May 28, 2016. http://www.christianpost.com/news/new-research-highlights-major-flaw-in-many-christians-thinking-opinion-164521/. Brendan Pierson, "New Jersey pastor, Florida programer convicted of bitcoin

musing about whether he could latch onto all the laws protecting the Catholic "seal of the confessional," or the content of sermons, to shield communications between investors and such a fund from intrusive government scrutiny.[70]

Nick had drawn the line, though, at the suggestion from Laura's PR firm that he start pitching a "be kind to animals" theme in his weekly sermons to soften the CIS image. He didn't want to soften the image. He wanted to polish the image diamond-hard, to make CIS a vehicle that was used by 10 percent of the population and loathed by the other 90 percent. Loathed enough to persuade public opinion that something needed to be done to tamp down the whole religious privilege racket. Being loathed, though, wasn't that much fun. Not many people recognized him on the street, but the faces of those who did registered far more consternation than approval.

At least Laura and Gene fucking Tucker weren't pushing him for exemptions from any discrimination laws—the lowest hanging fruit in privilege-land. Maybe thirty years ago, exemptions from racial, ethnic, and sexual orientation discrimination would've been a money-maker, but America now was a place where such discrimination was (for the most part) uncool and unprofitable. Still, Nick thought, churches could discriminate to their hearts' content against women, gays, blacks, cripples, divorcees, anyone who struck their fancy—and there was nothing anyone could do about it.[71] On top of that, courts had largely

---

exchange scheme," *Reuters*, March 17, 2017, http://www.reuters.com/article/us-cyber-jpmorgan-idUSKBN16O2EP.

70. Charlie Butts, "At issue: The privacy of the confessional," *OneNewsNow*, August 17, 2016. http://www.onenewsnow.com/church/2016/08/17/at-issue-the-privacy-of-the-confessional. "A victory for the seal of Confession in Louisiana," *CNA/EWTN News*, November 1, 2016. http://www.catholicnewsagency.com/news/a-victory-for-the-seal-of-confession-in-louisiana-52284/. "Highlights from in and around the world of Texas politics," *Associated Press*, March 3, 2017. https://www.apnews.com/0148f63147f444208aeb2d40dd9dca70/Highlights-from-in-and-around-the-world-of-Texas-politics ["The Texas Senate has unanimously approved prohibiting government entities from compelling pastors and other religious leaders to divulge the contents of their sermons in civil legal cases."]

71. Fiona Ortiz, "More colleges seek exemption from LGBT anti-bias rules, rights group says," *Reuters*, December 19, 2015. http://www.reuters.com/article/us-usa-lgbt-education-idUSKBN0U20K720151219. "Federal judge: Religious schools not required to serve students with disabilities," Martha Woodall, *Philly*.

erased the distinction between churches per se and for-profit outfits like Matteson Enterprises that were simply devout, so a high-powered law firm like G&H should be able to bulldoze the civil rights laws on their behalf without breaking a sweat. Nick had caved in meekly on daycare—how would he hold up if Laura and/or Earl and/or Gene fucking Tucker figured out a way to increase profits by discriminating?

Much more to Nick's liking was an idea someone had posted on Facebook several weeks back, which Nick had only just gotten around to reading. Pauline Franz was a roadside convenience store checker, whose parents had both died of lung cancer. She hated selling cigarettes, especially to the truckers who hit on her. Nick thought this was a winnable case. Muslims, after all, didn't have to sell pork, or even touch it.[72] Catholic pharmacists, in many states, didn't have to sell contraceptives.[73] Why should someone have to sell something a lot worse for you than that?

"Winnable," though, didn't seem to be enough anymore. "Return on investment" was the new mantra. How, exactly, would letting someone *not* sell cigarettes boost the CIS bottom line? Earl didn't smoke, and as far as Nick knew had no financial interest in tobacco sales. But the absence of a negative didn't equal a positive.

Nick trudged down K Street, cold rain stinging his face. Could this

---

com, April 03, 2016 http://articles.philly.com/2016-04-03/news/71997955_1_sky-suit-disabilities-act. Charles Touting, "Religious School Held Exempt from Discrimination Laws," *New Jersey Law Journal*, April 4, 2016 http://www.njlawjournal.com/id=1202754040451/Religious-School-Held-Exempt-from-Discrimination-Laws?slreturn=20160416135308. Anne Hilt, "'Religious Freedom' Means Putting LGBT Americans Back in the Closet," *The New Civil Rights Movement*, September 10, 2016 http://www.thenewcivilrightsmovement.com/annehilt/1_religious_freedom_means_putting_lgbt_americans_back_in_the_closet Joe Davidson, "Civil rights or religious liberty — what's on top?", *Washington Post*, September 9, 2016 https://www.washingtonpost.com/news/powerpost/wp/2016/09/09/commission-says-religious-liberty-should-not-top-civil-rights/.

72.   Hazel Sheffield, "Costco sued for discrimination against Muslim former employee," *The Independent*, March 3, 2015. http://www.independent.co.uk/news/business/costco-sued-for-discrimination-against-muslim-former-employee-10082098.html.

73.   Richard Wolf, "Supreme Court may be converting on religion," *USA Today*, July 30, 2016 http://www.usatoday.com/story/news/politics/2016/07/30/supreme-court-religious-liberty-freedom-abortion-contraception/86819172/.

be sleet already, so early in the year? He waited at an intersection in front of a pen store. A pen store! Nick thought in amusement. Where hotshot lawyers could buy thousand-dollar pens to show off to their billionaire clients. If any of them knew a thousand-dollar pen when they saw one. Nick preferred stealing pens whenever he could. He had half a dozen from the Mayflower alone.

Maybe if he repeated Natalie's daycare rationalization another fifty times he'd start to buy it. As he was working through how he might explain the big picture to Sammy Boone's mother, or maybe give her a thousand dollar pen to make her feel better, he stepped off the sidewalk into a six-inch deep puddle. His week was off to a roaring start.

*****

The elevator to G&H's offices went up, but Nick hit the down button to reach the CIS headquarters in the building's basement. As he turned the corner at the end of the hallway, he saw a young woman sporting a spectacular pile of blonde hair standing outside his office door.

"Hey!" she sang out, her incandescent smile lighting up the dreary hallway. "Mr. Fratelli! I'm your new intern!"

"My what?"

"Your new intern!"

"I'm sorry," Nick said ruefully. "I wish you were. I don't have any interns. Maybe you're supposed to go to the law firm upstairs."

"No, I'm working for *you*. Are you just going to stand there and drip, or are you going to let me in?"

Fumbling for his keys, Nick asked, "Did Earl send you?" She looked like someone who belonged on Earl's "staff."

"No, I don't know anyone named Earl. I'm here on my own—just for you."

"Well, then there's some sort of mistake. I don't have any time to spare this morning."

"Oh, there's no mistake," she said as she pushed past him into the barren office foyer. He hadn't gotten around to sprucing it up yet, since no one ever came there.

Nick showed her past the empty reception desk to his own dimly lit office, piled with discovery binders and endless memos he hadn't gotten around to reading yet. As he hung up his soaked coat, he snuck a closer look at his visitor. Not what Pop would call "stacked," but a slim Keira Knightley build, an unblemished, wholesome face, playful blue eyes, and that gravity-defying Hollywood hair. Even if he hadn't seen her, Nick would have been smitten by her voice: a rich southern accent with a hint of a question mark at the end of every sentence—never a lawyerly period. Positive attributes aside, Nick frowned as he settled into one of the chairs in front of his desk and motioned her to sit in the other. "I only have a minute, ok? So, why are you here?"

"I'm going to be your new intern! I just know I am. It's like you say in your sermons, and in *Inspired Spirituality*. The Divine Spirit has spoken to me, and through me, and I am destined to serve him. And you."

Nick stared at her, not sure how to react. Finally he hit upon, "Uh, what's your name?"

"I'm sorry!" She blushed, and girlishly clapped her hands to her face. "I'm Melody."

Perfect, Nick thought, for that voice.

"Melody Lapin. I'm from New Orleans. Near there, anyway. Maybe you guessed?" She giggled. "You must think I'm just awful, throwing myself at you like this."

"Oh, no," said Nick, a little too quickly.

"Here's my story. I'm twenty-two. I almost finished junior college back home, but there was this guy ... you know." She rolled her eyes and shook her head. "Hank," she said softly, staring at the floor as she wrung her hands. White, soft hands. "Anyway, he told me I was too dumb to be in school. But I'm not! He's the dumb one."

Nick nodded in vigorous agreement.

"So I had to get out of there. Come to the city—the big city, not just New Orleans. And I'm not here aimless. That would be dumb, wouldn't it? I thought it all through and planned it out before I came. 'Melody, old girl' I said, 'how can you truly make a difference? How can you truly serve God?' And then I saw one of your videos. Hank, he works out on a rig in the Gulf, and his company belongs to your church, so that's how I saw it. And I was just blown away! So I went and watched every one of them—some of them two or three times. And now, here you are in person! I can't believe it. I met Justin Bieber once, but you're much better."

Nick continued to nod rhythmically throughout her explanation, like a bobblehead doll. He blushed mildly at the Justin Bieber comment.

"I can help here. I can do anything you want. Open your mail, type your letters, you name it. I'll show them! And besides, your spiritual message. I need to help you get the word out!"

"The thing is," Nick answered, "we don't really have a budget for any interns. And if we did, we'd want a whole hiring process, pick the best one, and all that."

"Oh, I don't need a budget. I mean, a salary. Daddy's just happy I'm away from Hank—he'll support me. He might even want to make you a contribution—he loves what you've been talking about, especially on healthcare. And I'm the best one you'll find. The Divine Spirit calls me! Has anyone else come here to help? Don't you think that means something?"

An unanswerable point. Nick chewed for a moment on his thumbnail. Earl wouldn't mind—he'd give Nick a wink and a poke in the ribs. Peter wouldn't acknowledge her existence. Natalie was the issue. She could be a little catty. Her irritation at the episode with Prissy stemmed, as far as Nick could figure, from the calculation that if she were going to be a celibate money-making machine, then Nick should be too. Especially since so much of the money Nick was generating wound up in Natalie's pocket. Still, she could be sold on the idea of getting work done for free. But what work? It could be more hassle than it was worth just coming up with things for an intern to do.

"Well, I can't just haul off and hire someone, even for free. I've got this board of directors ... "

"But I thought *you* were the man in charge." Her eyes doubled in size, and started to glisten.

"I am, but—"

"Oh don't send me away!" She threw her head onto Nick's shoulder, grasping his forearm with one of her hands and stroking his bare hand with the other. She smelled like orange blossoms. "You don't understand how much this means to me. I can't just go back! Not after the way I stormed out of there. God wants me here with you! I know it!"

At Melody's touch, Nick's glandular system seized instant command over several small but rather important muscle valves regulating local blood flow near his pelvis, resulting in an immediate and prominent bulge in his trousers. He turned beet-red when Melody blurted out, "Look at those pants!"

To Nick's relief, she pointed not at his crotch, but at his right cuff, still dripping from the K Street puddle.

"I was thinking too much while I was walking in," he offered lamely.

"Now you just wait right here," she commanded, jumping up. "What size shoe do you wear?"

"Uh, ten? Ten and a half?"

"I'll be back in a jiffy, with some dry socks and some nice warm slippers for you. You'll catch your death! There's a shoe store not a block from here. And some Starbucks, too. I'll get you my favorite flavor—I know you'll just love it. Then we'll get down to work. And after we're done, you can just tell that old board of yours what's what. Don't ask 'em—just tell 'em! You're the man here, not them."

With that, she fluttered away. Maybe there really is a Divine Spirit after all, thought Nick.

October 20: Tidal Basin

Nick fell hard.

A year of failed passes at Natalie, broken only by the week in Puerto Rico with Prissy, left Nick helpless against the charms of a woman whose delight in life seemed to be trying to please him.

It wasn't just Melody's looks. That was only 80 percent of it. In truth, other than the hair, she had none of the classic beauty of Natalie Parks. She was more the helpless waif type.

But whenever Nick entered the room, the sun rose in Melody's face. If she'd been a pet dog, her tail would have been wagging furiously.

She hung on every word of Nick's sermons and always offered praise after he was finished. ("Wow, that was such a great talk!")

She laughed at Nick's jokes. She laughed once when she thought he was joking, even though he wasn't.

Two days after Nick uncharacteristically ordered a salad for lunch, she marveled that he looked like he'd lost ten pounds. He'd lost two, in an effort to impress her. She brought Nick brownies one day. Another day, watermelon soup. Pecan pie. Shoo-fly pie. Nick liked the shoo-fly pie the best—the highest concentration of sugar per bite. Nick gained back the two pounds rather quickly, plus five more, none of which she seemed to notice.

Melody was no dumb blonde either. She wasn't overly sophisticated, and couldn't spell to save her soul, but she wasn't dumb. Nick reminded himself of that regularly. A dumb person would not have picked up so instantly on the nuances of what Nick was trying to communicate, or offered such helpful and insightful comments as, "That is so awesome!"

She went gaga over Nick's monthly haircut and said things about his dress like, "You're wearing the blue shirt! That's my favorite. You look so, so commanding in it."

Her own clothes were a refreshing break from law firm severity. Her skirts were short and flouncy, her blouses cut low.

"Don't sleep where you eat." Nick had received this sage advice once from Kyle, of all people. He couldn't remember the context, but he did remember the words, and the prudent consideration behind them. They compounded his reluctance to put a move on Melody.

Until the day, that is, when Nick moved from being 98 percent hooked to 110 percent. He'd spent the morning trying to put a dent in his email backlog, with little success. Melody eagerly accepted his invitation to lunch. Nick ordered an open face cheesesteak with extra onions. Melody asked for a small Cobb salad.

"Can you believe they call that a tomato?" she asked, when their food arrived. "It's gray. Not even orange, much less red like it ought to be."

"They pick them when they're green and hard," said Nick. "Easier to ship that way. My brother Luca runs a produce department at Sav-A-Lot, he knows all about it. Then they run 'em through some kind of gas, to redden 'em up. Didn't work on that guy, though. You can get real red tomatoes from a greenhouse, but they cost more. Double. Place like this, they don't want to pay double."

Melody wrinkled her nose. "Yuck. I won't eat something like that." Pushing the tomato wedge to the side of her bowl, she added, "There ought to be a law."

With his raised eyes in a patronizing way, Nick replied, "Don't think that would get too far. If you want good tomatoes, you gotta pay for them. A law won't change that."

"Well what about a religious rule? You get around everything else."

"Sorry. Don't think I can get around supply and demand."

Nick took another bite, and chewed for a long time as he stared out the window. "You know..." he said, voice traling before turning to address Melody directly. "There *are* some religious dietary rules. Like kosher food, for Jews. There's nothing about tomatoes, but there could be."

Melody eyes shone. "Oh, you are so smart! Like what?"

"Well, lemme think."

Before he'd thought for very long, Melody said, "How about 'Food like God made it?' He didn't make that gray tomato, that's for sure."

"That's it!" said Nick eagerly. "Hold on. It couldn't be for everybody. But like prisoners, they definitely get the right to demand kosher or halal food.[74] It should be easy for us to say hey, we require *fresh* food, like the Divine Spirit made it. Nothing canned, or frozen, or processed like that shitty tomato. Fresh, natural food. That's our religion! That'll catch on like crazy."

---

74.   Mike Brodheim, "Tenth Circuit Rules Denial of Halal Diet May Violate RLUIPA," *Prison Legal News*, November 15, 2011. https://www.prisonlegalnews.org/news/2011/nov/15/tenth-circuit-rules-denial-of-halal-diet-may-violate-rluipa/.

This fit the Secret Plan so precisely, Nick was kicking himself for not having thought of it sooner. If people wanted to eat kosher or halal food, fine. All they had to do was stay out of jail. But once you're in jail, the point is to *lose* freedoms, right? Including the freedom of what you're going to eat. What better way to highlight the absurdity of religious privilege than to demand (and probably win) the right of prisoners to better food than most average working people ate themselves?

"In prisons?" asked Melody dubiously.

"For starters, yeah. That's the easiest case. But the military, they can get kosher and halal food, unless they're in the middle of combat or something. Students in a lot of public schools, same thing. Meals on Wheels for old people? Subsidized nursing homes? I bet it's the same, but I'd have to look it up. There was even a guy who won a ton of money from an airline for not getting the kosher meal he'd asked for."[75]

"But wouldn't fresh food for all those people cost more?"

"Sure. But it doesn't matter. Kosher and halal food cost way more, too.[76] But once you've established the principle that government has to pay higher prices for food to satisfy one religion, or two, even better, then the sky's the limit."

Melody clapped her hands. "Gosh, you're incredible! How can we celebrate?"

Nick was forming a precise idea about the answer to that question. An idea Kyle surely would have disapproved. But he held back.

"Tell you what. I think we're done for the day. One idea like that is more than enough. Have you been down to the Tidal Basin yet? FDR Memorial?"

"Gosh, no. I haven't even seen the Washington Monument up close yet."

Was that a hint of suggestive sly in her eyes? Probably not. Probably not.

"Well, this is one of the last pretty days of the year. So let's take a

---

75. "Brazilian Jew wins $1,400 from airline for not being served kosher meal," *Jewish Times*, March 30, 2016 http://www.jta.org/2016/03/30/news-opinion/lufthansa-ordered-to-pay-damages-for-not-providing-kosher-meal-to-passenger .

76. "Jew on death row sues to keep kosher after chicken dinner," *Associated Press*, July 25, 2016 (Kosher meals cost prisons 72 percent more to prepare). https://www.apnews.com/23acb57523dd4fc595ddda5179093be8/Jew-on-death-row-sues-to-keep-kosher-after-chicken-dinner.

walk. The office is officially closed. I decree it! Let me tell Natalie and Tonetta so they don't freak out." Nick punched keys on his cell phone for a moment, then read out: "We're off researching. Brilliant new plan. See you tomorrow."

They walked to the Jefferson Memorial, with a view of Hains Point in full autumn thrall. Did the trees look like that every year, or did Melody make them more vivid? They wandered through the maze of the FDR, where Nick read the inscriptions aloud in his best attempt at a New York patrician accent, adding his own rhetorical flourish. As the sun began to droop, Nick guided Melody to a bench facing southwest to watch the sunset. She sat nearly touching him, though she had room to sit further away. She snuggled closer. "Brr, it's getting colder," she said. It wasn't, but Nick laid his arm over her shoulder anyway.

"So where would you like to have dinner?" asked Nick, after a time. "There's a French place on Connecticut that has a marvelous wine selection. Plus—I bet—some wonderfully fresh food, like the Divine Spirit made it!"

Melody looked up at him demurely. "I have a better idea. I'm not dressed to go out. Let's wait until tomorrow night, and instead of going to a crowded restaurant, I'll pick up a big steak and bring it over to your place to cook. You get the champagne. Then we'll have a real celebration." She wasn't looking quite so shy anymore.

One of the best parts of that plan was that it would give Nick a few hours to clean the place up before she arrived. Clean sheets were a must.

October 21: Takoma Park

Friday was donut day at Guilder & Hersh. Nick always picked up a couple from the G&H kitchen on the way in. He was pleasantly surprised, though, when Natalie paid a surprise mid-morning visit, bearing a plate with another half a dozen. "Thought I'd share the wealth," she explained. "And see what this exciting new research project is all about."

Nick launched into a description of the fresh food play with his mouth half full of maple glazed donut. He gave Melody full, even overstated credit for her role. Natalie seemed impressed. "Is there any way for us to make money from religious food rules?" she asked, "Other than just getting more members?"

"I think so," Nick replied, swallowing. "Inspectors. Rabbis and imams get paid plenty to certify food as kosher or halal. So we need to have our certifiers get paid plenty, too. In fact, we may need to make it a little more complicated than just 'not frozen or canned,' to give them something more to inspect. We might even want to specify what people *shall* eat, not just what they shalt not eat. Like artichokes or something. Then we could work some sort of sponsorship deal."

"That is so brilliant!" Melody gushed.

"Mm-hmm," said Natalie, nodding in agreement. Turning to Melody, she said, "I just love that blouse. Did you get it around here?"

"This old thing? No, this is from back home. I haven't even looked for any stores downtown yet."

"Oh, my," said Natalie, with exaggerated shock. "This won't do! We have to take better care of you. Nick, shoo yourself back to your office. Get some work done. And close the door—we have some girl things to talk about."

Nick dutifully complied, happy to escape the next fifteen minutes of giggling he heard through the door. Natalie was sure in a good mood, he thought. She hardly ever acted like this. In fact, she'd been downright frosty the few times Nick had seen her interact with Melody. Go figure. Maybe the little white lie as to how responsible Melody had been for the food initiative had paid a bigger than expected dividend. Natalie did appreciate good work.

For the next couple of hours, with little Googling effort, Nick began to discover just how exciting religious food legal privileges could be—and to berate himself even more severely for not thinking of them sooner. The religious food certification game was so lucrative, even the Hindus were trying to get in on the act.[77] And they covered far more than prisoners—federal regulations had been proposed for all nursing homes to be required to honor their residents' religious dietary restrictions.[78] There were well over a million nursing home residents—how many of them would prefer fresher food? Nick tried but failed to recollect the name of the asshole nursing home owner back on Peter's boat on the Fourth of July, the one so solicitous about funding for Alzheimer's patients. How would he react to being forced to fork out more money for special food for CIS residents? His homes would make an ideal location to recruit plaintiffs for the first legal test case.

Despite his excitement, Nick couldn't keep his mind off tonight's date with Melody. She was such a gem in every way. Natalie had definitely grown warmer to Nick now that he was succeeding, but at some point you just had to give up on anything more than that. Could Melody turn out to be more than a one-night hookup?

Shortly before noon, another visitor arrived to disturb Nick's reverie. This time it was Tonetta. "Mr. Spillman needs to see you immediately. You need to come upstairs with me right now. Just you. It's urgent."

"What is it, Nick?" asked Melody anxiously.

"Beats me," Nick replied. He told Tonetta he was on his way out to lunch, and asked if he could stop upstairs afterward. She shook her head and just said, "Now."

When they reached the eighth floor, Tonetta told Nick to go see Natalie first. "Couldn't he just have called me?" asked Nick. "Why'd he have to send you down to get me?"

Tonetta shrugged and said she was just doing what she was told.

Nick found Natalie's office and eased into the chair in front of her desk. "What's up?"

Natalie looked like she'd just swallowed a toad. "Have you fucked her?"

"Excuse me?"

---

77. "Hindus want religious food certification," *The Indian Diaspora*, August 4, 2014. http://theindiandiaspora.com/news-details/diaspora-news/general_news/hindus-want-religious-food-certification.htm

78. Alejandra Cancino, "Nursing homes starting to offer more individualized menus," *Associated Press*, May 2, 2016. http://bigstory.ap.org/35245ce0e04248cf84c60a91c41299e9.

"You heard me. The little whore downstairs. Have you fucked her yet?"

Nick drew himself up indignantly. "That's none of your business! And I don't appreciate the question. Or your tone."

"Oh, it's very much my business," she replied, eyes blazing. "Indeed it is. This may be my big chance to break into criminal law. Here," she said, spinning her laptop around to face Nick. "Recognize anyone?"

The picture was definitely Melody, looking especially dolled up, with professional makeup and lighting. But the name above it read Melody LaPelletiere, not Melody Lapin.

"She's ... she's married?"

"No, you idiot, she's not married. Her name is LaPelletiere. Always has been. Does that name ring a bell?"

Nick had seen the name many times. "There's a LaPelletiere who runs one of the Christian health sharing scams we modeled Inspiration Health on. Bartimaeus, I think."

"The one and only. Also known as 'Daddy.' But please don't call it a scam. You're in enough trouble already."

"But why would she ... I don't get it."

"Look at the birthdate, Nick. Lower right, small print. And in case you forgot, it's 2022."

"December 4, ... 2005? She told me she was twenty-two!"

"Mmmm," said Natalie, feigning surprise. "Did she, now?"

"Then she's only ... no ... NO!" Nick jerked back so hard that he nearly toppled over backwards.

Natalie's chin jutted out, her gaze fixed. "Everything you say here is protected by attorney-client privilege. But I need the absolute truth or I cannot help you. Have you had sexual relations with that seventeen-year-old girl?"

"No," Nick croaked, voice barely above a whisper.

"Anything? Oral? Fingering? Through the clothes? Whacking you off? Anything?"

"Natalie ..." Nick groaned. But he knew he'd better answer. Eyes glued to his hands on his knees, he said "No. Nothing. I was scared she might, she might disappear if I tried anything. So I didn't. It might have been tonight, though."

"Tonight?"

"She's coming over to cook dinner at my place after work. Said she'd bring the steak if I got the champagne."

"Sounds cozy. I can see why she might not have wanted to get the champagne. So while you were getting the champagne, you were going to pick up some condoms, too, just in case?"

Nick continued staring at his hands. He'd done an extra careful job clipping his nails, just this morning. Finally, he asked, "How'd you find out?"

Natalie pushed out her right cheek with her tongue, calculating for a moment. Then she held up a cellphone. "I looked at her phone. There's a whole trail of chatty emails with her best friend, Tracy. She's been a bad girl, Nick, and Daddy caught her in the act. Said the only way she could redeem herself in the eyes of the Lord was to use her evil temptress powers for something pure and good. Like sending the Antichrist to jail." She held up the phone. "It's all right here."

"You stole her phone?" asked Nick incredulously. "That's a crime!"

Natalie's eyes narrowed in contempt. "They stole yours, didn't they? You'd rather I let you walk into the trap? So I was proactive. I'll turn it in to the building's lost and found, and she'll never know. There was just something about her that didn't seem right."

"Yeah, that a woman liked me," said Nick bitterly. "That's a dead giveaway for a fake, all right."

"That's not what I meant," Natalie responded quickly.

"Yeah. Right. So how'd you get into the phone you stole? Isn't there a password?"

"I watched her type it in. It's her birthday—120405."

Nick was too overwhelmed to speak, so Natalie continued. "Your little fling would have shattered everything we've built up over the past year. No one would touch us. Not to mention, probably three to five years in the DC pen for you. Judges are hard on pedophile priests."

"I'm not a pedophile!"

Natalie shrugged. "You would have been, once the prosecuting attorneys got through with you. After they put poor little teary-eyed schoolgirl Melody on the stand. Maybe they even would have put her in a pleated jumper and pigtails. 'Oh, it was so awful,'" Natalie simpered in a thick Southern accent. "'Ah jest stopped by to drop off some papers, 'n he was all over me! It was turrible!'" She daubed away an imaginary tear.

"She might not have done that," said Nick softly. He was in the "denial" stage of grief.

"Oh, no? She's quite the actress, you know. I've been looking her up, now that I have her proper name. She starred as Juliet in the junior class play, just last spring. And here's another one I think you'll like.

It's from August." She took back the laptop, hit a few keys, and spun the screen back to face Nick.

It showed the front page of the Viviers Parish Courier, covered by a picture of Melody sporting a sash and tiara, with the headline "Melody LaPelletiere Named Praline Queen."

Nick sunk even lower in his chair. "Is there anything else?"

"There was something odd in the emails. Do you know a priest named McIntyre?"

"Yeah, sure. Father Bob. My old chaplain at college. He came to see me last summer."

"To try to talk you out of CIS?"

Nick eyed Natalie intently.

"They paid him twenty thousand dollars to lobby you."

That ended the "denial" phase, as Nick surged straight into "anger." He sprang from his chair, stomping back and forth, clenching and unclenching his fists. "I can't believe it! The motherfucker!"

Natalie poured on a little more gasoline. "He wanted twenty-five. He finally settled for twenty up front, plus ten more as a success fee. Which I guess he didn't get."

Nick had been the weakest kicker back on Coach Dave's under-eight soccer team. But Coach Dave would have been impressed by the mighty blow Nick now gave Natalie's plastic trashcan, which soared through the air before crashing into her bookshelves. Had it hit plasterboard instead, it may have wound up in the next office.

"Hey!" said Natalie. "Watch it! I didn't do anything to you. Just calm down, then go downstairs and fire her. But don't hit her! Maybe I should come with you."

Nick was still pacing, grinding his fist into his palm. "Motherfuckers," he kept saying. The kick, though, had helped him past "anger," and into "bargaining." Or, more precisely, into the fierce stage of revenge. That an old mentor he'd idolized would betray his affection for cash seemed at that instant even worse than what Melody had done, perhaps because she hadn't actually done it yet. Upon calmer reflection later, Nick decided it was a silly apples-to-oranges comparison, like Peyton Manning vs. A-Rod. Right now, though, there was little room in Nick's brain for any conceptualizing other than "Somebody, somewhere, is gonna fucking pay."

"No, that's not what you do," he snarled. "Haven't you ever read a spy novel? When you find the spy, you don't just arrest him, or shoot him. Especially if the spy doesn't know you're onto him. You turn him. Or use him to spread disinformation. Or something cool and devious like that."

Natalie looked at him like he was speaking in Bulgarian.

Nick had wandered over to the window, watching the foot traffic on K Street pick up as lunch approached. His toe throbbed. "Tonetta said it was Peter who wanted to see me. Does he know about this?"

"No. I just wanted to make sure you came up. I thought you might ignore a message from me. Your attention seemed otherwise occupied."

This drew a long exhale. "It was that obvious?"

Natalie drooped her head in disgust. "I can't believe how close you came to destroying everything. For one little romp."

Nick redirected his anger for a moment. "Look, I'm just a guy, ok? A pretty woman seems interested in me, says she's twenty-two, looks like she's twenty-two, I'm not gonna hire a private eye to check her out. Ok? You may be the great ice queen, but I'm not."

"Ice queen? Is that what you think of me?"

"Oh, I'm sorry," said Nick sarcastically. "I forgot about you and Gene."

Natalie's jaw dropped. "Gene! Gene Tucker? That little suck-up? That's what you think? I wouldn't care about him if he were the last man on earth. You, you're not perfect—God knows you're not perfect—but at least you're a ... something. Your own man, with your own agenda, twisted as it may be. You do things. Gene Tucker? Give me a little credit, would you?"

Nick's brain chugged slowly. A glimmer of a thought tried to struggle its way to the surface. Could there have been more than one reason prompting Natalie to steal Melody's phone?

While Nick struggled with this, Natalie continued. "I've explained this before, but let me try one more time. I don't want to spend the rest of my life pressing shirts, like my mother. This," waving her hands at her office, "is my way out of all that. My way out of this—"

She undid the button on the left cuff of her blouse sleeve and pushed it up, revealing a grotesque scar. The burn she'd mentioned back on Peter's yacht last Fourth of July that Nick had tried to joke about. "You may not care about financial security, your vegetables before your dessert, but I do. Ok? I do."

This mix of good news with not-so-good news was too much for Nick to process. There was a logical flaw in an either-or choice somewhere, he dimly perceived. But right now, when he was trying to figure out how to turn this near catastrophe to his advantage, he locked the door to that brain compartment, walked back to the chair, righted the trash can, and said "Fine. Ok. What I need right now is two things. First, I need a place to work up here this afternoon. With a computer I can use. Can you get me that?"

"Uh-huh. Peter's in Denver today."

"And I need you to get that phone back to Melody, because I may want to call her, or text her, or something. She's probably freaking out already. Can you do that?"

Natalie looked dubious.

"Come on," he urged. "Wait—I got it. Go back down there, tell her there's a big emergency, and I've got to go straight to the airport with Peter. And I'm really upset about not being able to have dinner with her, and I wanted you to tell her that personally. Then you do your sleight of hand thing, and put the phone back in her bag, or wherever. After you've wiped your prints off it. Easy as pie."

Natalie grimaced. "Do you want me to give her a big kiss for you while I'm at it?"

"No," Nick said evenly, not wanting to stir up another outburst. "Just show me how to get onto Peter's computer. There is one more thing, though. I know I'm pushing my luck, but … could you bring me back a double roast beef sandwich and some cookies? Stress makes me hungry."

*****

Nick settled into Peter's office and reproduced Natalie's search for information about Melody LaPelletierre. He found little other than the Miss Praline contest and a not very active Facebook page. Studying her picture, he weighed more carefully the pros and cons of his first fleeting thought after Melody's true age became known to him. All he needed to do was hold off for a few weeks until she turned eighteen, and all would be well.

Bad idea, Nick. Bad, bad, bad idea.

How about claiming a religious exemption from the statutory rape laws? Didn't Muslims marry little girls all the time? Didn't Mormons have a case pending to legalize polygamy under RFRA?[79]

---

79. Maura Irene Strasburg, "Can We Still Criminalize Polygamy?", 2016 *U. Ill. L. Rev.* 1605, Sep 28, 2016. https://illinoislawreview.org/print/volume-2016-issue-4/can-we-still-criminalize-polygamy/.

More bad ideas.

With a puff of his cheeks, Nick turned to a study of Raymond LaPelletierre. At first he couldn't imagine any father using his daughter like that. Then he reflected on how many girls were essentially sold into marriage in Hindu and Muslim cultures, and even among the Amish.[80] Then there was the biblical story of Jephthah, the Jewish general who made a deal with God that if he could just win glory in battle, he'd happily sacrifice the first living thing he saw when he returned home, which turned out to be his daughter. But Jephthah did feel awfully bad about slitting her throat, which made it all ok.[81] Nick bet that Raymond LaPelletierre was highly familiar with the story of Jephthah.

Nick began watching some LaPelletierre videos. What a snake. His favorite subject was hell fire, and who deserved it, which turned out to be lots of people. If Melody had been brainwashed with this since birth, then maybe she wasn't responsible for her actions, and maybe Nick's still-forming plan for revenge was overly cruel. Then he thought again about the sound a cell door made when it slammed shut, at least in the movies. Keep going.

Natalie finally returned, and dropped a white paper bag on Peter's desk in front of Nick. "Here's a salad. No cookies. You're getting fat. Clean up your mess when you're done. The phone's back, and your message is delivered. She needed a whole box of Kleenex to wipe away the tears."

As Natalie closed the door on her way out, a little harder than necessary, Nick muttered, "You better watch it, or you'll be number two on the revenge list."

Sick of LaPelletiere, Nick tried to learn more about Bartimaeus, the health non-insurance company he operated. This proved difficult. Since there were no public reporting requirements, all he could find was the PR website, featuring pictures of thirty-five year old suburbanites, most of them blonde, grinning stupidly at their laptop screens, or at their central casting children (boy ten, girl eight), or

---

80. "Amish shocked by parents accused of 'gifting' girl," *Associated Press*, June 24, 2016. http://www.cbsnews.com/news/amish-shocked-by-parents-accused-of-gifting-girl-lee-kaplan-daniel-stoltzfus-savilla/.

81. Judges 11:29-40. https://www.biblegateway.com/passage/?search=judges+11%3A29-40&version=KJV.

at their golden retriever, thrilled at the blessed assurance of blissful health that Bartimaeus provided. Nick had suffered through enough actuary meetings with Laura Boess about the real world of Christian health sharing that he wanted to puke.

Nick's mind, which wandered far too easily, asked his fingers to click on his own Inspiration Health site for a quick comparison. The ad agency Laura Boess had picked took a totally different approach. Hip twenty-five year olds, of a variety of races, including two guys holding hands, communicated the simple message: "Pay for what you need." Not what you don't. You need coverage for accidents, for having or preventing babies, for sexually transmitted diseases, or for the one-off serious disease. At least for a few months, until you could switch to a traditional plan, which couldn't reject you or decline to renew you for a pre-existing condition, like Inspiration Health or Bartimaeus would. All for a dramatically lower monthly premium than even Bartimaeus charged—a helpful comparative pricing table was prominently displayed on the front page.

Slick, Nick thought. No wonder they'd already broken into six figures of customers. No wonder LaPelletiere was panic-stricken enough to sacrifice his daughter's—well, not her virginity, which was apparently long gone—but her, her what? Her freedom of choice in sex partners? She still had that, of course, except for the minutes she'd have to spend gratifying fat old Nick. Little bitch.

But what to do? How to use Natalie's illicitly gained intelligence to trash this sanctimonious turd?

Nick stared at the screen. It stared right back. His eye wandered around Peter's sumptuous paneled office, with its diplomas (Harvard B.A., Georgetown J.D.), lawyer prints, and ship's clock, which he understood better now. He was tempted to root through Peter's in-box, but decided against it. The desk drawers were locked. Peter wasn't such a bad guy, once he decided he could make money off you. He couldn't have been nicer during Nick's recuperation. What would Peter do in this spot? Silly question—he would never be in this spot. What advice would he give? Drop it, most likely. Deep freeze her for a couple of days to confirm she hadn't noticed the temporarily missing phone, then make up some reason why she had to go.

Which was why Peter was boring Peter, and Nick was changing the world. Keep thinking.

He idly Googled "What to do?" and received a list of Washington tourist attractions in return. This was all too hard to sort out while deadeningly sober. Two thirty—the day was almost over! he rejoiced.

Nick dialed Jay's cell phone, got a canned "Please leave a message," and slammed the phone down in in disgust. Ungrateful bastard. There really wasn't much other choice, though. He needed Jay's nose for the newsworthy, honed to perfection by years of selling stories where he got paid by the internet hit. Even more than that, he needed to spill his guts to somebody who would at least nod every now and then and pretend to give a shit. He needed the anti-Natalie.

He redialed Jay's number. "Yo," he said to Jay's robot. "It's Nick. I got the scoop of the century for you. Word. But it's gotta be now. NOW, asshole, or I go straight to AP and Reuters and you get shit. No Pulitzer, no nada. Call me, asshole. Or else."

There's a time for subtlety, Nick thought. And this wasn't it.

Nick threw up a clock on the computer screen, and watched the seconds tick by. As he was trying to figure out a reasonable deadline for Jay's return call, and more importantly what he would do if it passed, his phone buzzed. Thank you, Divine Spirit.

"I'm at a Senate hearing," said Jay. "What's up?"

"You got wheels yet?"

"Yeah. Not nice ones, but she runs. Why?"

"You're welcome. For the car. Which you wouldn't have but for me. You gotta come pick me up, right now. I don't wanna take a chance being seen on the street, 'cause I'm supposed to be out of town. So you drive into the garage underneath the G&H building on K Street, call me, and I'll come right down."

"What's going on?" asked Jay.

"Wouldn't you like to know? Can you be here in fifteen minutes?"

After a brief hesitation, Jay said "Thirty. This better be good."

*****

The prospect of movement unclogged Nick's brain. By the time Jay arrived, the framework of a plan had emerged. Over the course of many beers at a dive in Takoma Park near Jay's place (where Nick had already decided he would crash), Nick and Jay polished the façade.

Around ten o'clock, still at the bar, Nick finally pecked out an email on his phone. Jay proofed it—making several corrections—but Nick didn't trust his judgment, and asked the redhead at the next table to check it as well. She found no problems.

Melody:

I am so sorry! You can't believe how much I was looking forward to being with you tonight. But we've got big problems in New York, with state insurance regulators all over the health care operation there, threatening to shut us down. We're at the Plaza tonight—boy I wish you were here!—heading up to Albany tomorrow. We're going to try to grease a few political palms there, and make this go away. I'm hopeful, so long as everything stays quiet. Nobody knows about this investigation yet, so it should be easy to squash. In fact, if we pay enough under the table to get extra chummy with Goldstein over this, we might even get listed as an option for the New York state employee health care system. Awesome! Anyway, I'll let you know how things go. I think we'll be back Monday. And we'll have some unforgettable celebrating to do then!

Nick

October 24: The Mayflower

Late Saturday morning, Nick was sprawled on Jay's couch, fully clothed, in "never again" mode with regard to the consumption of alcohol. He spent that afternoon and evening learning more than he really wanted to know from Jay's undersized television about the state of college football. Sunday, Jay drove them out to the paintball range, where Nick discovered that the year layoff hadn't improved his game any.

Early Monday, Jay drove them to a Victoria's Secret store in Wheaton, where they had a delightful time picking out a negligee. Nick was fond of a fluffy pink one, but Jay correctly pointed out that black lace would provide better contrast on-screen.

Shortly before noon, working from a Wheaton Starbucks, Nick set up, but did not yet send, the next email to Melody:

> Success! Investigation will quietly disappear—less $$ than we thought. And Goldstein is very interested in future relationship, if we can keep the money flowing. I can't wait to see you, but it takes forever to get home from here. Won't hit Reagan till after 8pm. So here's the deal. I've reserved us a room at the Mayflower—they have terrific service, and you can check in whenever you want. This weary pilgrim is desperate to see you. As a special treat for both of us, I've ordered a package that will be waiting at the front desk for you. If you can be wearing it when I finally stumble in, I promise you a night you'll never forget.
>
> Nick

This, he knew, was the point of no return. If he wanted to chicken out, he still could. Just tell her nothing had happened in Albany, that the board thought having an intern was a bad idea, and it was all very nice but goodbye. This email, though, committed him.

Nick tried to picture where he'd be right now if Natalie hadn't been so nosy. When would the arrest have happened? Would Melody have given Nick a night to bask in the glow? Or would she have run screaming into the street in front of the Watergate, clothes meticulously disheveled, crotch full of "evidence?"

He'd have spent the night in lockup. Maybe the whole weekend, too, waiting for a hearing to set his bail. Nick had no idea how these procedures worked, and no desire to learn.

He mashed the "Send" button. Hard.

Nick had been checking the *Christian Crusade* website every few hours since Friday evening. He was only slightly disappointed that Marshall and LaPelletiere's vehicle hadn't run anything yet based on the Friday morsel. He assumed they had been waiting for confirmation. Now they had it. It shouldn't take long, now.

Less than two hours after Nick's message, the story appeared.

NY Fraud Investigation Derailed

A Christian whistle blower in the New York Attorney General's office is deeply concerned about the apparent cancellation of an investigation of fraudulent practices of the so-called "Inspiration Health Sharing" (IHS) company.

"I smell a rat," said the source, a devout Christian who now fears for his job. "Yesterday, we're closing in on the worst con men ever to hit New York. Today, Arnie Goldstein takes an interest, and poof, it's gone."

State Rep. Arnold Goldstein, a Democrat from Brooklyn, serves as speaker of the New York assembly. Goldstein, who is Jewish, consistently opposes the Christian legislative agenda. A number of New York assemblymen over the past decade, some of them Jewish, have been accused or convicted of bribery.

IHS has been called a mocking imitation of successful Christian health cost sharing programs, such as Bartimaeus Health. Unlike Bartimaeus, IHS provides no coverage for cancer, the most costly health issue for millions of Americans.

"I have been deeply disturbed about IHS for months," said Bartimaeus Director Richard Henry Marshall. "They are nothing but a scam, and they tarnish our whole movement. Bribery? I'm not surprised. They are criminals, they will stop at nothing. Shame on New York! But praise the Lord, we have a president willing to stand up for Christian principles. I predict there will be a federal investigation of the bribery here. Trust in the Lord, for He shall smite the foe."

On Nick's ten-point scale of possible outcomes, this ranked pretty close to a ten. The bigger they come, the harder they fall.

He thought about alerting Laura Boess, the IHS management team, and the sharks in G&H's New York office to the slam-dunk libel case present he'd just handed them, wrapped nicely in an anti-Semitic bow. Could they squeeze a seven-figure settlement out of this? Probably. But there was no need to tell them. They'd find out soon enough, if they hadn't already, and letting them identify the opportunity for themselves was likelier to result in action than any suggestion from a hick non-New Yorker.

He sent a text to Jay to go ahead with the Mayflower delivery as planned. Then he headed by Metro to the National Zoo, always a great venue for head clearing. At the Great Apes house, he tried not to picture the male staring in quiet rage from the corner as Richard Henry Marshall. But he couldn't shake the image.

Two Big Macs for dinner, then a single slowly nursed beer to pass the time. He was still cowed by Saturday's hangover, and wanted to keep his head clear in case something went wrong.

*****

Eight forty-five. Nick donned a stocking cap he'd borrowed from Jay and stepped into a taxi. "Mayflower Hotel, please. Back entrance, on Seventeenth Street."

Jay was there when Nick arrived, looking grim. "She checked in at seven," was all he said. Nick wordlessly pointed toward the elevator. He'd made some effort to identify the actual rooms where Jill Exner, Monica Lewinsky, and Ashley Dupree had stayed, but management was reluctant to reveal that. Oh, well.

They reached the door. Jay checked his camera settings for the fourth time in the last five minutes, then nodded.

Nick rapped out a cheery "Shave and haircut" knock and called out, "Hey, Melody, open up. It's me." He quickly slid sideways down the hall, to where he could see Jay but Melody could not see him.

Jay's video was perfect. Not only was Melody wearing the black negligee Nick had purchased that morning and had Jay deliver to the front desk, but she had one shoulder strap alluringly off. Jay had to blur out that breast to avoid a child pornography rap. Her first expression on opening the door was a naughty simper with an index finger to her lip. A second later—and Jay had borrowed a super slo-mo camera to catch it all—there was consternation. She tried to slam the door, but Jay had thought to wear his father's metal-toed construction boots, one of which was planted firmly inside. As the video rolled, Melody shrieked and ran back toward the bathroom. The whole episode lasted just under six seconds in real time, twice that in slow motion: just about aligned with the typical internet viewer's attention span. As Melody moaned "Who are you?" from behind the bathroom door, Jay shut off his camera, removed a package from his jacket pocket, calmly tossed it on the bed, then turned and quietly closed the door behind him as he left.

The package contained five pralines. Nick hadn't been able to resist eating one of the original half dozen himself.

October 25: The Watergate

After three nights on Jay's couch, Nick was more than ready to get back to his own comfortable bed, safely behind an extra security guard he'd hired to cover his Watergate hallway while things were hot. He knew Jay would be up for at least another eighteen hours flogging the story. His sympathy was restrained, though, after Jay mentioned the six-figure fee he'd been promised by one of the tabloid sites if the video was good enough—as it most certainly was—with Jay reserving full rights to all the stills.

Jay's text had already been largely written. It was accurate, except for the little lie Nick had told about the source of his tipoff. Natalie figured not at all; the tip, Nick said, was from an anonymous "senior member" of LaPelletiere's church who was appalled at the prostitution of an innocent young girl. May as well launch an internal witch hunt while I'm at it, Nick reasoned.

Some but not all of Jay's pieces speculated as to whether LaPelletiere had violated the pimping laws of the District of Columbia, and if so whether he was subject to extradition. He probably hadn't, but it was an interesting conversation to set up.

Nearly all of the stories included a photo of a building security form Melody had signed as "Lapin," with a big black circle around her 2000 fake birthdate. Jay had to Photoshop the handwriting a little to make it clearer, but there was no doubt that the last digit was never a five.

Jay deliberately waited until late in the day to take a second bite at the apple, this time linking the busted honey trap to the malicious lies *Christian Crusade* had told about IHS and Speaker Goldstein just a day earlier. It would have been hard, Jay noted, for anyone to bribe Goldstein in Albany, since he was in the middle of an anniversary cruise down the Danube with his wife.

Nick spent Tuesday comfortably behind closed doors at home, ordering in food and pacing. If he'd been wearing a Fitbit, he might have made his ten thousand steps for the day. He polished off a dozen Krispy Kremes and a quart of coffee, watching it all unfold. Half the chattering class thought he was a flaming asshole. What about Daddy? Why aren't they bitching about him? Shoot the messenger, why don't you. Many of the rest, though, heaped abuse where it belonged: on the cunning little slut and her despicable father. A few, from the atheist and secular humanist world, decried the larger issue of why Bartimaeus or IHS were allowed to exist at all, and speculated how much they would drive up premiums for average ratepayers if allowed to continue unchecked. Hardly anyone, though, concentrated on the aspect Nick found most riveting: how close a (fairly) innocent young man had come to being brutalized in prison for a crime he wouldn't even have known he was committing.

October 26:
Janet Harmon's Office

Nick sauntered into the G&H office around eleven Wednesday morning. Tonetta gasped audibly. "Natalie in?" he asked, as casually as he could muster.

"I'll let her know you're here," Tonetta gulped.

"Oh, don't bother," said Nick as he moved down the hall, letting himself in with the security card he'd forgotten to return on Friday. Nick knew such behavior would never, ever have been tolerated for anyone less than an A-list star in G&H-land.

Natalie was on the phone. Nick had been pondering clever openers all morning, but "How's tricks?" was the wittiest he could manage as he leaned in.

"Excuse me," she snapped immediately at the telephone. "I'll call you back."

"You!" was her even less witty reply. But then, she hadn't spent as much time working on it.

"Where have you been?" she demanded. "Close that door."

"Oh, no," said Nick. "I'm not falling for that one. I need to see some ID first, before I get caught alone in here with you." He'd spent time polishing that one, and thought it wasn't bad. It even drew a flicker of reprieve, at least in the eyes, before she launched back into the tirade she'd been working up.

The gist of it, as anticipated, was Nick's woeful lack of team player skills, or at least his willful intransigence in that direction. Matched only by his unconscionable failure to return her dozens of increasingly frantic calls, texts, and emails, and his unthinkable rudeness in simply walking out without a word on Friday.

Nick was a big fan of Muhammad Ali, and his favorite Ali triumph was the "rope-a-dope" bout with George Foreman. So he hunkered down against Natalie's onslaught, shrugging and occasionally even semi-agreeing, waiting for her to grow weary as Foreman had. This took longer than he had thought—she had an extraordinary amount of anger energy at her disposal. Finally the torrent slowed, and he sprang his counter-attack.

"Team player? Hey, I just scored a triple-double with fifty points, and we won the game, going away. Hell, we just won the fucking championship, of the universe! Anybody who really cares about the team, and not her own self-importance, ought to love that."

"Championship? Just look at all this press." She shoved half a dozen of the worst pieces, already printed out, across her desk at him.

Nick glanced through them dismissively. "Yeah, I've seen all this. Here's my favorite, from *Christian Crusade*: 'Satan at Work!' And if you found all this, I know you found all the good stuff, too. Right?"

She declined to admit or deny this, so Nick continued. "We're not running for president, ok? Or even for *The Voice*. Majority support doesn't matter. What we're after is notoriety, and a solid minority behind us. What's our market share now? Fraction of a percent? What's even our brand recognition? Five percent, max? Well that was last week, babe. *Everybody* knows us now, do they not? And even if half the people—hell, three quarters of the people—despise us, this kind of splash can drive our market share into the millions. Millions! You want to put a dollar figure on that?"

Nick knew that Natalie was savvy enough to have already done this math on her own. It just galled her too much to admit it. So after a moment's stony silence, he continued.

"And as for not returning your calls, how hard is that to figure out? Friday afternoon, hey, I admit it, job number one was saving my own ass. But job number two was saving yours. You are now absolutely one hundred percent clear of this. Total, truthful deniability. If I'd had ten documented back and forths with you over the weekend, how much harder is that defense to make? Look, you've been scouring the web as much as I have this last twenty-four hours. How often have you seen your name mentioned? That would be zero, right?"

Natalie turned back to the subject closest to her heart. "All the 'millions' you're talking about," she said quietly, "that's just until Congress gets wise and shuts this all down. I know that's what you want. Then what?"

Nick rose and walked over to the window. The sky was mottled grayish. Not threatening imminent rain, but not a delightful fall day, either. Yesterday, when Nick had been stuck hiding out in his apartment incommunicado, the weather had been much lovelier. "I don't know," he said at last. "I just try to get through one day at a time. A year and a half ago, I'm just cutting and pasting leases at GSA, hanging out at bars with Kyle, trying to pick up what he leaves on the table. Which isn't much. Then I get this little email that the woman of my dreams wants to see me again, and all hell breaks loose. I'll tell you what, though. If you're half the sharp operator I know you are, you'll be rich off this long before the knuckle-draggers in Congress get around to doing anything about religious privilege."

On the windowsill Nick spied a Nerf basketball. He snatched it up before Natalie could stop him, turned and shot at the basket as she barked "Hey! Don't!" He missed the entire backboard, by a foot. "Triple double, huh?" she said.

"You distracted me," he accused.

Natalie pointed down at the ball on the floor and motioned for Nick to retrieve it for her. She pump-faked as Nick yelled "Hey!" and shot out his arms. As he realized he'd been had, she calmly sank a swish.

Nick bowed grandly. "You win. Lunch is on me. Any place but the Mayflower. They do owe me, big time, for putting them back on the map though. Tell your product placement lawyers to negotiate me a nice juicy commission on their sales uptick after this."

"Are you insane? I can't be seen on the street with you. You're toxic!"

"Toxic? Don't you mean Satanic? I like the sound of that better." He scrunched up his face in a Marshall imitation, and in a deep, troubled tone burbled, "Satanic!"

This drew an actual laugh from Natalie Parks.

"Look, we both gotta eat, right? It's almost one o'clock. We'll order in, if I'm too toxic. I'd like one of those divine piles of week-old soggy lettuce, like you got me on Friday. And you can have a big-ass lasagna. And we'll share. Besides, you're my lawyer, remember? And I need advice. Big time advice. Hours of advice."

"What you need," said Natalie, "is a punch in the nose."

"See?" Nick replied. "Good advice already. Except the punch can't come from you. Because you'd really mean it. Maybe a punch from your little friend Gene Tucker. I could handle one of those."

Before Natalie could flare up again, Nick raised his hands to damp the flames. "Just kidding. Kidding! Look—I'm in no shape to get any decent work done today, and frankly I don't think you are, either. So can we just order something in? I am a client, right?"

While they waited for lunch, they compared notes about what they'd each been doing since Friday afternoon. How Natalie had returned Melody's phone. How Nick had nearly fainted when he saw a Melody look-alike at the Starbucks. How ticked off Peter Spillman was over Natalie's inability to locate Nick. How methodical Jay had been, and how much he was likely to make off the story. "Worth every penny,"

Nick opined. "Especially since I'm not paying it." Natalie was amused by that, but not by the pralines. She didn't find those humorous at all. Still, the level of her friendliness seemed to rise, as always, with the level of his success, and even Natalie had to admit that this turn-the-spy operation had been a stunning success.

Over lunch, the talk turned back to law school, firm politics, and the coming midterm election, which most pundits thought was shaping up poorly for Bertram. "This little fiasco won't help him any," Nick suggested. "Makes his backers look like the idiots they are."

"Nice enemy to make," said Natalie. "President of the United States. Way to go."

Nick was flattered, but waved her off. "Nah. He's got bigger problems than me."

Natalie's phone buzzed. "Sorry to bother you, Miss Parks," said Tonetta, her voice loud enough for Nick to hear. "But there's a Mr. Gimenez here, and he's quite anxious to locate Mr. Fratelli. Do you, uh, happen to know where he is?"

Nick nodded and motioned to Natalie to send him on back. He checked his pocket and realized he'd left his cell phone at home. How did Jay know where he was? Because he was a sharp reporter, that's how.

Jay looked like hell—like he hadn't shaved, bathed, or slept since Sunday night. He didn't smell too sweet, either. It was a wonder Tonetta hadn't called security rather than calling Natalie. Maybe she'd done both.

Jay gaped wildly at Nick, then dubiously at Natalie. "What's up?" Nick asked him. "You all right? Go ahead—she knows everything. My lawyer, remember?"

Jay turned back to Nick. "Melody's dead. Hung herself yesterday afternoon."

Natalie drew her hands to her mouth. Her shoulders heaved.

"Is it on the news?" Nick asked. "I haven't been checking." Natalie's distress was making it harder for Nick to keep his own composure. Jay's eyes were red and raw.

"No," said Jay. "It's not going to be. They're hushing it up."

"Then how do you know?" asked Nick.

"Because I know," Jay snapped. "It's my job to know things, remember? In between killing little girls, that is."

That did nothing for Nick's poker face. Jay said, "Sorry. This is real tough. Can I get a chair somewhere?"

Nick jumped up and gave Jay his chair. He went to sit on the windowsill behind Natalie, his hand resting on her shoulder.

"Ok. So her dad's staying at a hotel out in McLean, ready to swoop in once she ... you know ... and help her through the whole police ordeal. We do our thing, and she races out there in a taxi. Once the follow-up story broke yesterday afternoon, about how we've ruined her dad by feeding her false information—actually, buddy, that's a 'you,' not a 'we'—she freaks out and runs off into the woods. When she doesn't come back after an hour, they go looking for her. Private security guard finds her, on a tree."

"Apparently, Daddy wants to hush it up. Hires a funeral home connected to Marshall's church to retrieve the body. No announcement, no coroner, no death certificate, no nothing. They're just gonna pretend she's on a trip abroad to hide her shame, some mission to Timbuktu, and never comes back."

Nick still wasn't convinced. "No death certificate? How can you know, without a death certificate?"

"Because I know!" Jay barked. "You think I wasn't desperate to find some reason, any reason, to believe it wasn't true, once I got the tip? That I didn't check with security at the hotel? That I didn't talk to my contacts back in New Orleans? That I didn't talk to the goddamn funeral home? Or the Fed Ex dispatcher shipping the coffin back to Viviers? That I didn't track down her friend Tracy, using a fake name, and find out she hasn't heard from Melody since noon yesterday, and she's frantic? Teenage girls talk more than they breathe, Nick. Melody isn't doing either one. I even went and checked out the fucking tree, Nick. They sawed off the branch to get her down. So don't even question whether I fucking know."

Natalie rose and left the room at a trot. Nick had never seen her so upset, which seemed especially odd since she had so despised Melody. Then again, he hadn't seen many people who had just learned they were responsible for a teen suicide, and was feeling pretty miserable himself.

"Some 'Ice Queen,'" Jay observed. "Were they close?"

"Not really," said Nick. Then he caught himself. "Well, some. But this is rough."

There was a long silence. Nick knew that Jay got paid per click for stories he posted, and this was a hell of a story. But still. "You're not going to ...?" Nick finally said.

Jay reacted in fury. "You're a scumbag, Fratelli! You really are. No, I'm not gonna cash in on this family's agony by writing a big exposé about something they want to keep private. Jesus Christ—how can you even think that?"

Nick pressed his wrists into the sides of his head, hard, as though to keep it from exploding. "I'm not thinking anything," he moaned. "I can't think. This is all horrible. Cut me a little slack, ok?"

The ice queen returned, face washed, makeup restored, hair brushed, and jaw set. She took her seat and addressed Jay: "Have you spoken to a lawyer? If you end up needing one, you'll need one quickly, and it will be better to have shared what you know with him or her in advance."

"Uhh, yeah," Jay said, drawing back. "I'm speaking to two of them right now. Aren't I?"

"Sure," said Nick. "I mean, not me, 'cause I don't know what I'm doing, but this law firm is the best. We gotta stick together. Maybe before you leave we should—"

"No," Natalie interrupted, sharply. "Absolutely not. There's a conflict. You two are not in the same position. As you've already pointed out, Jay, you were not involved in sending the false information to her father that may or may not have been a factor in her death. And another difference—I don't know if this is relevant or not—but I understand you received some, ah, cash payment for your role in this? Nick did not. That might or might not be important."

"I'm a reporter!" Jay cried indignantly. "I report news stories. Of course I get paid! Is there a crime in that?"

Natalie shrugged. "Reporting, creating ... who knows? Prosecutors love making new law whenever they can, especially against the press. Anyway, the point is, you need a lawyer who's looking out only for your best interests. So does Nick. And since we already represent Nick, we can't do you as well. No way. I've got your address, and I can send you some excellent referrals."

Knowing Jay since childhood, Nick could tell he was more than miffed at having to use a different lawyer, and at the thought that Nick and he might end up pointing accusing fingers at one another. But as Natalie was speaking, Nick recalled that Jay knew nothing of her initial role in stealing Melody's phone, and she was determined to keep it that way. So was he.

"I guess she's right," Nick mumbled. "But there shouldn't be any problem. It's just a safety thing, a belt-and-suspenders deal, to talk to a lawyer now anyway."

"Yeah," said Jay bitterly. "Right." He stormed out without a good-bye.

Silence prevailed for a long while. Nick remained at the windowsill, inches from Natalie. "I just can't believe it," he said finally. "It's so, so stupid. She had so much going for her. So what if she gets embarrassed?

Everyone will have forgotten that by next month. So, so stupid."

Nick was trying to be inoffensive, but failed. Natalie flared again. "Not everyone is a human computer. Like you. Women have emotions. Sometimes they act on them. You can call it stupid, if you want to feel superior. I don't."

This was too complicated for Nick to unpack right away, beyond a simple, "I do so have emotions!"

"No you don't," she snarled, eyes ablaze. "You have one emotion, not 'emotions,' plural. You want to get inside my pants. That's it. That's all there is. And when you can't do that right away, you try to make believe with someone else."

Unfair! And wrong. But not by a wide margin. And her argument failed to account for the fact that if he could just get past that first, important hurdle so many other vistas, emotional and otherwise, would open up. But it was all too hard to explain. "That's not right," was all he could muster. "But I don't want to talk about it now."

He leaned his forehead against the cold window. Rush hour was beginning to pick up steam on K Street and its sidewalks. Very few of these people, Nick thought, had killed any pretty girls this week. Or deliberately ruined any distinguished community leader's career, even if he was an asshole. Or turned his back on his lifelong best friend in his moment of anguish.

"I'm sorry," said Natalie after another long while. "I was out of line. Look, Janet Harmon's in today. She does criminal work, white collar mostly, but she can handle this. Let's go talk to her.."

*****

Nick followed Natalie down the hallway to Janet Harmon's office. She was prim, fiftyish and graying, with glasses perched on the tip of her nose like Mrs. Romany, his homeroom teacher back in sixth grade. Nick and Jay hated Mrs. Romany. He'd have to tell Jay he was lucky not to be stuck with Janet Harmon as a lawyer. But he knew Jay wouldn't believe him.

Natalie laid out the whole story, including her own role, matter of factly. Nick chimed in with a few details to try to seem important. Harmon took careful notes and emitted a physician-like "hmmm" every few minutes to prove she was still listening. When Natalie finished with Jay's evident distress, Nick opened his palms to indicate he had nothing further to add.

Harmon tapped her teeth with her pen for a moment, and said, "Well, if there's no death reported, there's no manslaughter. That's easy. The phone, invasion of privacy, you returned it right away ... I don't think a prosecutor would bother with that, if it ever came out. Which it will, if you're ever questioned under oath. Either of you. That was very foolish, Natalie. Even without a crime, there are legal ethics considerations."

"I know," she murmured.

"But if she hadn't ... " Nick volunteered.

"Sex with an intern?" Harmon snapped. "Or any other employee, client, or independent contractor? Of any age? Have you lost your mind?" Yep—Mrs. Romany, déjà vu.

"We've been through that," said Natalie, rising to Nick's defense. "He understands better now. If people didn't make mistakes, you wouldn't have a job, would you? So drop the sermon, and just tell us, what's the exposure? And what's your practical advice?"

Despite their age difference, Natalie's star was rising rapidly within the firm, while Harmon was at best treading water. That's why, Nick figured, she didn't respond to Natalie's impudence.

"Practical advice? Nothing you don't know already. Don't talk about it, to anyone, ever." With a Mrs. Romany look in Nick's direction, she added, "Pray—to your 'Divine Spirit,' I suppose—that LaPelletiere sticks to his plan to keep this hushed up."

Harmon was wearing a crucifix pendant around her neck. Nick made a mental note to chide Natalie, at some more propitious moment, for selecting a Christian bigot who evidently disrespected CIS. Would she have expressed the same disgust over a prayer to Allah, Shiva, or Yahweh? Nick's religion had hurt a lot fewer people than theirs had.

"As for your exposure," she continued, "I don't see much there. There are some cases of criminal liability for intentionally driving someone to suicide, but they're far more egregious and explicit than this. Still, there's a first time for everything. And if you get charged, even if you prevail, you still lose. You have no idea how dreadful a criminal trial can be for the defendant, even one who is entirely innocent."

Nick believed he did have some idea about that. And he resented the way she sneered on the word "entirely." But he remained silent.

*****

Nick and Natalie walked back to her office, and when they arrived she went in but Nick remained outside, leaning on the door frame. Through her window, he could see that twilight had ended.

"Ok," he said. "I guess that's it. Watch and wait. I'm gonna head home now, and I may not come in tomorrow. If you could get someone to take care of cleaning out Melody's desk and sending anything necessary back to her family, I'd appreciate it. I don't want to have to deal with them."

Natalie moved her head methodically from side to side. She motioned for Nick to come in, and circled with her finger to indicate he should close the door again.

Nick sat. Natalie sat. She remained motionless for a moment. "There's one thing I haven't told you. Or Janet."

By this point, Nick had more than his fill of revelations for one week. He'd have sooner heard a doctor say, "Son, you're going to lose that leg," than discover one more world-changing tidbit. "What is it?"

Natalie said nothing. She studied her desk, where her hands were folded. "She liked you, Nick. A lot. God knows why, but she did. She told Tracy that in her last long email, Thursday night, after you two came back from the Tidal Basin. She wasn't sure she could go through with it. She even talked about ... well ... not telling her father what you two had done. Or were about to do."

Revelation-wise, this was pretty major.

The sky outside Natalie's window was now pitch black. "Why didn't you tell me?" he asked at length.

She tried anger again. "Why didn't you call me back? What is there about, 'Nick, you absolutely have to call me back as soon as possible' that's so difficult for you?"

"Why didn't you tell me on Friday? When I was here, in this chair?"

She threw her hands in the air. "Oh, you're so impossible! I knew you would say that. I just knew it!"

Nick was having difficulty figuring out how he was being so impossible. Generally, he got it pretty quickly, but the "Why not on Friday?" question seemed eminently fair. How was he supposed to make the right choice if he didn't have the right facts? So he tried a variation: "If you didn't tell me on Friday, why would you have told me on Saturday or Sunday?"

"What I told you on Friday," Natalie said through gritted teeth, "was to fire her pretty little ass, immediately. *That's* what I told you to do. You wouldn't do it. Instead, you and Jay run off and start playing spy versus spy, and you don't call me back, and now she's dead."

Ponder-period number two commenced. The thing about Nick was, he could figure things out, even tricky interpersonal nuances, if he had the time to do it. Usually, he didn't, and wound up with his foot in his mouth. But Natalie wasn't pushing him now. She was on the defensive, which she wouldn't be if her conscience weren't tormenting her. It dawned on Nick that her anguish this afternoon, genuine enough, was more over her own guilt than over any deep remorse for the demise of Melody LaPelletiere.

Nick could no doubt use that cogent analysis to score some devastating debating points. Which would get him exactly where?

"I think ..." he finally started, "I think a bunch of things. Let me get to the end, ok, before you jump on me again? I think it would have been better if you had told me everything on Friday, and let me decide what to do based on all the facts. You didn't trust me enough to get to the right answer, and you should have. You know me as well as anyone. How often do I just follow orders? Like, never?"

"I think ... you were afraid that if I had all the facts, including what you just told me, I might not have just fired her pretty little ass, like you wanted. I might have ... I don't know what I would have done, frankly. But I didn't have all the facts, and as you say, now she's dead."

Natalie started to speak, but Nick raised his palm. "Ah—lemme finish. I also think that, fuck-up-wise, the mistakes I made were much worse than yours. A million times worse. We're both just trying here, ok? I don't know what all I'm doing and, at least sometimes, you don't either. Sometimes we hit it, sometimes we don't. So that's what I think. And one more thing. For real. I think I've had it for one day. So, unless you've got some other huge secret—which, please, please tell me you don't—I'm outta here. I just want to go be alone for a while."

"I don't..." Natalie half-whispered, staring at the door. "I don't want..."

"Huh?"

"I don't want to be alone tonight," she said more strongly. "My car is down in the garage. We'll stop and get you a toothbrush."

October 27: Arlington

Nick awoke around four a.m. The sound of Natalie's breathing was evidence that he had not been dreaming. Unless he still was, but he didn't think so. Hard as it was to believe, the universe had turned inside out. The "Why?" question that would bedevil Nick for a long time to come stood second in line right now behind the "What?" question. What, exactly, had just happened?

They had ordered a pizza delivery while Natalie drove home. Natalie claimed she was a good cook, but didn't feel up to the effort tonight. Nick was agreeable to that.

Natalie said she'd pick up a bottle of Chianti while Nick was buying a toothbrush, razor, and condoms. Nick was agreeable to that, too.

They watched television on a pathetically small screen while eating the pizza, and for a little while afterward. Both of them were conversationed-out. Nick had no recollection at all of what they had watched.

Natalie's Arlington condo was like her office. Neat as a pin, no dust to be found, one picture of her parents, lots of chrome and glass. But it had some delicious sweet scents Nick could not identify, which her office lacked. The array of spices and condiments in her cupboard when Nick went to look for napkins confirmed what she'd said about liking to cook.

The sex, it must be said, was not as Nick had so often imagined it. His daydreams had usually begun with an extensive investigation, by eye, hand, and tongue, of every square inch of her exquisite body. But Natalie wanted the lights out, and Nick was agreeable to that.

Nick's drained vitality created a second problem. If this had been happening at a time of Nick's choosing ... the night of the first G&H reception ... the night at Earl Matteson's house ... the night of the marijuana victory, or better yet the glorious Kansas fracking victory ... either Fourth of July ... he'd have been ready to service the Saudi king's harem, and leave them panting for more. But after today's events, his ego wasn't the only thing deflated. He performed, in a clumsy manner, rather quickly. "That's ok," said Natalie sleepily. "Just hold me." At least he was able to grab onto a handful of breast with his right hand, and never let go. His left arm, unfortunately, was pinned rather painfully beneath her shoulder, as he heard her settle into sleep. It grew so numb that Nick was afraid it might break off. But eventually Nick, too, began to doze, arm or no arm. When he awoke around four, she had rolled away and his arm was free. By the light of the digital clock, he was able to complete his visual inspection of Natalie's bare upper back. Which did not disappoint. Just listening to her breathing seemed to fulfill a lifetime of Nick's dreams.

Nick didn't want to awaken Natalie, but he had some hopes that in a second round before work, he could do a better job. No such luck. When her alarm rang at five, Natalie popped out of bed like a jack in the box. A robe materialized from nowhere, shielding Nick from the view he craved. "I'll drop you at your place on the way in. We shouldn't be seen together. And this is between us, ok? No bragging to your buddies. Or at the firm, especially not there. I could get fired for this. I mean it."

Nick nodded gravely, and reached out to grasp her hand. He was too slow.

December 10:
Guilder & Hersh Kitchen

By dint of repetition, Nick managed to convince himself over the next few weeks that he hadn't done anything wrong. Exhibit A was the first frame on Jay's video of Melody's face after opening the hotel room door. This was not a young woman experiencing inner turmoil. This was a she-devil.

Besides, if she had any thought at all of betraying her father to have a fling with Nick, all she ever had to do was say so. "Ah jest don't know what to do ..." with a single tear, and he'd have melted like a Hershey bar on the back seat. She had to know that.

Exhibit B was dear old dad. Maybe not admissible in criminal court, but he was a monster. How could he not even tell Melody's friends she was dead? Even Jephthah didn't hide what he'd done. So by simple genetics, she was half a monster, at least. Which explained the way she acted, during her weeks of sneaky seduction.

As for the suicide, how could anyone have foreseen that? Nick still couldn't believe it had really happened. He spoke to Jay at Thanksgiving, to see if there was any new information. Jay seemed distant, as though Nick had wronged him in some way. Nick couldn't see how. The legal rules against representing different clients on the same matter weren't Nick's fault. Anyway, Jay relayed that there was a fresh grave at the LaPelletiere family cemetery plot, with no headstone. "Convinced yet, asshole? Wanna go dig her up?" Jay had furiously asked Nick. Melody's Facebook page displayed a cheery message about how she needed some time to herself now, before she embarked on a mission for the Lord—just as Jay had predicted.

So teenage girls do strange, stupid things, Nick rationalized. News flash. If you lived your life fretting over every strange, stupid thing some wacko might do, you may as well hide in the closet. Unless hiding in the closet would set somebody else off, too.

Three, four times a day Nick repeated this analysis to himself. More when he drank too much, which was nearly every night now.

Sex with Natalie continued and improved. Every Friday, whether he needed it or not. Fridays didn't create any awkward issues about coming into work together the next morning, since Nick wouldn't be caught dead at work on a Saturday, and Natalie wouldn't consider being anywhere else. She seemed to enjoy these sessions, at least sometimes, and occasionally even participated. Nick was finally able to complete his thorough inspection of the temple he had worshipped for so long, committing every pore to memory. It had been worth the wait. And he kept his promise—which she reminded him of sternly every week—to keep everything secret. They ordered in some marvelous meals, but never went out where they could be seen together.

It didn't take long for doubt to begin to gnaw. It had begun chewing, in fact, about three seconds after it first sunk in that his goddess was proposing sex to him. If Dan Snyder had called and said, "Nick, I'd like you to start coaching the Redskins" ... if Bill Gates had called and said, "Nick, I found another billion under the couch, and I'd like you to have it" ... if Mrs. Romany had called and said, "Nick, I'm sorry about that C- I gave you in geography," he'd have been less surprised. With a toss of her head, Natalie Parks could have her pick of the sexiest (and richest) bachelors—or married men—in Washington. Why Nick?

The good reasons: Maybe she appreciated the devotion Nick had always shown. Maybe she wanted to open herself only to a known quantity. Maybe she admired his independence, his resolution, his creativity, his spunk. Maybe she could spot potential, like the baseball scout who signs the twelve-year-old pitcher. Nick *could* lose some weight, pump some iron, pay someone with exceptional creativity to do something about the hair, visit Peter Spillman's tailor, and hunk himself up. Maybe the sex had begun at a moment when she was overwrought, and continued because she liked it.

The less good reasons: The money Nick was generating was rocketing Natalie to law firm stardom. But the gravy train was at risk of derailment without notice, because its driver's brain was inconveniently located below his belt. His hormone pot needed to be emptied periodically, because he was an idiot male. If Natalie herself didn't do the job, then it would be left to ... well, she'd just seen what might happen. Everyone has their cross to bear.

Which was it? Could it be both? Could one morph into another? Brain-scrambling questions. The only answer Nick was sure of was that he really, really looked forward to Friday nights.

But there were more questions. When could the secrecy end? When the law firm changed its policy? When Natalie left the firm? When Nick changed lawyers? Never?

None of these were good answers.

The only good answer, Nick concluded, was when CIS got so big, and Natalie along with it, that there was a de facto exception to the G&H rule. That didn't seem too terrible. Until Nick considered that G&H numbered Google, Credit Suisse, and the government of Japan among its clients. CIS had about a thousand years to go to become more important than they were.

The realistic answer, of course, was that the affair would end before any of these things happened. Or, if she was being devious, she'd contrive to hook Nick up with someone "safe," then graciously step aside.

Did Earl have enough money to pay for such a person? Yes. Would he do that? Yes. Was keeping CIS going worth enough to Earl to justify that expense? Closer, but probably yes. On further thought, hell yes. Earl was making eight figures fracking to his heart's content. The mystery woman Nick started to fret about would cost a low six-figure number, if that.

Would Earl really do that? He seemed like a straight shooter. But after Melody, after Father Bob, after Rosie—who, Nick wildly concluded on zero evidence, was another plant—he decided to assume that the answer was yes. Nothing is simple, straightforward. Everything has twists, exceptions, loopholes. That's how CIS exists. Hell, that's how the rest of religion exists—a giant fraud, feeding thousands of mouths that would wither away if it weren't propped up by governments everywhere—which it, in turn, backed to the hilt.

But Nick liked sex with Natalie. A lot. So he kept doing it. He made some feeble efforts in the direction of improving his diet—at least the solid food part—to try to look better for her. He even signed on with an ex-Marine personal trainer she had recommended. After a few sessions with this guy, Nick began devising a CIS version of hell, just for him.

If Natalie ever suggested he should meet a woman friend of hers, his antennae would go up. Until then, there were Kama Sutra positions yet untried.

Maybe he was over-thinking. Maybe Natalie was just trying to get through one day a time, like he was, and didn't have a master plan. Maybe she had some feeling for him, but wasn't sold yet. But with a little time, a little patience, maybe she'd come around. She'd come this far, hadn't she?

Nick's best idea was that maybe there could be a religious exception to the G&H anti-fraternization rule. CIS was built on exceptions, wasn't it? Didn't the Holy Koran itself contain exceptions to accommodate the prophet Muhammad's libido? His exploration of this avenue, though, ran smack into an imposing obstacle: Earl Matteson.

The bad news came via a call from Tonetta, one Thursday afternoon in early December while Nick was counting the hours until his next encounter in Arlington. Twenty-nine to go. "Mr. Spillman would like to see you," she said. "For real this time."

Since Nick knew that Natalie was in New York with Laura Boess for the day, it was likely that Peter did, in fact, want to see him. Had word of his affair with Natalie trickled out?

"This is disagreeable," Peter began. He looked uncomfortable, not making direct eye contact like he usually did. "As a rule, creative people should be allowed to create. One cannot question your talent, or your success in generating, shall we say, growth in the law, which this firm has been pleased to assist."

Seven figures worth of revenue pleased, thought Nick. He was relieved, though, that the conversation didn't seem to involve Natalie in any way. Unless they had hidden cameras in her bedroom, "creativity" didn't seem to enter that equation.

Nick didn't think it was his turn to talk yet. After a brief scowl Peter said, "Let's get Earl on the line."

This took only a moment. "Hey, kid," boomed Earl's voice over the speakerphone. "How you feelin'?"

Nick hadn't spoken to Earl since his recuperation in Crisfield, so it was a fair question. What troubled him at the moment was whether he should acknowledge Earl's role—his *suspected* role—in avenging Nick's beating, which seemed ages ago now. Hallmark didn't have a card for that.

"Just great, Earl. How's the gang out there?"

Earl wasn't a small talk guy. "Lookit. You need to cut this shit out with the breaks. That's bullshit, and you know it. You're bustin' my balls."

Nick was mystified. "Brakes?"

"Yeah, shit for brains, BREAKS. Work breaks. Every goddamned two hours. My crews puttin' in rigs are gettin' all tore up by it. It's like a goddamned union. One guy craps out, and the whole crew shuts down for ten minutes. And the foreman tells me I gotta put up with it, 'cause I'm CIS. You gotta fix this—pronto."

If Peter didn't look so solemn, Nick might have split a gut. As it was, he had to cover his mouth with one hand. He'd made one passing reference to "serenity breaks" for employees in a sermon three weeks ago, akin to Muslim prayer breaks, and then watched Facebook explode as it developed a life of its own. The Secret Plan had found its own legs, and proud papa Nick glowed with his toddler's every independent step.

"Gee, Earl," he ventured. "You sound stressed. You might want to try a little serenity break yourself. Does wonders."

Nick was glad Peter wasn't armed. "Our young friend is attempting humor," he said gravely. "He finds this amusing, because he's not the one losing money. Yet."

"Aw, come on," Nick protested. "Losing money? Net-net, you're not losing anything. You're making tons. Giving those poor slobs a little work break now and then is nothing compared to what you're making from all the extra fracking you're doing."

"Net-net," Earl replied, "I'll break all your other fucking ribs, too. Now how you gonna fix this?"

An image of Doris flitted by in Nick's imagination. She wasn't smiling.

"Well?" demanded the speakerphone. Nick realized his pause had exceeded civilized limits.

"I can't just unsay it," Nick replied, shifting in his seat. "I mean, the Muslims do that. They have this abrogation deal, where there's two verses in the Koran that are totally opposite, and they just say Allah changed his mind or something.[82] But everybody knows that's horseshit, and I got enough credibility issues as it is."

"Muslims?" asked Earl. Nuance wasn't his forte.

This kind of problem, though, was right up Peter Spillman's alley. Finding common ground, distinguishing what the parties really needed from what they merely wanted, working things out—this is what he knew how to do. "Now, Earl," Peter volunteered. "Your crews work in shifts, I recall? Eight hours?"

"They only *work* seven and a half. They get a half-hour meal break. Paid. They get potty breaks, too. Also paid. Now they get these goddamned serendipity breaks on top of all that. Every now and then somebody turns a wrench, just to relieve the boredom."

"Serenity breaks," Nick corrected. "Not serendipity. Sort of like potty breaks to flush the waste from the mind. They do a world of good."

"I think," said Peter, "we may safely dispense with continued reliance on that particular metaphor. Forever. So Earl: if you get your your seven and a half hours of honest labor in, omitting the potty breaks,

---

82. Labib Mikhail, *Islam, Muhammad and the Koran*, Springfield, VA, Blessed Hope Ministry 2002 p.123-125. https://books.google.com/books?id=teikJgAACAAJ

I take it that it matters little whether that is spread over an eight hour period, or, say, an eight and a half hour period?"

Earl emitted something indecipherable, which seemed to acknowledge having heard the words Peter said.

"Now about your philosophy, Nick. From what I gather, you make frequent reference to some variant of the golden rule? Treat others as you wish to be treated?"

Nick knew that by the time Peter was finished with whatever logical pirouette he was spinning, Earl would have exactly what he wanted. He also knew there was nothing he could do about it. "Yeah. I guess." He considered suggesting the alternative golden rule definition, "Them that has the gold makes the rules," but thought better of it.

"And surely, anyone who is being paid for seven and a half hours of work should actually perform that quantity of work? Isn't that what anyone would expect, were the shoe on the other foot? Even if that requires remaining on the jobsite, for, say, nine hours?"

"Hold it right there!" boomed the speakerphone. "That's bullshit. It's only a few troublemakers wantin' these breaks. No way is everybody gonna stay an extra hour to accommodate these pussies."

"One step at a time, Earl. Nick, are you with me so far?"

Nick tried to mimic Earl's earlier acknowledgement grunt as precisely as he could.

"I am familiar with the culture of manual labor, Earl," said Peter. "As you may recall, I worked one summer at the marina, in high school. Dreadfully hot. Now, Nick. Suppose that in a given work crew, even though everyone is *entitled* to take serenity breaks, no one makes that choice. There would be no point in requiring such a crew to remain on the job site for nine hours, would there? They could leave after the usual eight. But in a crew where someone does request this religious accommodation, why, employees get their breaks, the company gets its seven point five hours, and all will be well."

Nick shook his head dismissively. "Until he gets beaten to a pulp, which should take about a day. You can't like, let employees vote on whether Muslims get prayer breaks or not, and by the way, everybody gets longer hours if you vote yes. Courts will never buy that."

"An excellent example!" Peter clapped his hands together. "For if you are speaking of Islam, its lawgiver has been deceased for what, a thousand years now? So Islam is frozen in time, and that's why it has such difficulty adapting to the modern age. But you, my friend, are alive and well, despite Earl's little joke. So it is within *your* power to fine-tune your religious teachings. What court could object to that?"

More silence ensued. Nick cleaned his glasses with a dirty Kleenex from his pocket, even though he didn't need them to visualize his Secret Plan toddler trying to walk with shackles on his legs.

Peter broke the silence. "We're all agreed then. Natalie will draft a 'clarification' for the website."

"Good," said Earl, and clicked off.

Nick stood up to leave, only to have Peter say sharply, "Sit down, please." He fell back heavily into the chair. The dark wood paneling of Peter's office reminded Nick of the wood at the Tune Inn bar, which was exactly where he needed to be right now.

Peter eyed Nick balefully for a moment, then said, "No, stand up. Walk with me. I need some coffee."

Coffee, at four in the afternoon. Why had he ever hooked up with people like this?

Nick couldn't remember whether Peter's bio had mentioned military service. But he seemed to be marching toward the kitchen, rather than shuffling, as Nick usually did.

"It is time for a new phase, as it were," said Peter, as he held his cup under the coffee spigot. Plain black, not Perfumed Vanilla or any of the umpteen other foofy varieties on offer. "At the outset of an enterprise, a certain degree of shooting from the hip may be necessary. But as the enterprise matures, so must its procedures. You understand, I take it?"

"Not really."

Peter stood straight, bending only his head to take a tiny sip from the steaming cup. Nick leaned against the doorframe, one leg crossed over the other, fidgeting.

"Your future initiatives, such as these so-called serenity breaks, must be vetted. They must be weighed in the balance with all you have done so far, and careful consideration must be paid to potential consequences."

"I do that already."

Peter blinked slowly, in exasperation. "I'm sure you do. With results like the kerfuffle we just witnessed. Trust me, if you had heard what Earl had to say an hour ago, before I calmed him down, you would have found it most disagreeable. Two heads are better than one, Nick. We must insist on more communication and cooperation."

Nick straightened, planting his hands on his hips. "And six heads are better than two. And you get to bill a lot more hours that way." Six heads, Nick knew, or even one head that wasn't his own, was exactly what the Secret Plan did not need. Nick's dream was to *fail*, not to succeed—at least the way all the overachievers at G&H defined success. Fail spectacularly, in an explosion big enough to engulf Marshall and his ilk, but fail nonetheless. It was hard enough to pull this off on his own without a bunch of eager beavers breathing down his neck.

"I'm afraid we must insist," said Peter, taking another sip.

"Insist?" Nick sneered. "Insist? And what happens if I don't? What're you gonna do? Break my ribs? I'll tell you who hates all the extra bureaucracy you're talking about. Earl Matteson—that's who. And he doesn't like it when my ribs get hurt. Not one bit."

"Your valiant defender," replied Peter drily, "expended quite some energy an hour ago demanding that you be 'shut down,' as he put it. Silenced. Like your predecessor the prophet Muhammad, perhaps. He has what he wants now, and sees little value in allowing you to foul things up any further. Though 'foul' was not the verb he used."

Nick's shoulders sagged. But for Earl, he'd still be at GSA. And without Earl's future backing, CIS had no capital source for future initiatives. There was some revenue flowing in now, but no solid base other than Earl. What Peter was telling him now fit uncomfortably well with the tone of voice he had just heard on the phone. Even the greatest generals had to retreat sometimes. Didn't they? Patton, Pershing, Grant, all their strategic retreats... hmmm ... maybe he should look up what those were. He couldn't think of any right off hand.

"Nick?" Peter asked, as he studied the repeating pattern on the floor tile.

"Ok ... ok. I'll try to do better."

Peter settled into a plastic chair at a tiny round table, motioning for Nick to join him.

"Now here is an example. You're familiar with some of the adverse reports about Zubitril?"

"A little." Zubitril, a/k/a "Prozac without the side effects," had been made available through CIS online outlets—managed by Laura Boess—to CIS congregants in good standing since early summer. The buzz on the internet, though, was that Zubitril taken with alcohol (as the packaging clearly indicated was *not* a permitted use) produced a marvelous high, followed by an occasionally shattering crash which had purportedly induced several suicides.

"Have you responded to these reports in any manner, written or oral?" asked Peter.

"Nah. You know, I was never sold on that shit. Zubitril was Laura's deal, all the way. Besides, we got it in a side corporation, so even if it goes bust we're still ok."

Peter glowed in triumph. "You make my point, far better than I ever could. It is so wonderful that you have never uttered a word in response to these charges. Because those words that I almost thought you just said—I'm certain I misheard you—are precisely, to the tee, what you must never say. You must never even think them. What if you should, perhaps, fall asleep on a train, and unconsciously utter deplorable words like those in a dream? What then? Communication, and cooperation: that is how we shall deal with the vicious atheist slander against Zubitril."

Leaving aside his natural resistance to being told what to do, Nick felt a twinge of relief. He had drawn a blank as to what to do about the Zubitril reports, so letting G&H worry about it was fine with him. He'd be damned, though, if he'd let them stifle the next brilliant idea he had—or someone had—like God-created food.

Peter emptied his cup and stood. "I don't want you shut down, Nick. Not at all. Your creativity is not only good for the firm financially, but it's intellectually fascinating. Far more than much of what we do. Believe me—and I know you don't, but it happens to be true—I am your greatest ally. And, I would like to think, your friend. We can soar to new heights together. But we require, as I say, communication and cooperation. No more surprises. Are we agreed?"

"Sure," Nick mumbled, as he clattered back his chair and turned toward the door. "Whatever." He peeked at his watch. Twenty-seven hours until Natalie.

January 5: Korean War Memorial

The November elections went poorly for Harry Bertram. Not only did the Republicans lose control of the Senate, but the thirty-two Republican seats lost in the House were disproportionately comprised of die-hard evangelical Bertram loyalists. At least a few Democrats had raised the issue of religious privilege, citing the CIS fracking cases and automatic weapons demands as an example of how out-of-whack the laws had become, and how it was time for the pendulum to swing back the other way. A bill to repeal RFRA and RLUIPA picked up twenty-four Democratic and two Republican co-sponsors.

Even more shocking, a few days after the election, came the announcement that the Republican governor of California—a guy who could raise big bucks—was forming an exploratory committee to challenge Bertram in the next Republican primaries. Since he knew he couldn't crack the evangelical base, he decided to confront it head on. "One people, one law. That's the way to get America back together again. No more special rules for special classes. Let's get past that, and get America back to work again." The first polls showed him running behind Bertram in recession-hit Iowa, but far ahead in less religious New Hampshire.

Nick loved all that, and knew that when the Cape Cod skyscraper story broke, the pressure for reform would only intensify. What he didn't love was the handwritten note he received from Shawnay, shortly before Christmas:

> Dear Nick:
> I'm sorry to do this, but DVH Productions is terminating its video contract with you at the end of the year. This is your two weeks' notice. I just feel so dirty, week after week. I told them they could keep either you or me, and they picked me. So it's over. Good-bye. Have a nice life.
>
> Very truly yours,
> Shawnay Jefferson

Nick knew there was no point in trying to talk her out of it. Or in offering her more money. Or in trying to explain to her the *Matrix*-like logic of the Secret Plan, where up was down and worse was better and Nick was accomplishing an ultimate good despite all appearances to the contrary. But he appreciated everything Shawnay had done, including her futile efforts to keep his feet on the ground. He shopped the internet for a good price on a hundred roses as a thank-you, not as a "Please come back to me," which he knew would fail. Before he hit the "Buy" button, though, he had another inspiration. It cost quite a bit more than the hundred roses would have, but shortly before Christmas a truck rolled up to the Jefferson front door, and two workmen unloaded a set of carnival-quality funhouse mirrors with a card: "For Ashante and Tyrell, the two favorite sons of my favorite producer." Maybe someday, Nick mused, Shawnay might understand the message that people are not always what they seem.

CIS, Nick realized as he resumed his online Christmas shopping, had a glaring omission. No holidays! Every religion worth its salt had some decent holidays. They couldn't result in days off work, though, or Earl would shit a brick. Maybe he could have people celebrate his own birthday? "Nickmas"? It would be worth floating that idea with Peter, if he could deliver it with a straight face, just to watch his jaw drop.

The whole issue would require careful thought. The right sort of holiday could generate litigation for G&H if employees who wanted to observe it were denied an "accommodation" by their employer.[83] It could also mean extra money in the pockets of federal employees who claimed CIS membership. Jews and Muslims who worked rather than attending church on Jewish or Muslim holidays got fat checks from the taxpayers for doing so—why shouldn't CISers get the same?[84]

And then, once he had finally come up with something brilliant, he'd watch it get picked apart by Peter's "communication and cooperation"

---

83. See Ron Zapata, "EEOC Sues Vonage Over Jewish Worker Firing," *Law360*, June 27, 2007. http://www.law360.com/articles/28041/eeoc-sues-vonage-over-jewish-worker-firing.

84. John Solomon, "Probes Find Improper Use of Religious Comp Time," *Washington Post*, October 12, 2007. http://www.washingtonpost.com/wp-dyn/content/article/2007/10/11/AR2007101102163.html. "EPA Needs to Better Control Religious Comp Time, Report Says," *FedWeek*, October 7, 2016. http://www.fedweek.com/federal-managers-daily-report/epa-needs-better-control-religious-comp-time-report-says/.

dictate. What a bummer.

Christmas itself was a blast. Natalie took off the whole last week of the year to spend at home with her parents, but that was ok, because another woman was also absent: Yvonne, Luca's ex-wife. She stuck around for Christmas Day, but after that she was off skiing with her latest boyfriend—precious children not invited. Luca was happy to have them, but he had to work. Uncle Nick was more than willing to come to the rescue.

The oldest, Jonas, was sixteen now and spent most of his time on his own. Except for the day after Christmas, when Nick took him up to paintball. Working together, they did ok—far better than Nick had ever done with Jay, who hadn't returned Nick's invitation call. Whoever Doris's paramilitary connections were, Nick thought, may want to consider grooming Jonas.

Monica, at fifteen, was a mystery to Nick. In part, this was because the pink-dyed hair on the side of her scalp that wasn't shaved didn't jibe at all with her little-girl voice, or with the academic awards Luca never tired of bragging about. But even more importantly, every time Nick looked at her, he couldn't fend off the arithmetic dating her so close in age to Melody. That was the beginning and end of his thought process regarding Monica, who rarely peeked up from her cell phone anyway.

And then there was Tony. Ten years old—the perfect age, as far as Nick was concerned. Old enough to be interesting, but not old enough to be obnoxious. Nick couldn't get enough of him.

"I'm just letting him win," said Nick, as Tony annihilated him for the fourth time in a row in the latest *Call of Duty* release.

"Yeah," said Luca, lounging on Pop's couch on Christmas afternoon. "Like I used to let you win at *Doom*."

"I never beat you at *Doom*. Never once! I'd've remembered something important like that."

"Correctamundo," said Luca. "Never. And you're giving Tony no more slack than I gave you."

Nick shot him a dirty look. Then lost again.

Tony gasped when Nick took him to see the Hope Diamond and the giant gold nuggets at the Smithsonian's mineral room. He spent the rest of the day conspiring with Uncle Nick about how they could break in at night and steal them. At the Korean War memorial, he imitated the postures of all the exhausted soldiers in the platoon, then spent the afternoon ambushing Chinese commies. At the Clara Barton office, he was enthralled by the story of how her Civil War missing soldier files lay hidden from the world for 130 years until their accidental discovery by a carpenter in 1996. He demanded that Uncle Nick boost him up so he could peer into the attic where the secrets were found; Nick was relieved when a docent wandered by and said, "Sorry, son, we don't allow that."

*****

Nick was actually tickled when his phone rang at six a.m. on the first Thursday after New Year's and he saw it was Luca calling. "Hey, bro. Any chance you could help me out here? They declared a fucking snow day today, even though—as you can see—it ain't even snowing yet. And I gotta work, and Yvonne's not back till Sunday. Jonas is, uh, not reliable, and Monica refuses to deal with Tony. So can you take him?"

"Sure. Although, if it gets too deep, you know, he might have to sleep over."

"Whatever. Can you get here soon?"

Nick checked the radar, and decided he could make it to Rockville and back before the storm hit in earnest. Tony had a bag packed that looked like he was planning to stay for a month. Nick figured he'd spend an hour or so in the office, then take Tony up the Washington Monument, to see what the city looked like in snow.

"This doesn't look like a church," Tony accused, as they pulled into the G&H garage. Nick had applied for a dedicated "Clergy" parking spot on busy K Street, and was primed for a lawsuit when the anticipated rejection arrived, but even religious exemption law couldn't make the District of Columbia parking bureaucracy grind any faster.

"You spend a lot of time in churches?" Nick replied. "Are you an expert on what churches look like?"

"Yeah, I am. And they don't look like this."

"Mine does. And we're growing a lot faster than everybody else."

When they got off the elevator and turned the corner to the CIS office, Nick saw a young man sitting cross-legged on the floor. He scrambled to his feet, trying to look stern. He looked a tad younger than Nick, with receding blonde hair and traces of leftover acne.

"Mr. Fratelli?" he squeaked.

"Yes?"

"This is for you." He handed Nick an envelope. "You've been served, and your attendance is compulsory." He tried to manage a sneer. "Latest convert?" he added, indicating Tony, then swaggered down the hall to the elevator.

"Are you in trouble, Uncle Nick?" asked Tony, wide-eyed.

"I don't know," said Nick. Truthfulness was a must around Tony. They settled in to Nick's office, and he opened the envelope.

"What is it?" demanded Tony.

"Shut up a minute." Plain speech was a close cousin to truthfulness.

Inside the envelope, Nick found a subpoena from the House Committee on the Judiciary. A subpoena? Nick would have paid money for the chance to give the folks on that committee an earful. So why a subpoena, forcing him to attend?

So they could look tough, obviously.

The only substantive clue given on the one-page document was the title of the hearing he was being ordered to attend: "Abuse of Religious Freedom Laws."

Nick gazed at the ceiling for a long moment. He wagged his hand toward the southwest, in the direction of the capitol, and gave Tony a wink. "No, I'm not in trouble, Tony. *They're* in trouble."

February 1: House Judiciary Committee

"Is this where they impeached Clinton?" Nick asked, gazing at the high ceiling and portraits of past committee chairmen adorning the walls of the House Judiciary Committee hearing room. He felt four hundred pairs of eyes fixed on him.

"I think so," said Peter Spillman tersely. "I would advise you to reserve your tourist gawking for another time, and focus on the business at hand. Remember: short answers. 'Yes, sir' and 'No, sir' are always good. When they hit you on the contradictions, just fuzz things over, like I'm sure you did in fifth grade when your teacher—are you listening?"

He wasn't. He was intent on the doorway, through which Marshall, McCarthy, and half the RFF board were filing in. Nick thought it unfair that they didn't have to stand in the same line as hundreds of the hoi polloi, but he knew they'd be here to watch him twist in the wind.

"Pay attention," said Peter. "If there's even a hint of any criminal allegations, we jump straight for the Fifth Amendment. We can handle the fallout later, but we can't undo any mistakes you make if you fumble an answer. I'll be right next to you—you won't have to do a thing."

Nick moistened his lips, his eyes darting nervously about the room as he wriggled out of his backpack. There was very little room behind the witness table, much of it filled with lighting that Nick knew from his studio experience would soon have him drenched with sweat.

He'd debated with himself nonstop about the next step, then decided to trust his gut rather than the conventional logic that had been drilled into him. The smugness on Marshall's face had pushed him over the edge.

"Look," he said, leaning in close to Peter's ear. "I appreciate it, but I don't want you to sit next to me. It's too ... I'm too overloaded as it is, and I won't be able to think straight if I've got you here. I need to focus."

"You're not supposed to think," Peter snapped. "You're supposed to do what I tell you. Short answers, 'yes' or 'no' whenever you can, and don't interrupt when I break in."

Nick scrunched up his eyes and rubbed his forehead. "No, man, I can't do it. You can't sit here. Go on to the back."

"But I'm your lawyer!" Peter said through clenched teeth.

"And I'm your client. Trust me, it's better this way. Or don't trust me, I don't care. You just have to go. Do it now, because I don't want to embarrass you in front of the committee once this starts."

Peter opened his mouth, but said nothing. Shuddering in resignation, he turned, waved to signal an imaginary colleague, and left the witness table. Nick laid his backpack on the seat that had been reserved for Peter, to give himself some space.

*****

The hearing began ten minutes late. Chairman Gustavus Randall, a Tea Party darling from Kentucky, rambled through his opening statement. He started with the Ten Commandments, trembled through the stormy ocean crossing that landed the Puritans at Plymouth Rock in search of religious freedom, recited the phrase "our beloved Christian nation" half a dozen times, and took credit for RFRA even though he hadn't been in Congress when it was enacted.

Nick was sure he would say something to create an opening, and Randall did not disappoint. "But today we are confronted with a conspiracy to defraud the American people, founded on a blasphemous scam perpetrated in the name of almighty God. This hearing—"

Nick jumped to his feet. "Mr. Chairman!" he called loudly. The microphone was designed for use only by a seated witness, so he needed to shout.

"Sit down!" barked Randall. "I will remind you that there are legal penalties imposed for contempt of Congress. You will have ample opportunity to explain your disgraceful conduct once I am finished."

The Little Blue Engine sat back down, clasped his hands to chest, and feigned his best simulation of shock while leaning in toward the microphone. "Contempt? Me? Oh, no, sir. I have no contempt for Congress at all. Like ninety percent of the people do. I'm in that *other* ten percent that thinks you guys are doing just great. You've passed some wonderful exceptions to the laws, and we're using them. To the max."

Back in the third row, Peter Spillman pinched the bridge of his nose and squeezed his eyes shut. From the back of the audience, Nick detected a snorting laugh.

"Mr. Fratelli," said the chairman sternly, "we are well aware of the intent of the laws we have enacted, which is to protect the free *and sincere* exercise of religion. The question here is sincerity. You have none. You are mocking not only this committee, but every God-fearing

American. The purpose of this hearing is to determine the sincerity of your so-called beliefs."

"Congressman, it sounds like you've already made up your mind, so it's hard for me to understand *what* the purpose of this hearing is. Or, not so hard, I guess." Nick turned in his chair and swept his hand at the assembled cameras, to more guffaws.

Bang! went the chairman's gavel. "Silence! Committee counsel shall take note of the witness's conduct and consider appropriate action regarding a citation for contempt."

Washington is a septic tank, Nick had heard once. The biggest chunks rise to the top.

He stood again. "Mr. Chairman, I request to call a witness."

"Sit down!" the chairman shouted, with yet another smash of the gavel. Nick wondered whether those things ever broke. That would be a hoot. "You don't call the witnesses here! We call the witnesses! Counsel, take further note of the witness's contempt."

Nick grasped the table with both hands and loaded as much dignity as he could muster into the act of resuming his seat. He held the pause as long as he could, and began as calmly as he could. Biathlon, he reminded himself. A ridiculous sport, combining cross-country skiing with target shooting. It made no sense at all, except that when you had just finished a ski run in the bitter cold, your heart was racing, and a racing heart made shooting a rifle at a target vastly more difficult. Nick would never, ever have made a good biathlete. But he had rehearsed this moment in his head so many times he thought he could pull it off.

"Questioning a man's sincerity is a grave matter," he began. His voice was almost too soft to be heard, so he leaned in closer to the microphone. "Especially questioning his sincerity about the religious principles he holds most dear, that form ... the core of his soul. If you will not even let me defend myself, you may indeed become worthy of contempt. I won't delay these proceedings, or go off on a tangent. I request only a single witness, who—by chance—is already here in the room. Sincerity is a relative notion—I simply wish to compare the sincerity of my beliefs to the sincerity of others."

Nick wondered whether actual steam was shooting out of Randall's ears. "The witness is reminded, for the final time, that he does not call the witnesses here. *We* call the witnesses. Period. Now, Mr. Fratelli, let us *finally* begin. I wish to call your attention to an email purportedly written by you on September 7 of last year, a copy of which appears on page ninety-six of the hearing binder. Please turn to that page, and tell the committee whether you are the author of this document."

Nick did not touch his binder. Instead, deliberately too close to the microphone, he said, "I call as a witness ... the Reverend Richard Henry Marshall."

The crash of the chairman's gavel was nearly drowned out by the collective gasp of four hundred members of the audience. "Counsel!" he bellowed. "That's three!"

Nick had only been fishing a few times. He liked the part where you got to sit on the dock and drink beer, acting like you were doing something, hoping that no wiggly little animal would disturb your reverie. He definitely did not like the part about slicing open the fish's belly and getting brown goo all over your hands. Richard Henry Marshall would be a hell of a catch, though, and he'd relish squishing his every entrail. Nick visualized a stream of bubbles from Marshall's nose as he eyed Nick's bait.

Marshall rose majestically. "I have no fear of this man," he boomed. "I shall testify of the Lord today, and tomorrow, and every day. Gus—I mean, Mr. Chairman—let us humor this charlatan. Let us proclaim the good news of Jesus Christ, so that all may hear."

YANK! Reel-reel-reel, then yank again!

"Mr. Chairman—" Nick had to raise his voice above the din. "Mr. Chairman, Reverend Marshall wants to testify. I want him to testify. The American people want to hear us out. Surely, sir, you do not want to disappoint them?"

And miss a shot at tonight's lead story on Fox News?

While the chairman huddled with his staff, Nick tried to remember to breathe, and pulled from his shirt pocket a picture he had brought of Clarence Darrow seated next to William Jennings Bryan at the 1925 Scopes "Monkey Trial." Nick knew that transcript backwards and forwards, and had watched *Inherit the Wind* many times. It was even more preposterous for Clarence Darrow, the defense lawyer, to call as a "witness" William Jennings Bryan, the prosecution's lawyer, than it was for Nick to try to drag Marshall into a congressional hearing, the sole purpose of which was to roast Nick alive. Yet Darrow's trick worked, because he knew that neither Bryan nor the presiding judge could resist such a chance for glory. Bryan had said, "I want the Christian world to know that any atheist, agnostic, unbeliever, can question me any time as to my belief in God, and I will answer him." Not exactly Marshall's words, but close enough. The world had changed a lot since 1925, but the eagerness of politicians to bend rules for personal aggrandizement remained constant.

"Consider yourself on a short leash, Mr. Fratelli," said the chairman. "Very short. Reverend Marshall may answer your questions if he wishes, but if you try to turn this hearing into a circus we *will* prosecute you for contempt."

"Thank you, Mr. Chairman. No circus—I promise." The judge who had presided at the Scopes trial had been defeated when he ran for reelection, Nick knew, and he devoutly hoped the same fate would befall this asshole.

Nick pushed the backpack off the chair that would otherwise have been occupied by Peter Spillman, flush with his own. He proffered a hand, which Marshall disdained as he clambered over knees and wires and settled heavily into it.

Nick thought he spied pancake makeup softening the bags under Marshall's eyes. Could that be? Had Marshall anticipated this might happen? Nick wished Natalie were there. She could help him with questions like that. But Peter had vetoed her presence, with a dismissive reference to "camera bait." Such a timid mind. Peter always saw only the downside, never the upside. He would never have allowed Nick to try a stunt like this.

"So, Reverend Marshall, good to see you again. For the record, you are affiliated with the Southern Baptist denomination?"

"I am."

"And the Southern Baptist majority view, which you share, is in the inerrancy of the Bible. Is that correct?"

"That is what true Southern Baptists believe. All true Christians, for that matter. I am a true Christian, and a true Southern Baptist. Not a fraud."

Whoops from the back of the room.

Nick opened a dog-eared paperback Bible he had brought with him. A dozen yellow Post-It notes stuck out from its sides. Nick found the one labeled "judge not," opened to that page, and read out: "'Judge not, that ye be not judged.' That's Matthew, chapter seven. At the top here, see?" He shoved the book under Marshall's nose. Marshall did not budge.

"That's inerrant, right? Just generally, could you explain what the inerrancy of the Bible means?"

"God said it. I believe it. That settles it. That's what it means."

More whoops and some applause. Not a lot, though. Nick wasn't facing the back, but it seemed the whoops were coming from just one guy.

"I've seen that bumper sticker," said Nick. "So you believe the literal words of the Bible are all true. Correct?"

"My God doesn't lie. I can't speak for yours."

Nick knew that Darrow had lured Bryan into the ridiculous. Genesis said that God condemned the snake to crawl on his belly as punishment for deceiving Eve. Darrow's sucker punch was, "Have you any idea how the snake went before that time? ... Do you know whether he walked on his tail or not?" But Nick thought Marshall may have read the transcript too, and anyway, might be too smart for that. So he'd worked out a different tack.

"I've always wondered, Reverend: do you hate your father?"

Marshall jerked his head. "Now see here!"

Nick flipped to another Post-It note page. "'If any man come to me, and hate not his father, and mother, and wife, and children, and brethren, and sisters, yea, and his own life also, he cannot be my disciple.' That's Jesus talking, in the gospel of Luke.[85] See, they've got the actual Jesus words here in red ink. So I'll repeat the question: Do you hate your father?"

Titters from the crowd, which was beginning to lean in Nick's favor.

"No, I do not hate my father. You are taking that quotation completely out of context. It's about the need for placing God above all men."

"Well, it says what it says, and you insist it's literally true. If Jesus had wanted to say 'Place God above all men,' I bet he could've managed it. But he didn't. The man said 'hate your father.' But, just one follow-up. Do you hate your children? I know you've got a bunch of them. Do you hate them?"

"I will not dignify that insult with an answer."

"'Cause when the same idea is repeated in both the Old Testament and the New, it's gotta have some extra oomph, right? And in Psalm 137, it says 'Happy shall he be, that taketh and dasheth thy little ones against the stones.' Wow! Have you ever done that?" Nick didn't need to read from his marked page for that one.

"That Psalm, Mr. Fratelli, concerns the struggle of God's chosen people against the ungodly, as you well know."

"Maybe I should wear a helmet." More laughter. "But let's get back to the father thing. Do you, Rev. Marshall, sincerely believe in the

---

85. Luke 14:26. https://www.biblegateway.com/passage/?search=Luke+ 14:26&version=KJV

inerrant truth of the book of Exodus? Or not?"

On fleeting occasions playing paintball, Nick had seen a look in a trapped player's eyes that said I know what's coming, but not from where, and I can't do anything about it anyway. A gob of red paint would look great on Marshall's nose.

"Of course I do, when it's properly interpreted."

Nick grandly flipped the page, and recited: "'For I, the Lord thy God, am a jealous God, visiting the iniquity of the fathers upon the children unto the third and fourth generation.' That's Exodus.[86] Do you sincerely believe that?"

Marshall glared at him. Before he could reply, Nick said, "Now my Pop, he isn't perfect, but he's pretty ok, and I'm not worried about being stuck with anything he did. At least *after* he got married." Pop would get a kick out of that. "And Grandpop, I don't know much about him. But his dad, who Exodus says I'm stuck with, I heard he got out of Naples in a big hurry, for something. I don't know what it was, but it had to be pretty bad. So do you sincerely believe, that when I get to the Pearly Gates, I'm gonna hear all about that, and they're gonna say, 'Sorry, fourth generation kid. The down escalator's over there'"?

"Unless you repent of your fraud, Mr. Fratelli, that analysis may not prove necessary."

Another lonely hoot from the back. Thinking more quickly than usual, Nick said, "Not much use in repenting, if I'm screw- if I'm stuck paying for great-grandpa's sins anyway. But let's move on. A simpler question. Yes or no. Can anybody see God? While they're alive, I mean."

Marshall looked at Nick like he had two heads. What Nick had gleaned, from studying clips about Marshall for years, was that he knew a lot about politics, but of all things was actually a little weak on the Bible. A lot of other God experts would have spotted the trap right away.

"Here's a clue." From a page he'd already turned to, he read: "'And the Lord spake to Moses face to face, as a man speaketh to his friend.'[87] Here's a second clue—am I generous, or what? 'For I have seen God face

---

86. Exodus 20:5. https://www.biblegateway.com/passage/?search=Exodus+20:5&version=KJV.

87. Exodus 33:11. https://www.biblegateway.com/passage/?search=Exodus+33:11&version=KJV.

to face, and my life is preserved.' That's Genesis, chapter thirty-two.[88] So some people, at least, have seen God?"

"I am familiar with the Bible. And I believe it."

"So you *also* sincerely believe the New Testament, gospel of John. 'No man hath seen God at any time.'[89] Here, you can look at it."

"You are once again taking things completely out of context!" cried Marshall, above the crowd's buzz.

"No, I'm not," Nick snapped. "This is exactly, precisely *in* context. A minute ago you said you 'sincerely' believed one thing in the Bible, and now the Bible you say you 'sincerely' believe says exactly the opposite thing. That just puzzles me, especially when you go criticizing *other* people's sincerity, and calling 'em frauds." He paused an instant before the kill, like a matador before a spent bull. "Say, can you cross your eyes? A kid named Barry back in third grade could do that. Maybe sincerely believing you can see something and not see something at the same time, maybe that was his trick." Unbeknownst to Nick, within minutes, doctored photos of a cross-eyed Richard Henry Marshall began flooding the internet. He never lived them down.

The laughter finally diminished after repeated smashes of the chairman's gavel. "Time to wrap this up, Mr. Fratelli," said the chairman. "None of this is relevant."

Nick thought it was a million percent relevant, and he had a dozen more sticky notes on his Bible. If this were a high school debate, without the annoying time limits, and with judges who have to sit there and pay attention, he could have cruised to an easy victory. He especially liked the one about the four mutually exclusive versions of the number of women who were said to have arrived at Jesus's empty tomb, one in each of the four gospels.[90] How could you "sincerely" believing in four opposite stories at the same time?

But Randall wouldn't let him go on forever, and the crowd would soon tire of too much theology. He flipped through his sticky notes in desperation, realizing he needed a deus ex machina in a big hurry if

---

88. Genesis 32:30. https://www.biblegateway.com/passage/?search=Genesis+32:30&version=KJV.

89. John 1:18. https://www.biblegateway.com/passage/?search=John+1:18&version=KJV.

90. William Henry Burr, *Self Contradictions of the Bible*. Library of Alexandria, 1923. https://books.google.com/books?id=FteYvvt7bncC

he wasn't going to squander the amazing opportunity that Marshall's hubris had given him.

Looking down at his book, Nick's glance fell on Marshall's shoes. They looked a lot like Peter Spillman's, with buckles and a squarish pattern embossed in the leather, or snakeskin, or whatever it was. Nick hadn't the faintest idea what the material was, but he did suspect that those shoes cost more than his monthly rent.

"I love those shoes," Nick heard himself saying. "Must've cost a fortune. Say, Reverend, how much do you make? I mean, not total—that's personal—but just off Bartimaeus. You don't even do anything there, from what I see. Just get kickbacks, or commissions, or something like that. 'Course, it's all top secret. But—am I right?—you make over a million dollars a year from these kickba- whatever you call them. Is that right? A million bucks a year?"

Nick had no more idea how much Marshall made from Bartimaeus than he had about the brand of Marshall's shoes. But in every basketball game, right before the quarter or halftime buzzer sounds, a player will heave a shot at the basket from the backcourt. ESPN will replay, over and over again, the couple of times each year when such a shot swishes through the net. On top of that, Nick had absorbed the urban legend that Lyndon Johnson had spread rumors accusing his opponent of fornication with pigs, on the theory that "I just want to hear him deny it."

Which is not what Marshall did. He instead turned a brilliant purple, while struggling to formulate a response to this despicable pipsqueak. He was hampered by not knowing exactly how much he really *was* making off Bartimaeus. The number was certainly large, and his total income was in the mid-seven figures. But what proportion came from Bartimaeus, as opposed to his regular salary, his church lease payments, his book royalties, his television residuals, his investment properties, his whatever else, he couldn't say. And if he didn't know, how did this blasphemer know? Or did he?

Worse yet, Marshall couldn't employ the time-tested political tactic of attacking the accuser. "Your health insurance scheme is worse than mine!" ... "No it isn't—yours is worse than mine!" was exactly the kind of mud-slinging Bartimaeus did not need.

"I want you to know ..." Marshall began to sputter, after too long of a stunned pause. "I want you to know, I want the world to know, that I am proud of what we do at Bartimaeus. It's not about the money. I'm proud to support Christians helping Christians. I'm proud of every little Christian baby we help bring into the world. I'm proud ..."

"So you do make a million!" Nick interrupted gleefully, twisting the knife as hard as he could. "All off denying benefits to sick people. What a racket!" Laura Boess would have a cow over that, but he'd deal with her later.

"Why, you ...!" Marshall roared, rising suddenly and shoving back his chair so hard it nearly toppled. "Mr. Chairman, if you can't control ..." He blinked in disgust, not wanting to pick a fight with Randall. Instead he turned on Nick, shaking a fist inches from his nose. "You are of Satan! I am PROUD of everything we do, and I'm not going to stay here and be bullied by Satan himself."

He turned his back sharply on Nick and stormed off. At least, that's what he intended to do, and what he would have done, had he not inadvertently inserted his expensively shod foot inside the strap of Nick's backpack. Down he went, nose to the floor, taking a television light and a pitcher of water with him.

"I guess pride goeth before fall," Nick deadpanned into the microphone. The room erupted in laughter. C-SPAN even caught Chairman Randall covering his mouth with his hand, before banging his gavel and declaring the hearing in recess until further notice.

"Mr. Chairman, before you start questioning my sincerity," Nick shouted furiously, "you ought to explore the sincerity of this guy. I'm not sincere? Give me a break."

More people would have heard him, had his microphone not been switched off.

Nick turned to find Peter Spillman, but he was gone. He noticed instead a Fox News reporter, with her unmistakable blonde hair, waving frantically to attract his attention for a quick interview. As Nick made his way toward her, he brushed past Jay, who was holding a microphone and looking for his own exclusive, with a quick "Hold on."

February 4: Watergate Garage

The humiliation of Richard Henry Marshall attracted plenty of television coverage that evening, but had to compete for media attention with the latest atrocities in the Turkish civil war and the Supreme Court hearing on reversing *Roe v. Wade*. Nick was not at all surprised when he flipped on his computer the next morning to find a two-word message from Peter Spillman: "See me."

As he rode up the elevator, Nick assured himself he was dealing from a position of strength. No way even Peter could bitch about how that turned out. He knew deep down, of course, that he was fooling himself. Peter could always find something to complain about.

Instead of the anger he expected, though, Nick heard a note of dejection in Peter's voice. The normally immaculate desk he sat behind was cluttered with papers and a dirty coffee cup. This was not a meeting that called for the bonhomie of the living room setup in the corner.

"Communication and cooperation. That's what we agreed to. Do I recall that correctly?" Peter asked. Natalie, seated to the side of Peter's desk, avoided eye Nick's eyes.

"Yeah," said Nick defensively. "And that's what I've been doing. I've been sending every sermon through Natalie to get wordsmithed, and I haven't started any new initiatives on my own. I'm working on a new idea for corporate religious exemptions from the immigration laws with Natalie and Ramon that ought to be a good one. If the Divine Spirit calls a person to hop from one side of the Rio Grande to the other, why should government get in the way of that?[91] And why should a devout

---

91. Ryan Lucas, "Deep In The Desert, A Case Pits Immigration Crackdown Against Religious Freedom," *NPR*, October 18, 2018. https://www.npr.org/2018/10/18/658255488/deep-in-the-desert-a-case-pits-immigration-crackdown-against-religious-freedom. See generally Luis Granados, "The Sanctuary Scam," *TheHumanist.com*, October 2, 2014. https://thehumanist.com/voices/rules_are_for_schmucks/rules-are-for-schmucks-the-sanctuary-scam. Statutory exemptions make it easier for religious workers than for other persons to enter the United States legally. "Special Immigrant Religious Workers," US Citizen and Immigration Services, https://www.uscis.gov/working-united-states/permanent-workers/employment-based-immigration-fourth-preference-eb-4/special-immigrant-religious-workers.

CIS corporate member have to pay big fines for employing a member of its own religion? Earl would jump at the chance to hire more low-paid immigrants in his operations, wouldn't he? But I won't announce it until everything's approved, 'cause I'm cooperating." He turned to get some affirmation from Natalie, but received none. He hadn't even run by her yet his brilliant idea that would let Earl fire Democrats, or employees dumb enough to complain about safety conditions, that he was pretty sure could work.[92]

"Now yesterday—I assume that's what you're worried about—that was different. I had a plan, and once Marshall walked in I *knew* it could work, and I knew I had to be really, really on to make it work. And I couldn't do that with you breathing down my neck. So, I'm sorry. But hey—you can't argue with how it turned out! They thought they had me dead to rights, but now look who's squirming!"

Peter had both hands pressed down on the table. Before he could speak, Nick squeezed in "I bet Earl loved it! Don't tell me he didn't!"

"Yes, Earl says he enjoyed it," said Spillman softly. "But that's not ultimately the point, is it? Earl Matteson knows his business, and I know mine. I've been around this game a long time, Nick. And the fellows I learned my trade from were around even longer."

Peter waved at his corner office window. "You don't succeed in this town by leading with your chin. You don't succeed by making a lifelong enemy of a man like Chairman Randall. When you are attacked, you hunker down. You give a little ground. You live to fight another day."

"But I won," said Nick, genuinely puzzled. "No way do they restart that hearing. They know now that whatever they hit me with, I'll just come back with how some mainstream religion is even worse. 'Unnamed sources' on the committee staff are already admitting that."

---

92. "SF archbishop asks lawmakers to respect his right to hire those who uphold Catholic teachings," *Associated Press*, February 19, 2015. https://www.foxnews.com/us/sf-archbishop-asks-lawmakers-to-respect-his-right-to-hire-those-who-uphold-catholic-teachings Michael Gryboski, "Judge OKs California School's Requirement That Employees Have a Pastor for a Reference," *Christian Post*, March 26, 2015. http://m.christianpost.com/news/judge-oks-california-schools-requirement-that-employees-have-a-pastor-for-a-reference-136418/. Joanne Levasseur, "Winnipeg church fires woman after health and safety complaint lodged," *CBC News*, May 1, 2015 http://www.cbc.ca/news/canada/manitoba/winnipeg-church-fires-woman-after-health-and-safety-complaint-lodged-1.3057494?cmp=rss

"You won a battle, Nick," Peter said wistfully. "Like Pyrrhus did. Not a war. Al Qaeda no longer exists for all practical purposes, does it? While Hamas and Hezbollah continue to grow and thrive. Why is that? Because Al Qaeda bit off more than it could chew. Not that I'm calling you a terrorist, but the strategic error is fundamentally the same. The same error Hitler made by attacking the Soviet Union, and Tojo made by attacking Pearl Harbor. Lee on Cemetery Ridge. Get my drift, Nick? Hubris—uncontrolled hubris. Even Icarus, flying too close to the sun, if you want to go back that far. Pigs get fat, Nick, but hogs get slaughtered."

Nick knew all those references, and when he had a chance to review the bidding later he was impressed that Peter did too. Overwhelmed right now though, he turned to Natalie. "Is that what you think?"

"I think Peter knows what he's doing. That's why I joined the firm—to learn from people who know what they're doing."

Thanks for nothing, Nick thought. "And I don't? How'd we get this far if I don't know what I'm doing?"

"We got this far with careful, thorough lawyering," she snapped, giving him more eye contact than he really wanted. "You waltz in here out of la-la-land, with one off-the-wall idea. One." She held up her index figure. "We turn it into something. Then, right at the critical moment, with everything at risk, you deliberately ignore the best, most experienced minds in the business. Won't even hear what we have to say."

She's just sucking up to the boss again, Nick decided. Tomorrow night I'll find out what she really thinks. Meanwhile, it seemed a good moment for him to change the subject.

"So, are you guys going to appeal the Bradford County case?" A local judge in Oklahoma had just handed Matteson Enterprises a stinging defeat on a fracking exemption case, pointedly disagreeing with the decisions from other jurisdictions that CIS qualified as a religion. As he was finishing the sentence, Nick realized it sounded like he was implying "See, you guys aren't always so smart," even though that wasn't his intent.

"We have no choice but to appeal," Peter replied. "And I am confident we shall prevail. We must all return to work now. There is little point in asking you to agree to cooperate with us more closely in the future. You already agreed to that once, and we see the result. I only offer, as a data point in your constellation of considerations, that this firm was getting things done in Washington long before you were born, and we will be here long after you are gone. If you continue to ignore our advice you will have only yourself to blame for your own failure. Good day."

*****

The hammer fell the following week, when Nick flipped on his custom search engine one morning and found a stunner.

Inside CIS—First of a Series
By Jaime Gimenez

A hatchet job, start to finish. The first installment focused on Nick's impudent college atheism, to cast doubt on the sincerity of his current religious devotion to CIS. It quoted heavily from Father Robert McIntyre and students from his comparative religion classes whom Jay had dug up. It was too painful for Nick to read carefully, so he just skimmed it once. Then he jerked up the telephone receiver, without even thinking first about his renewed commitment to "communicate and cooperate."

"Hello?" said Jay.

"What the fuck, man? I mean, what the fuck!"

"Good morning to you, too."

"What the hell are you doing?" Nick sputtered.

"I'm reporting. My job, remember?"

"Your JOB! You're castrating me! Is that your job? Your best bud from third grade? The guy who gave you your big break, made you the hottest journalist in DC? And now you're turning on me. That's your JOB, asshole?"

"Oh, you don't need me anymore," said Jay evenly. "You're a heavy hitter now. You've made that abundantly clear. Why, you have Fox News. You don't need little Jay Gimenez anymore."

"Fox News? Is that what this is about?" The Fox report on Nick's confrontation with Richard Marshall, in fact, had shown only a few unflattering seconds of Nick's interview, the part where he was flustered and stammering. Then three more minutes of talking heads in the studio tut-tutting about America's roots as a Christian nation. "Look, I was coming right back to you at the hearing, but you were gone. And I couldn't pass up ... shit. I can't believe you're doing this. Without even talking to me."

"Fair and balanced, Nick. Fair and balanced. That was the old Fox

News line, wasn't it? I've given you plenty of puff pieces. Now I'm tilting back to get to fair and balanced. Worked for them, right? And as for talking to you, oh, I have plans for that. On camera. One take. With some thought-provoking questions I just know you'll enjoy. The viewers will, anyway. Unless you're afraid to talk to me."

Nick had supreme confidence in his ability to handle Marshall and the dim bulbs in Congress. But a loaded-for-bear Jay, who knew so much about what Nick was really thinking, was another matter altogether.

A light dawned. "Are you getting paid for this?" Nick demanded.

"Friendly reminder, Nick. Nothing you say to a reporter is off the record, unless the reporter agrees it is. Which I don't. Of course I'm being paid. I'm a professional reporter, remember? It's not a hobby, like mocking people's heartfelt religious beliefs."

"You bastard. You know what I mean. Is Marshall paying you? Or RFF? How much?"

"Oh, my," said Jay, chuckling softly. "It sounds like you're offering me a bribe. Trying to nail down my price, so you can offer me a dollar more than you assume I'm being paid by your opponents. Is that what you're doing, Mr. Fratelli?"

Nick actually hadn't thought that far ahead yet, but it didn't seem like a half-bad idea. Anything was better than this article, and what seemed poised to come. But the "on the record" warning had him spooked.

"I wouldn't pay a shit like you a nickel. For anything, ever. Fuck you." And he hung up.

Now came the worst part: the realization that he would have to explain to Natalie, and maybe even to Peter, why he had once again hauled off and failed to pass every syllable through eight levels of litigation exposure analysis and PR bureaucracy before uttering it.

Natalie was less annoyed than Nick had expected, perhaps because he hadn't been entirely candid with her about all that had been said during the call. She didn't even cancel tomorrow night's date, as Nick had feared she might. Nick stayed later at the office than usual, trying to get his work done, but largely failing. He couldn't get his mind off Jay's articles, which could be devastating. He needed a quiet drink or three. Or better yet, some solid advice from the Divine Spirit.

*****

In the cold weather, Nick had taken to driving the few short blocks from the garage in the Watergate to the garage in the G&H building. As he locked his car door in a dimly lit corner of the Watergate garage after arriving home, what he first took to be a scrawny teenaged boy in a baseball cap and dark leather jacket stepped from behind a neighboring car.

"Hey, Nick."

Melody's soft southern drawl was unmistakable.

Nick slammed back against his car as though he'd been physically shoved. "What the—"

"Don't worry," she said, with one of those rippling laughs that had melted his heart. "I'm not a ghost. And I'm not going to hurt you. Ever again. Just the opposite."

Nick had no words. His every brain cell, including those normally assigned to managing his heart and lungs, was consumed with the task of matching what he remembered of the shape of Melody's face, separate and apart from that cascade of hair, with the face under the brim of the baseball cap, fringed only with a short black bristle. Which was all a pointless exercise, because there was only one voice like that in the galaxy.

"Look," she said urgently. "I can only stay a minute. I'm not supposed to be here. I'm in witness protection, ok? That's where I disappeared to. It was all a big trick. And that reporter friend of yours"—her eyes flashed with anger—"he's not as smart as he thinks he is."

"W-Witness protection?" Nick burbled. "But that's only for, like, witnesses. Like the Mafia, stuff like that."

Melody seemed to look right through him. Nick had never seen that kind of hard stare from her before. She seemed quite grown up.

"Me?" Nick stammered. "I haven't committed any crime. Everything I do is legal! That's the whole point!"

"They're out to get you, Nick. You've really made them mad. They … they've even talked to the president."

"Bertram?"

"Uh-huh," she nodded. "You're in a lot of trouble, Nick. Seriously. I don't know what you can do about it, but you're so smart, maybe you can figure somethin' out. I just had to warn you, that's all. But if they ever find out I did this … you don't know how bad that would be. I probably *would* kill myself then. I just couldn't stand it, with Daddy, and all the others … Please promise me, Nick. You hurt me once, and maybe I deserved it, but I don't deserve it now. Please promise you'll never, ever tell anybody I was here. Please!"

"Ok," said Nick, without thinking. Melody committing suicide was firmly planted in his brain as a Bad Thing, to be avoided at all costs.

Melody's eyes were beginning to water. "Good-bye, Nick—forever!" she said, and began to stride toward the exit ramp. Nick remained rooted on the spot. When she was six cars away, she suddenly turned and cried out, "I do love you, you know!", then sprinted away at full speed.

Nick could never have caught her even if he tried. Which he didn't.

February 5: The FBI

The main reason Nick didn't make it into the office until Friday mid-afternoon was not the hangover, or the shattering headache that accompanied it. He'd dealt with those before, although this one threatened some longstanding records. The main reason was he had no idea what to do once he got there. So he hung around his apartment all morning, cleaning. Things had to be desperate for him to take measures as drastic as that.

Communicate and cooperate? How the hell was he supposed to do that? He thought long and hard about whether he could tell Natalie about the visit from Melody, even if he swore her to secrecy. After all, she felt as guilt-ridden about a suicide that never happened as Nick did. Didn't he owe her the courtesy of telling her? He would spend all night in bed with the woman. He had to keep the secret even then?

Then there was Jay, who seemed to have come completely unhinged since the incident. Without any means of corroboration, though, Jay would simply disbelieve Nick. He would assume it was a trick to get him to cut off the exposé series.

Overarching all that, of course, was the promise he'd made to Melody. Nick had no clue whether this latest encounter was just another ploy. If it was simply a ruse for making his head spin when clear thinking was a must, it was brilliant. But if it was real, if she had taken great personal risk to give Nick a warning ... The bottom line was, Nick had felt so terrible the first time he believed he was responsible for Melody killing herself, he couldn't go there again. That removed one variable from a viciously complex equation.

All of which left him with no clue what to do about Jay's articles. And no clue what to do about the prosecution threat Melody had warned him about, for an unknown crime he hadn't committed. And no clue how to prepare to meet such a threat. And without revealing Melody's secret, no way to get any help from the pros at G&H in that preparation, even though he was at the highest level of anxiousness to "communicate and cooperate" he had ever been. "Uh, Peter, I had this sort of dream that the feds were after me, and I was wondering if we could, uh, game plan a little for how to react to different tacks they might take?" That would go over well.

After a couple hours of bathroom, kitchen, and refrigerator effort—he couldn't even remember what was under the half-inch of mold in the blue Tupperware—he tried going back to bed. It made more sense to roll over and press a cool pillow to the side of his aching head than to go into an office where it was highly unlikely any good news awaited.

*****

The only remote wisp of good news, once Nick finally hit the office, was a voice message from Kyle, who had also left a message two days earlier. It would be a relief to hang out with him for a while, even if he couldn't tell Kyle everything. Or anything, really, because Kyle's eyes would just glaze over and he wouldn't care. Which would be refreshing, after so much stress dealing with all these folks who cared so deeply about everything. Everything, that is, that had enough trailing zeroes. But tonight was not the night to see Kyle, partly because it was Natalie night, and partly because Nick's temple still had a giant wedge stuck in it. It hurt so much Nick even skipped lunch, a rare event indeed.

Staring at the computer screen brought neither relief nor any answers. Nick started flipping through some vacation websites. It had been nearly a year since Puerto Rico, where he had met Prissy and gotten snookered into those outlandish "vestments." That memory shot another jolt of pain from one temple to the other. But Natalie surely wouldn't take time off work, and he didn't want to go anywhere by himself. He even checked out a few porn sites, which did nothing for him. The possibility that he was so wiped out he might have difficulty performing with Natalie tonight added one more layer of misery.

*****

A little after four o'clock, he stepped out to the restroom. Two burly men in business suits strode toward him down the hall. "Niccolò Fratelli?" one of them asked.

"Yeah?"

"I'm Agent Sanderson. Federal Bureau of Investigation." He flashed Nick a badge of some sort, inside a wallet. "This is Agent Bowers. Would you please come with us, sir?"

"Am I under arrest?"

"No, you are not. We want to talk to you, that's all. Please come this way."

"But I've got ... how long will this take?"

"Not long, sir. The car's waiting."

Sanderson was maybe forty-five. He had a reddish crew cut, sprinkled with gray, over a ruddy face. He was an inch or so shorter than Nick, with a barrel chest that had pumped quite a bit of iron. The hand he had wrapped around Nick's forearm was unusually large.

Bowers was several inches taller, black, with a moustache/goatee surrounding his mouth. J. Edgar Hoover would not have approved. Both men looked like they hadn't cracked a smile in years, and would need special rehab classes to help them figure it out.

"Well, I've only got a few minutes. I've got stuff to do tonight. You're sure this won't take long?"

Sanderson kept his iron grip on Nick's forearm, while Bowers moved to Nick's other side and eased him along with a powerful hand in the small of his back. They rode up the elevator in silence. As they emerged in the lobby and headed to the door, Nick tried to lighten the mood. "So, is this a perp walk?"

"No," said Agent Sanderson. "We do those on Mondays, when we can get more press."

Nick had read a Grisham novel about fake FBI agents, and he hadn't examined Sanderson's badge closely. But the black car with government plates illegally parked in the "No Parking or Standing" area in front of the G&H doorway was one clue these guys were legit. The bigger clue came ten minutes later, when they pulled into the garage underneath the massive FBI headquarters on 10th Street.

By that point, Nick didn't need reminding that his original, unfulfilled mission on getting up from his desk had been to take a leak. When they reached the seventh floor, he asked to be excused. Permission was granted, but only with Agent Bowers standing directly behind him, which disrupted the process a bit. Nick pondered demanding the religious privilege to pee in peace, but thought better of it. He also weighed the pros and cons of whirling in mid-pee, spraying Agent Bowers, and using the ensuing distraction to escape. But he thought better of that, too.

The room they ushered Nick into was small and overheated, but brightly lit. This made things easier for the two video cameras Nick spied in the corners. One wall sported a large mirror, which Nick knew from all the cop shows he'd watched was actually a one-way window. He thought about something outrageous he could do in front of the "mirror" if he was ever left alone. An extended nose-picking campaign might do the trick, but he lacked the nerve to try it.

Which was too bad, because he was left alone in that room for a good forty-five minutes before anything happened. At least, it seemed like forty-five minutes. He couldn't tell, because right before entering, Agent Sanderson asked him to empty his pockets, remove his watch, and place everything in a plastic bag.

"What for?" asked Nick.

"Sir," Sanderson said wearily, "this will go a whole lot easier for everyone if you let us ask the questions. It's standard procedure. I suppose they don't want suspects communicating with co-conspirators during questioning. Just put your things in the bag, sir."

"Communicating? With my comb? And now I'm a suspect? What am I suspected of? And how long is this going to take? I already told you, I only have a few minutes."

Sanderson snapped open the bag. "In here, sir."

Nick still demurred. "Well, you can't search through my phone. You don't have a warrant, and I do not give you permission. Understand? You do not have permission to search through, or even turn on, that cell phone."

Sanderson shrugged, removed a paper from his jacket pocket, and handed it to Nick. "This is the warrant for your person and personal effects, sir. Agents with warrants for your apartment, car, and office are on the scene now. Put the items in the bag voluntarily, or we will have to commence the full body cavity search. Maybe you'll enjoy that. Most people don't."

Nick put the items in the bag. And sat. And sat, and sat. At one point he rapped on the secret window, yelling "Hey, I gotta get going," but the window did not respond.

*****

Finally Agent Sanderson returned, with a new face. "This is Inspector Morales from the Federal Election Commission. He has a few questions." Sanderson withdrew a plastic card from his shirt pocket. "Before he begins: Niccolò Fratelli, you have the right to remain silent. Anything you say here can be used against you. You have the right to an attorney. If you cannot afford an attorney, one will be provided to you."

Nick's agitation, already simmering as he conjured up worst-case scenarios through the long delay, boiled over.

"Federal Election Commission? You've kept me here all this time, for the Federal Election Commission? That's ridiculous! I'm not running for office!" Nick rose quickly from him chair. "I told you I didn't have much time when we started. It's been nice meeting you. Call me next week, and we'll do lunch. I'm outta here."

As Nick moved toward the door, Agent Sanderson blocked his path and said, "I'm not sure that's wise."

"You're the font of wisdom now?"

Sanderson waved an imaginary headline through the air: "'Pseudo-priest refuses to cooperate in money-laundering investigation.' Not too propitious a public relations moment for that right now for you, is it? With the Gimenez articles, et cetera?"

"Money laundering! I don't even know how to launder money!"

"Then this shouldn't take very long, should it? Sit down."

Nick sat down heavily. "I really, really need to leave very soon. Ok?"

Inspector Morales asked, "When did you first meet Zoltan Fiola?"

An electric shock coursed down Nick's spine. Zoltan? Money laundering? Holy crap. At least this wasn't about the church. If Zoltan were mixed up with something fishy—which seemed entirely possible—Nick could quickly establish that he had nothing to do with it, and get this particular problem off his plate.

Morales walked Nick through the details of his initial phone calls and meeting with Zoltan. He peppered Nick with questions about other individuals with foreign-sounding names, none of which Nick recognized. One by one, he asked Nick about the congressional candidates on whose behalf the church had placed advertisements. After going through an identical set of questions about five of them, Nick burst out, "Look, I don't know anything about any of them, ok? These questions are ridiculous. We had a chance to associate the church with prominent statesmen, in a legal way, and we took it. Free speech, ya know? You heard of that one?"

Inspector Morales appeared as interested in responding to that challenge as he was in the shade of green paint on the wall. "The sixth name on the donee list is Rep. Ramona Doolin, of the fourth district of Florida. Please tell me when you first became familiar with the work of Rep. Doolin."

Nick slumped and repeated the same answers he had given about the first five. He jerked back to attention when Morales asked, "When did you first meet Marco Boyers?"

Marco Boyers ... he knew that name from somewhere, but couldn't place him. "Politraffic," Morales offered helpfully.

"Oh, yeah," said Nick. "That guy." He described, as best he could recall it, the session he'd had with Boyers in the office above the Chinese restaurant, with the A list candidates and the B list candidates, though he couldn't remember which was which. "'Mumbai Mafia,' I think he called one of the groups."

Morales produced a printed list of candidate names, with dates and contribution amounts, divided into what Nick vaguely remembered was the A list and the B list. "Do you recognize these transactions?"

"No."

"They are taken from independent expenditure reports filed with the FEC, sir."

"Could well be. I don't remember details like that."

"Sir, do you notice any difference in the nature of the amounts involved in the transactions on the A list and the transactions on the B list?"

Nick snatched up the paper. "Well, the B list ones are all round numbers, usually even multiples of $100,000. The A list ones are all over the lot."

"When did you first notice this pattern, sir?"

"About three seconds ago, when you showed me this paper."

"How odd. Such an obvious pattern. Tell me sir, when did you first become involved with the Bharatiya Janata Party?"

"Come again?"

"The Bharatiya Janata Party. The BJP. The ruling party in India. When did you first become involved with that party, sir?"

"I didn't! I've never heard of them. Well I've heard of them, but—"

"Excuse me," said Morales. "You are, or are not, familiar with the BJP? Please try to stick to one story."

"I'm not sticking to any story! I'm just telling you, I—"

"So you say you're not sticking to your story," said Sanderson, the first words he'd uttered since Morales began. Sanderson winked at Morales and said, "You're good! It usually takes us longer to break these guys down."

Nick tried to regain his composure. "You're twisting my words. Yes, I have read about the BJP. No, I've never had any contact with them. I wouldn't know a BJP guy if I fell over him."

Morales spoke like an automaton, never flinching or moving a muscle beyond what was absolutely necessary throughout the questioning. "No contacts, sir? According to the reports—they're all right here, if you wish to refresh your recollection—you received BJP funds from BJP operatives in 127 separate transactions last year, totaling nearly

$60 million. At the direction of you co-conspirator, Zoltan Fiola—who is being quite cooperative in our investigation, I must say, since we promised him full immunity—you then acted as a willing conduit for the expenditure of foreign funds to influence federal elections. In violation of 52 US Code section 30121."[93]

"What's that," asked Sanderson casually. "Three to five?"

"Yes," replied Morales. "One hundred and twenty-seven separate felony counts, at three to five years sentence each."

Sanderson leaned back in his chair and re-crossed his legs. "Of course, Nick, there's always parole. If you're at minimum security down in Alabama, you'll have a fair shot with the parole board there. Good Christians, all of them. I'm sure they'll go easy on a man of the cloth."

Nick was too stunned to respond with anger. "I don't know anything about BJP and that money," he squeaked. "But if you're threatening me with prison, well, I need a lawyer."

"But you *are* a lawyer, Nick," Sanderson said with a sneer. "A very famous one, from what I read. A regular trailblazer. Say, Morales, you know any Miranda cases where somebody who already is a lawyer walked because he couldn't get *two* lawyers on his side?"

Morales shook his head. "Nope."

"Me neither," said Sanderson with a shrug. "Maybe you could trailblaze that one, too? How about it, Nick?"

Nick hadn't the faintest idea how such a theory would stack up under what was left of the *Miranda* principle, after years of Supreme Court nibbling at the edges. Finally he said, "Look. I'm done answering questions here. Courts have said religious people don't have to answer government questions about their religious practices, ever, even if those practices involve laws like child labor.[94] You said I'm not under arrest, but you won't even tell me what time it is, and I'm probably late already. So, good-bye."

"Off to the fuck fest?" asked Sanderson, leering. "Guilder & Hersh

---

93. For a story about enforcement of this law, see "Florida man admits helping funnel 2012 foreign political contribution," *Reuters*, July 25, 2016. http://www.reuters.com/article/us-florida-crime-election-idUSKCN10527V

94. Shadee Ashtari, "Judge Cites Hobby Lobby To Excuse Fundamentalist Mormon From Child Labor Testimony," *Huffington Post*, September 18, 2014. http://www.huffingtonpost.com/2014/09/18/hobby-lobby-testimony-mormon-child-labor_n_5844696.html. Perez v. Paragon Contractors, D.Utah 2014 https://ecf.utd.uscourts.gov/cgi-bin/show_public_doc?213cv0281-121.

will just love those tabloid headlines, won't they, Morales? 'Felon flees FBI for final fling with lover/lawyer.' And the tabloids, Nick. They'll eat that chick up. Photogenic? Are you kiddin' me? We're talking eight-page spread! You sure can pick 'em."

The room spun around Nick's head. "How did you—?"

"Oh come on, Nick. We're not the Keystone Kops. And you're not exactly James Bond sneaking around, either. Is he, Morales?"

"Uh-uh. More like Inspector Clouseau."

"That's a good one, Morales. Inspector Clouseau! You seen him, Nick? Here's another one for you. You ever seen *The Wolf of Wall Street*? Where they take the guy they're gonna fire and have two goons stand over him while he cleans out his desk, then usher him out the front door? Is that how they do it at G&H when they fire somebody for breaking their rules, and all the rules of legal ethics while she's at it? Walk 'em right out the door into that mob of reporters, all trying to get a shot of the hottest babe in town? I got it—instead of *The Wolf of Wall Street*, how about—*The Sex Kitten of K Street*?"

"That's a good one," Morales agreed. "Her mom and dad back in Paterson will love it. Where she'll spend the rest of her life lugging laundry bags, since no law firm will touch her with a ten-foot pole."

Nick was too shattered to formulate any words. He was also too busy replaying Melody's warning from last night. "They're out to get you, Nick. You've really made them mad."

"Look, kid," said agent Sanderson, spreading his palms. "We got no beef with Natalie Parks. We never use half the dirt we find on people, because it ain't right. Usually, anyway. Frankly, we got no beef with you, either. You know how things go. They start out with big threats, then the lawyers go back and forth a while, then things settle out, and unless you're a poor black kid you never wind up doin' any time. But to do that, we gotta find out what the facts are first. The lay of the land. Then the AG knows how to start negotiating with your bigtime legal eagle buddies at G&H. Here's the deal, man to man: you play straight with us, quit pissing and moaning all night, quit talking about wanting a lawyer, and just tell us the fucking truth. And we leave Natalie Parks out of it. Deal?"

Nick hadn't the slightest reason to believe that Sanderson would honor his end of any "deal." But he'd promised Natalie secrecy, so many times, that he saw no choice but to grab onto the sliver of hope Sanderson offered and try to live to fight another day.

"Ok," he croaked.

"Progress at last!" Sanderson chortled. "More good news, Nick. Morales, you're done, right?"

"Yes, sir."

"Then we can click right along, and finish up in no time. Send in Rickman when you leave, ok?"

Special Agent Rickman was from the Food and Drug Administration. He grilled Nick about Zubitril for what seemed like hours. Every detail about the men Nick had met in New York—whose names he couldn't remember. Every detail about the reports he had and had not seen of the side effects people were blaming on Zubitril. Every detail of the independent research Nick had done, or was aware that someone else had done, about the safety and efficacy of Zubitril. That was a short conversation, because there had been none.

When Rickman left, Nick asked Sanderson if he could get some food and some aspirin. "I haven't had a bite all day, and I'm not feeling too well."

"Sorry, that's not the procedure. Funny you should mention food, though. Because next up is officer Koster from the US Postal Service, mail fraud division. Of all things, he has an interest in your eating habits."

Officer Koster plunged quickly into a close comparison of Nick's ringing sermons on fresh food, the way the Divine Spirit made it, with other data points. For example, the contents of Nick's cupboards and his credit card pizza delivery bills. "It's supposed to be a personal choice," Nick moaned. "That's all I ever said. If you think the Divine Spirit wants you to eat fresh food, you should be able to do so."

"Yes," said officer Koster, "but on December 11, at three minutes and fifteen seconds into your weekly talk, transcripts of which were later sent through the US Mail, you said ..."

After Koster came Shannon Pilsner, a lawyer from the Securities Exchange Commission. "The SEC?" wailed Nick. "I'm not a stockbroker. Can we please, please take a break, and let me come back tomorrow? I'll be here whenever you say. I promise."

Ms. Pilsner grilled Nick on the contents of a brochure advertising time-share units at the Cape Cod "temple." It seems the company Laura Boess set up was already collecting deposits on units in a building that not only wasn't built yet, but hadn't even received zoning approval, based solely on the "expectation" that such approval would have to ultimately be granted pursuant to RLUIPA. "I don't know, I don't know,

I don't know," said Nick. "I've never seen that brochure. All I did was explain RLUIPA, which lets churches build what they want, where they want, and Boess ran with it it from there. Talk to her. You two have a lot in common."

To the extent Nick had the energy to think independently at all rather than just respond to questions, he wondered why he hadn't been grilled by anyone from the IRS yet. There was no need to strain his brain on that one, though, once Agent Amar Singh arrived. Singh's agenda was easy to reverse-engineer. IRS maintained a list of "factors" to determine whether a church was tax exempt or not, which Nick had built CIS around.[95] You didn't need to satisfy every test, just most of them—which CIS did, thanks to Nick's careful construction. Singh, of course, harped incessantly on the ones CIS didn't satisfy, like "schools for the preparation of its ministers," to try to pull some damaging admissions that could be used against CIS's tax exempt status. In his weakened state, Nick gave up more ground than he would have with a snarling G&H attack dog at his side. But not that much more, he didn't think. Besides, tax exemption wasn't critical to the success of the Secret Plan—most of what he wanted to accomplish could be done without it.

Then Singh began wandering down a more treacherous path: Nick's CIS expense reports. Rather, the lack of them. No, Nick didn't remember how many people had been at the $1,200 dinner on May 7, or what theological point had been discussed. Yes, he did think $700 was a fair amount to pay from church funds for Armani shirts, but no, he didn't remember how many he had gotten for that amount. "And in March," asked Singh, "there is a a $400 item from San Juan, Puerto Rico, where the memo line simply says 'Prissy.' What is 'Prissy?'"

Fuck!

Next up: Investigator Russell Nesbit, from the Hudson County New York Fire Marshal's office. Investigator Nesbit had dozens of questions about what Nick knew about the fire that destroyed the St. Mercurius retreat center last June. As wiped out as he was, Nick would rather take on a dozen Nesbits and Sandersons than cross Doris. He stuck diligently to his line about not knowing anything about that fire other than what he'd read in the newspaper. He probably committed

---

95. *Internal Revenue Service*, "Tax Guide for Churches and Religious Organizations," page 33. https://www.irs.gov/pub/irs-pdf/p1828.pdf

the federal crime of obstructing justice by lying to the FBI when he repeatedly swore he knew of no one else who might have information about the fire.

After Nesbit left, Sanderson said, "Good news, Nick. We've reached our last questioner. Detective Rogers should be here in just a few minutes, and when he's done you'll be free to leave. While we're waiting, what can you tell me about the Glorification Temple?"

"Huh?"

"Glorification Temple. Out of St. Louis. Fellow who founded it says he's a former member of CIS."

"Mystery to me," said Nick truthfully. "Never heard of it."

"How about Pilgrim Covenant Congregation, down in Miami? They're connected to a law firm, like you are."

"I've got no connection to a law firm. I'm just a client. And a tenant. And I've never heard of Pilgrim Covenant Congregation, either."

Sanderson shrugged. "I hope you're telling the truth. If you're not, we'll find out."

"Never heard of either one."

Sanderson left, and returned a few minutes later with Detective Rogers, a broad-shouldered officer of the DC Metropolitan Police Department. He came straight to the point. "Mr. Fratelli, I'm here to ask you some questions about the murder of Melody LaPelletiere."

Nick fainted.

When he came to, with the aid of glasses of water splashed in his face, he had the presence of mind to demand a bathroom break. "I need a stall, not a urinal," he insisted. "With the fucking door closed." Seated on the toilet, he tried to sort through the ramifications of the alleged murder of someone who wasn't officially even dead, but who at least some people like ace reporter Jay Gimenez *thought* was dead, who sported a freshly dug grave, but who most definitely was not dead. At least she wasn't twenty-four hours ago. But Nick had already firmly decided he would never tell anyone, ever, about seeing her alive, which could make a murder defense a tad more challenging.

Could these guys have planted someone else's corpse in the grave Jay found? From what Nick had seen of agent Sanderson so far, that didn't seem farfetched.

Shit. Shit. Shit. That was as far as Nick's rational thought process could carry him on this one.

Nick obstructed justice with the first words out of his mouth, that the last time he had seen Melody was the Friday morning he had learned she was only seventeen. He added a count to the crime when he covered for Natalie by saying he'd received an anonymous call from someone claiming to be a member of Raymond LaPelletiere's congregation suggesting he check out Melody LaPelletiere's Facebook page to verify her age.

"There's no phone record of such a call that morning," said Sanderson.

"You know, you're right," said Nick, who was past caring by now. "I remember now. It was actually a guy who came up to me on the street when I came in that morning. And before you ask, no, I don't remember what he looked like. Actually, yeah, I do remember. He looked a lot like you, agent Sanderson. Remarkably like you."

"Nice one, Nick," said Sanderson. "You're a regular trailblazer, you are."

The detective's questions petered out after that, as Nick simply kept repeating, "I don't know. Last time I saw her was Friday morning at the office. I didn't even see her that Monday night at the hotel. I just heard her voice." He attempted to reverse-engineer from the questions what their theory of a murder might be, but could not do so. All the questions focused on Nick's whereabouts during the time period shortly after the Mayflower scene. None of them implied that anything had happened to her since last night, so that risk seemed crossable off the list. While on the toilet seat Nick had tried to decide whether it made sense for him to act surprised and/or dismayed that Melody was dead. But it was just too complicated trying to sort out whether he should, or should not, act like he knew about the fake suicide. So he just stuck to his marvelously persuasive alibi about spending the entire day Tuesday secluded in his apartment, munching Krispy Kremes.

When Rogers eventually tired of hearing the same answers repeated, Sanderson slapped Nick on the back. "First round, all done! We'll let you know when we need you back. But don't leave the country." As they reached the door, Sanderson handed Nick the plastic bag of his belongings.

His watch said 2:45 a.m.

February 7: Guilder & Hersh Main Conference Room

Sleep kept Nick from having to think about what to do next until the middle of Saturday afternoon. After he woke up, the next hour was spent staring at the ceiling, which was as blank as his mind. After that, a large Domino's with everything, which he polished off quickly. A week of college basketball was backed up on the Tivo, and he tried to make a dent in it but couldn't remember who won ten minutes after each game finished.

Sunday morning, he finally picked up the telephone and called Natalie at her office.

"Hi. It's Nick."

"Nick who?" she said coldly.

"Please don't," he said softly. "I have to talk to you. You're still my lawyer, right? It's billable."

"You know where I am." Then she hung up.

*****

Other than the encounter with Melody, Nick laid out everything that happened as accurately as he could. "I know I should have had a lawyer there," he pleaded. "And I tried. But with what they said about hurting you ... I didn't know what to do. I tried to do the right thing, but I probably got it wrong. I get everything wrong. Big surprise there."

Natalie had been typing notes on everything Nick said directly into her computer. It was more efficient that way. She stopped now, and chewed a bit on a strand of her hair. "You were on the spot. We should never have ... "

That didn't bode well for next Friday night.

"Why didn't you call me yesterday?"

"Yesterday?" asked Nick incredulously. "I spent yesterday wondering whether Melody had it right when she hung herself. I don't think I can deal with all this anymore." An exaggeration, but he wanted to overkill the non-existence of his encounter with the live Melody on Thursday night. And yesterday he had been even less amenable to questions beginning with the words "Why didn't you" than he was now.

"Oh, don't be a baby," she snapped. "I don't know if I ever mentioned it, but this law firm, we know what we're doing. Ok? We've gotten people out of plenty of bigger jams than this before. The government's got very little, when you boil it down. Half of what they were harassing you about is total bullshit."

"Half. That's comforting. So what am I looking at—only 150 years?"

"You're impossible." Nick knew why Natalie had chosen law over medicine. Her bedside manner was atrocious.

Nick pressed his fist on Natalie's desk. "Let me tell you what's impossible," he said, the whine gone from his voice. "What's impossible is for me to hear, even once, from your boss Mr. Spillman about my failure to 'communicate and cooperate.' If I hear that one more time, I will jump right through his fucking window. I'm not kidding. I put up with Sanderson and his goons all night for you, but I am *not* gonna put up with that again."

Natalie held eye contact with Nick for a very long ten seconds. Then she rose and stalked silently past him, out the door.

Half an hour later she returned, calm as ever. "I've told Peter about us. He's not happy, but I'm not fired. He said it was better to come clean than to keep it hidden. Especially," slumping her shoulders, "since it's not all that hidden. Janet's on her way in, with a couple of the other folks from criminal. All hands meeting at two. You'll need to go over everything again there, slowly. I just gave him the bare bones outline. Go get yourself some lunch—and bring me back a salad."

*****

For the first time, Nick had a chance to meet in the showcase conference room behind the main reception desk, where he had mistakenly thought that first encounter with Peter Spillman a century or so ago would occur. Was that a real Matisse on the far wall? All in all, conference room class notwithstanding, this was a meeting he could have done without.

Unburdening himself to Natalie had been a relief. Repeating everything to his new inquisitors was a chore. Especially because they, unlike Natalie, needed to be educated on the intricacies of matters like why, exactly, he had ever thought that defying the FDA by selling untested Zubitril to American customers could be a good idea. Or what great mission he was accomplishing by plunking a high-rise in the middle of the Cape Cod beach, where two of his appointed defenders had second homes. They kept going until nearly six p.m.

"Don't be so glum, Nick," said Peter as the meeting wound down. "When you look at each tree individually, instead of the forest you were confronted with on Friday night, it's really not that bad."

All of a sudden, Nick realized that despite his careful attempts to repeat everything as exactly as he could, he had left out the one detail that proved it really *was* that bad. A detail he couldn't tell them about. But a detail he *had* to tell them about.

Nick groaned and looked up at the ceiling to prevent a mist from forming in his eyes. "There's one more thing. Natalie, I didn't even tell you this. I ... shit. Look, I can't tell you where I got this. But it's for real. The FBI guys, and the others, they're doing this for a reason. It's the president, Bertram. He's out to get me. *He* gave the order. This isn't run of the mill. It *is* a fucking forest, not just the trees."

"That sounds a bit paranoid, Nick," said Spillman, once the shock wore off. "What leads you to this conclusion? We're your lawyers, remember. Any secret you have will remain completely safe with us." He'd have made a decent doctor, thought Nick.

"I can't tell you. But it's true."

"Nick," said Natalie impatiently, "cut the crap. Either you got this from somewhere, or it's another figment of that hyperactive imagination of yours. Which is it?"

Nick raised his palms helplessly. "It's from a 'reliable source,' as Jay would put it. Just humor me, ok? Pretend it's true, that these attacks are ordered, straight from the top. Does that change your thinking any?"

The assembled lawyers looked at one another uncomfortably. Janet Harmon finally broke the silence. "The 'run of the mill' cases you refer to are the only ones we have experience with. We live under a rule of law, Nick, in which presidents—at least ones not named Richard Nixon—don't go around saying 'Get this guy.' A rule of law which, some people say, you've been hell-bent on undermining since day one of your, shall we say, 'enterprise.' But be that as it may, all we can do is use the statutes and precedents to defend each separate charge as it is made. Unless you tell us the secret source of the conspiracy you allege."

Nick, tight-lipped, shook his head. "Just do the best you can. But be aware what you're up against. It's the president, for shit's sake."

As the meeting broke up, Peter asked Nick to stay for a moment. Here comes the leave-Natalie-alone lecture, Nick thought. As usual, he was wrong.

"Natalie has informed me of your aversion to the phrase 'communicate and cooperate.'" Peter's eyes danced playfully. "So I won't repeat it. I think you are beginning to understand it yourself. But we have to go a bit further now. We need to trim our sails. No more new initiatives, at least for the time being. I know you've been working on a new immigration exemption, and I think it has great merit. Keep working, but nothing new can be announced until we have a handle on things. Both from a legal standpoint and from a PR standpoint with your friend Mr. Gimenez. Do you disagree?"

"No, I totally agree." More than you know, thought Nick. He'd had the misfortune to come up with yet another brilliant idea lying in bed yesterday, that he really didn't want to pursue. Catholic hospitals were free to turn down cases they didn't agree with—vasectomies, tubal ligation, etc., because they violated their religious dictates.[96] What kind of cases would other hospitals like to turn down? Cases for homeless people who couldn't pay? Easy, but maybe too easy. It could be a little tough coming up with a theological justification for that, even for someone as creative as Nick. But with a little more refined thought ... The first area to explore would be heroin overdoses. Nick suspected these were net money-losers for a lot of hospitals. "I'm sorry, sir. Please stop shuddering, and here's a rag to clean up your vomit. We do not handle suspected drug overdose cases, because the Divine Spirit tells us not to. There is a Catholic hospital twelve miles from here that might. Here's a map. Oh, and here's a CIS tract you can read, about the perils of improper drug use. There's a five dollar off coupon for Zubitril on the back page."

Lucrative? Absolutely. And it fit the Secret Plan to a tee. If only Nick could work up the stomach for it as easily as he'd been able to do a year ago. An official directive to shut down the new initiative skunk works was the out he needed right now.

"And chin up, man!" Peter was saying. "We can handle this. We can't afford to have anything new go wrong—our plate is quite full,

---

96.   Bob Egelko, "Catholic hospital can refuse sterilization requests, judge says," *San Francisco Chronicle*, January 14, 2016. http://www.sfgate.com/news/article/Judge-Catholic-hospital-can-refuse-requests-for-6759627.php; Anna Maria Barry-Jester and Amelia Thomson-DeVeaux, "How Catholic Bishops Are Shaping Health Care In Rural America," *FiveThirtyEight.com*, July 25, 2018. https://fivethirtyeight.com/features/how-catholic-bishops-are-shaping-health-care-in-rural-america/?ex_cid=538twitter

as you know—but everything you told us today, even the possible conspiracy, I must say I believe we can deal with it all, as this firm has done so many times before. So show some proper fighting spirit, and perhaps in a few months' time we can return to the offensive. Agreed?"

"Yes, okay. And ... thank you."

As Nick rose and turned toward the door Peter added, "Even your Secret Plan."

Nick whirled around, dumbfounded.

Spillman's teeth were on full display, his eyes aglow. "I wasn't born yesterday, my friend. Your agenda has been as obvious to me from the outset as it evidently has been to Marshall and the RFF, though I didn't learn the actual phrase 'Secret Plan' until Natalie's confession today. But I hope you ultimately prevail. I truly do. As one who respects the law, the current religious privilege regime disgusts me."

"But ... I thought you were just ... "

"You thought I just wanted to create more work for the firm? Oh, I do. Absolutely. But the wheels turn slowly in Washington, and it will take at least a decade, probably more, for you to achieve your dream of even-handed law. By which point I will be more than ready to hand over the reins of leadership to young Mr. Tucker, who is already angling to push me aside, and spend my remaining days extracting rockfish from the Chesapeake Bay, one by one."

Nick opened his mouth to speak, but no words emerged. Peter shooed him off with two waving hands, and a "Back to work!"

February 10: The Sports Bar

Nothing bad happened on Monday. There were more individual meetings with members of the defense team. Potential defense team, since he hadn't been charged yet. Not for complicity in foreign funding of American political campaigns, or securities fraud in the sale of condo units at the Cape Cod pseudo-temple, or mail fraud for promoting dietary habits he didn't really believe, or the arson at St. Mercurius, or the murder of Melody LaPelletiere, who was still alive. Or for the obstruction of justice crime he really had committed, in lying to the FBI about Doris, Natalie and Melody.

Then there was the friendly call with Peter and Earl, who said he was willing to fund whatever defense was necessary. It hadn't occurred to Nick whether that might be an issue.

On Tuesday, Jay's second story broke. No secret revelations, just a general smear job accusing CIS of being a money-minting sham, quoting numerous holy men who solemnly agreed. After the first half hour of a root canal, you become inured to it all. It is what it is, and it will end when it ends. That's where Nick's head was now. He couldn't stand looking at any other news stories after that.

Wednesday Nick treated himself to a stroll around the zoo, which was empty and bleak on a winter weekday. Spending time with creatures that hadn't been reading Jay's articles eased his nerves. Besides, worrying would only make things worse. Just deal with whatever they serve up tomorrow, he told himself. For tonight, the single best way to get his mind cleared would be to return the calls from Kyle, who'd been pestering him for a week now. It was hard to believe it had only been eighteen months since he shared an office with him at GSA. "Big news, Rev. Can't wait to tell you. Beer's on me." Nick had been bone dry since his night at the FBI, and a beer or two would hit the spot.

*****

"Yo, Reverend Nick!" Kyle called out, as Nick entered the Wisconsin Avenue sports bar he'd picked for their rendezvous. "Looking good, man. You been working out?"

"A little, yeah. I've got this personal trainer now, since November. A Marine. He's evil incarnate. I hate every goddamn pushup. But it's

Natalie—she says I've got to look the part."

"Look the part?"

"You know. The weekly sermons, client meetings. People take you more seriously if it looks like you take yourself seriously. I don't know, she's probably right."

"Who says you gotta be buff to be a preacher? Look at Buddha, man. You think he did pushups?"

Bless you, Kyle. Nick felt better already. Just being here, with the six giant screens, the occasional cheers from a corner, the smell of good honest bubbling lard, the endless peanut refills—this was living. Nick would take this over some posh five-star where they served up three cold asparagus spears and called it dinner any day of the week.

"The guy you're thinking about—the fat, happy guy—that's not the original Buddha. It's Maitreya. He's different. Anyway, it doesn't matter. Natalie says jump, I say how high?"

"Man, are you pussy whipped. Anyway, that's what I want to talk to you about. You, Mr. Reverend Fratelli, have personally saved my life."

"Please don't call me Reverend. I am so sick of that."

"You, Your High Exalted Eminence, have saved my life. Hallelujah! I have been saved. Amen! Everything's on me tonight." Kyle called to the woman working behind the bar on her way by. "Could we get two beers, please? In those three-foot glasses? We got a special occasion here."

"Two yards, coming up." Nick knew the bartender's warmth was pasted on, but at that moment chose not to think so. A pretty girl, acting friendly, bringing him a three-foot beer—for which he would not only not have to pay, but would have the extra pleasure of watching Kyle squirm when Nick held him to his promise. On top of that, the Wizards were up by twelve at halftime. This was going to taste good.

"So who's the lucky girl?" asked Nick. "You've found true love, I take it?"

Kyle laughed so suddenly he accidentally disgorged a couple of peanuts. "Not exactly! I don't think 'lucky' is the word she'd use. It's me who's lucky. Lucky to have a friend like you, who has saved my ass. Hallelujah!"

The yards arrived. Kyle stood up from the bar stool, solemnly raised his glass with two hands, bowed his head. "To my spiritual leader."

"Cut it out, would you? Sit down, and tell me what's going on."

"Yes, master. You remember Cindy? The blonde at OPM, with the big boobs?"

Nick made a concerted effort, but couldn't call up a Cindy from the

Office of Personnel Management. "Anyway, she calls me up a couple weeks ago and says. 'I'm pregnant.' That's it. No hello, no nothing. Just blurts it right out: 'I'm pregnant.'"

"And you're the father?"

"That's what she says. Who knows? This is a no shrinking violet, trust me."

"I trust your judgment on that, at least. But if she says you're the father, she's the one who'd know."

Kyle drained the top foot of his three-foot glass. "Maybe yes, maybe no."

"So is she going to have it?"

"Hell yes. That's what she says, anyway. Then she starts right in on the money. Does not miss a beat. I'm going to have to pay for this, I'm going to have to pay for that. She's gonna have to take time off from work to pop out the kid, and I'm supposed to cover that, too. Like I don't know OPM's already got maternity leave covered, greedy bitch."

That part did sound a little greedy, though the rest of it didn't. "Wasn't she on the pill?"

"Said she must have missed one or something. Or it was a fluke—'just one of those things.' She doesn't remember. 'Just one of those things,' she says. Like I'm supposed to ruin my life for 'just one of those things.'"

"Didn't you use a condom?"

Kyle flashed irritation. "I don't know, Nick. I don't remember which side of the bed I was on, either. We were a little busy, you know?" Natalie would have made Nick wear two condoms if she'd thought of it. Nick was sorry his friend had gotten himself into this mess, but it was his own doing.

"Well, if you play, you gotta pay. Are you thinking of getting married?"

Kyle chortled indulgently. "Nick, Nick, Nick. You don't read your own shit, do you? I'm *exempt*. I've been a dues-paying member of CIS since day one. Well, since you won the pot case, anyway. A buck a week to old buddy Nick—no problem, man."

Nick sat perfectly still. "Exempt? *What* are you talking about?"

"Your inspired scripture, man. It's a hoot! And I watch your sermons every week, log in just like I'm supposed to. Here's a tip Nick: tell everybody to smoke a joint while they're watching. You get really, really funny that way."

Nick moved not a muscle. Kyle took another long swig, and wiped the foam from his mouth.

"I memorized part of it. To tell Cindy. That first epistle you filed, with the DC pot court." Kyle put on a basso profundo voice. "'Children are the *greatest* gift from the Divine Spirit. Children are a gift to *all* humanity, not just to their biological parents. The raising of children is the responsibility of all humanity, not just of the temporal vehicles through which the Divine Spirit transmits a new soul to earth.' Temporal vehicles—I loved that shit! Where'd you get that? You make that up? You should've seen Cindy's face when I told her we were just temporal vehicles!"

Nick just gaped.

Kyle took another long gulp. His yard was nearly gone, before Nick's had been touched.

"And then the pay dirt: 'No man shall override the collective duty of all humanity for the Divine Spirit's gift of regeneration by absconding with responsibility for any single child himself.'" You write clear as a bell, Nick—Myers always said so. My religion won't even *let* me pay for the kid—the government's gotta do it!"

Nick vaguely remembered writing the words. He did it to show off to his brother, to whom he'd bragged, a lifetime ago, that Luca could get out of paying child support to Yvonne. But he hadn't shown it to him, because he knew his brother would never go for it. Luca loved his kids too much and was too leery of rocking the boat with Yvonne to risk any craziness like this. Besides, much as he wanted to show off to Luca, the logic was a stretch, even for *Doctrines of Inspired Spirituality*. He also remembered—more clearly by the second—hitting the "block delete" button at the last minute to take that silliness out before filing the *Doctrines* as an exhibit to the motion at the DC court. Could he possibly have confused his versions? Or not saved the file correctly?

No! It was Natalie. Meticulous Natalie. She'd screwed it up. She was the attorney on the case, she was responsible for assembling the filing, and she had filed the wrong version of the document. It was her fault, not his.

That comfort lasted about second and half. He'd still written it. He'd still get the blame for it, if this ever leaked out. Which it had better not.

Nick wondered whether Mark the gospel writer, if he was up in heaven, ever had the same sinking feeling. "I meant to take out that bit at the end about the snake handling. How'd that get back in? Did somebody go through my trash or something? Look at all those

Luis Granados

people getting bitten, and blaming me for it, when it's not my fault." [97]
Scripture writing was a trickier business than most people realized.

"Kyle, you can't do this. No court will buy it. It was a mistake that was supposed to be taken out before it was filed. I'll testify to that. Letting fathers out of paying child support? Are you nuts?"

Kyle was dead stupid most of the time, but not all of the time. He had, after all, graduated from law school and passed the bar exam on his first try. When it was his own ass on the line, he could be downright astute.

"No, Nick, I'm not nuts. And neither were you, when you wrote it. You were looking right at *Hobby Lobby*. I was there, remember? Sitting behind you, in our little shared office at GSA? Alito writes as clearly as you do. He said that even if government has a compelling interest—which maybe it does, when it comes to the welfare of children—it can't burden a religious belief if there is any 'less intrusive means' of furthering that interest."

"And you have a religious belief."

"I most devoutly do! I can't tell you how deeply I feel that it's morally wrong to pay that bitch a nickel for this kid. 'Just one of those things.' Wrong! So Alito says—as you well know, since you're the one who told me about it—that if it's just money we're talking about, then the 'least intrusive means' is not to force anybody to pay for something against his religion, but for government to pay the bill itself. Home team wins!"

Nick rested his face on his hands, elbows propped on the bar. He knew exactly where this was going.

"So if the government's gonna pay for contraception—which, if she'd used it, we wouldn't even be *having* this conversation—then it can pay for braces for the kids God sends into this world via 'temporal vehicles' who happen to be good CISers living their faith. What do you call your members, anyway? I never figured that out."

"You cannot do this," moaned Nick, through his hands. "Judges are human beings. They have at least a little bit of heart. They're not going to let some kid starve because a deadbeat dad refuses to pay."

"Nobody's starving here. Cindy makes more than I do. She just wants to stick it to me. Plenty of single moms out there. It's no big deal."

"It's a huge deal, damn it." Nick slammed his fists on the bar, jarring several peanuts out of their bowl. It was hard to be mad at Kyle, though.

---

97.   Bart Ehrman, *Misquoting Jesus*. San Francisco: HarperCollins 2005 p.67.

Especially when, in fact, Kyle had tracked Nick's own thinking from that first night with Luca at the soccer stadium exactly. There was a big difference, though, between just writing down a devilish idea and acting on it. Wasn't there?

"Besides," Nick said, "no judge will buy it. You can't possibly win."

"Now there you are mistaken, counselor. Fact is, I've already won. I've already had it out with Cindy and some lawyer cousin of hers. I told them how if Hobby Lobby won, and Matteson won, and people are buying M-16s and Zubitril right and left, and all the other shit you've got going down, and I'm the asshole buddy of the big boss—who helped him put the whole deal together—she didn't stand a chance. She'll spend more money fighting this, and losing, then she'd spend raising the kid. So she caved. We did it!" Kyle gleefully smacked Nick on the back.

"You cannot do this," Nick repeated wearily. "Let me try this slowly, so you get it. You—can—not—do—this. You have no idea the shitstorm I'm already in. I've got investigators crawling through my books, and you know how bad I am with even balancing a checkbook."

"True," nodded Kyle.

"I've got poisoned dogs turning up outside my door. I've got Christians calling me the Antichrist, the sign of the end times. I've got atheists calling me a right-wing nut job. How can I be both? I've got both Jews and Muslims saying I'm mocking them. First time they ever agreed on anything. You know what happens to people who mock Muslims? Oh, and that reminds me. I've got the Westboro Baptists saying they want to picket my funeral. My funeral!"

"Are you dying?"

"I am now!" Nick roared, halting several conversations around him. "I may as well. If this gets out, I'll have every woman in America on my case. This isn't the straw that broke the camel's back, Kyle. It's the goddamn asteroid that broke the camel's back. You know who I've got on my case? The F-fucking-BI. You heard of them?"

"What did you do?"

"I don't know what I did," said Nick, shutting his eyes in pain. "And I don't know what I'm doing. All I know is—just wildly guessing here—I'm not up for any kind of medal. Kyle, please. You've got to fix this. Call Cindy. Tell her you found an angel or something. I'll pay for the kid. Through college! I've got some money now. Just don't let this get out, I'm begging you." He joined his hands in supplication. He'd have dropped to his knees if the bar stool weren't so high.

Kyle cocked his head to one side, with a rueful look. "You should have returned my call last week when I first wanted to get together, Mr. Bigshot. Since then, man, well it got on Facebook, and Twitter, and today, it's like viral. Everybody's talking about it. I'm everywhere, man. So are you. We're a *meme!*"

"Ooooooooohhhh!" Nick threw his arms down on the bar and buried his head in them. Due to some Newtonian force of physics he only dimly understood, this sent his still full yard of beer crashing to the floor behind the bar, where it shattered into a thousand shards. Like his life.

February 10: Motel 6

"Excuse me, sir. Are you all right?" This from the three-hundred-pound manager, not the pretty bartender. Nick's head remained buried in his arms. He knew that the manager didn't really care whether he was all right or not. And that the English translation of his words was, "Get the hell out of here, drunk."

"Sir?"

Nick raised his head and stood up. "He's paying," he snapped, jerking a thumb at Kyle. He couldn't bear to look at Kyle's face. He walked out the door and straight to his car. More of a trot, technically.

His mission was to not think about anything. There was nothing he could think about that would do any good. One plan worked: turning the speakers up full blast. His top-drawer sound system rattled every thought out of his head.

By chance he had parked the car facing north. So that's the way he headed. Maybe if he reached the North Pole, Santa Claus could give him his life back. Aaack! Don't do that. Don't think. Just drive.

After an hour, not far from Frederick, Maryland, Nick admitted to himself that just driving would not actually solve anything. He needed to spend the night somewhere, away from everyone, with his phone turned off. He followed the signs for a Motel 6. That would be perfect.

He sprawled on the bed for half an hour, staring blankly at the stucco ceiling. To his dismay, Nick realized he wasn't even hungry, despite having only eaten a handful of peanuts. When his childhood pet Bernie the beagle had stopped eating, Pop had taken him to the vet and come back alone.

The voice in his head kept saying: "Oh, don't be a baby."

Natalie had fairly spat those words at him the first time Nick had mentioned wanting out. Nick could see her eyes blazing when he closed his own. She was ready to fight to the last drop of Nick's blood. So long as it was billable.

Nick had avoided thinking about Natalie since the all hands meeting at G&H. The back of his brain sensed that any reassessment of their relationship would not leave him happy—a premonition that turned out to be spot on.

Nick had puzzled endlessly over her motivations for their weekly rendezvous, but now he let himself see the truth. The only mystery was why it had taken him so long to figure out what was so obvious. They called lawyers whores for a reason—but Natalie took the metaphor seriously. She had no more affection for Nick than she had for her ATM. If it took sex to keep him on the reservation, then sex it would be. That was all there was between them, and all there would ever be.

But blaming someone else for his misery wasn't what had terrified Nick's subconscious into not letting him think the Natalie issue through for all these weeks. The dark truth so painful to process was that it was Nick himself who had turned this good woman into a whore. If he hadn't been so ... so what? ... so *impossible*, she'd still be just an honest workaholic.

Then again, it does take two to tango, doesn't it? It was all too complicated. The only thing that wasn't complicated was that Nick didn't want to think about Natalie any more. Or see that impeccable, imperious face, ever again.

A drink was what he needed now, to help him think things through. No, that was a bad idea. He'd drunk an ocean of booze since this wild trip began. All it had brought him was more trouble. He'd had enough of liquid courage, the kind that led to one audacious step after another, just to see what would happen. Now he knew. Tonight was a night for water.

"They put felons in jail, son." That was Earl's solemn wisdom when he agreed to cover the defense costs. Yeah, Earl, you know a lot about that, Nick thought. Maybe we could share a cell. If I go down, you're coming with me, big guy.

"I don't know about jail," Peter had said later. "First offender, novel prosecution theories, there's a strong argument for lenience. You can forget about any kind of legal career, though. Even if you keep your law license—and I'd give that less than a fifty-fifty chance—who'd ever hire you? Who'd want to have to guess whether their attorney is telling them the truth, or just gaming them? Would you hire you?"

No, I wouldn't, thought Nick. Not in a million years. I don't even want to be me, much less pay me money for being me.

A bottle of sleeping pills could solve a lot of problems. But he'd be killing Mama along with himself, and she didn't deserve that. She deserved a decent, loving son. Well, two decent loving sons. She already had Luca. Who had it made: steady job at the grocery, a pleasant new girlfriend to replace Yvonne, two above-average teenagers, a budding ballerina, and a ten-year old smartass who never ceased to amaze. Plus maybe more coming after he remarried.

Besides, the Numbnuts, his fantasy basketball team, were in third place and with Montell coming back from the hamstring injury he had a shot at the title. He needed to live at least long enough to see out the season.

"We'll crush you, you little shit. You don't know who you're dealing with here," Nick imagined Marshall telling him. "You're mocking the sacred beliefs of millions of people. By the time we're done with you, you're going to wish you'd never been born."

Though he'd never actually heard those words, the thought of them turned Nick's despair to ire. Let Marshall and those smug RFF bastards win? No fucking way. He'd beaten them before, and he could beat them again. Somehow. Spillman would think of something. Anyway, *they* were the ones who'd perverted the law, *they* were the high and mighty who God put above everyone else—or so they claimed—and who'd gotten away with it for way too long. What Nick had done to push the privilege system past the breaking point would turn out to be a good thing, in the long run. He was sure of that.

Well, maybe not "sure." That was a strong word. He wasn't really sure of anything anymore. And in the long run, as Keynes had said, we're all dead.

Had Marshall already won? Did Nick wish he'd never been born? A Scotch would help with a knotty question like that, but he'd already decided against that. The question, he concluded, didn't make any sense, because he actually had been born, so wishing one way or the other was pointless. He did most definitely wish, though, that he did not have to face Peter Spillman in the morning to figure some way out of Kyle's insanity. Pondering the epistemological meaning of "sure," he decided that he really was sure of that.

One thing Nick hadn't gotten around to doing yet was looking up the two names agent Sanderson had mentioned: Glorification Temple and Pilgrim Covenant Congregation. He pulled out his smartphone, and a quick search revealed what they were: CIS copycats. The nerve! Glorification had lifted sections of the *Doctrines of Inspired Spirituality* almost verbatim, maybe enough to be a copyright violation. Its members, among other things, claimed to be exempt from jury duty. Which was copycatting even more, since Jehovah's Witnesses already had that one.[98] Pilgrim Covenant was miles ahead of CIS on religious immigration

---

98. https://www.jehovahs-witness.com/topic/77528/why-no-jury-duty

exemptions—the main thing they seemed to be about—though from what Nick had learned so far he didn't think they were doing it right. Then again, maybe the immigration lawyers at G&H were being overly conservative.

Once Laura Boess realized that every other hotshot on Wall Street could (and would) start competing with her with the latest and greatest twist on a religious exemption business niche, she was liable to have a stroke.[99]

Those poor RFF bastards were going to have to start playing Whack-A-Mole with every entrepreneur who ever attempted to read a law book, Nick consoled himself, and Agent Sanderson was going to have a lot of late nights. O, what a tangled web we weave, Nick thought with a smirk, when first we start letting everyone make up laws for themselves.

The mole named Niccolò Fratelli, though, had enough of being whacked, and wanted to stay in his hole.

The back of the motel door had a notice about checkout times, fire escape routes, etc. Nick couldn't make out the words from where he was lying, but he did study the rectangle for a while.

He picked up his smart phone, and touched the little green icon for, of all things, making a call. But the dial tone unnerved him, so he put it back down.

On the stand next to the bed sat a TV remote control and a game controller. He wondered whether the games available were any good, and whether you had to pay extra to access them. The TV was about a quarter the size of the one he'd bought to replace the one the RFF thugs had shattered. No matter what happened, they'd have to pry that baby out of his cold, dead fingers. He could give up the car, but not that the big screen TV.

Nick picked up the phone again, tapped the green "Call" icon a second time, and listened to the dial tone until it shut off.

Not from indecision, though. From the realization that this needed to be handled in person.

---

99. For an article about a real-life incubator of fake religions seeking privileges and exemptions, see Everton Bailey, Jr., "Spreading religion or evading taxes? An Oregon nonprofit clashes with feds," *The Oregonian*, November 24, 2016. http://www.oregonlive.com/portland/index.ssf/2016/11/south_beach_missions.html.

*****

Thirty minutes later, he pulled up in the parking lot of the Sav-A-Lot store where Luca worked. This felt so, so right. He didn't know whether Luca would be working this late at night or not, but he felt lucky. By the law of averages, *something* had to go right. And it did. There was Luca, back in the produce department he managed, working on some sort of repair to a bin full of cantaloupes.

"The high and mighty have returned!" Luca boomed. "To what do I owe the honor? You're not starting up some sort of broccoli religion, are you?"

Nick studied his brother's face for signs of bitterness or envy. He found none. It looked like Luca was happy to see him and just making a joke because that's what Luca did.

"No, definitely not. In fact, I just quit. The whole religion business. I'm done."

"How can you quit? I thought it was your, uh, church, or whatever it is."

It was cool in the produce section. Cool but well-lit. Just the opposite of the dark, overheated motel room where Nick had spent the final moments of his clergy career.

"Quit as in, I'm done. They can keep it." Nick was confident that if he hired a non-G&H lawyer, a cease-fire could be arranged in which both sides would just walk away. Nick would have nothing further to do with CIS or any other religion, and the government would turn its prosecutorial attention to all the other moles that needed whacking, sparing itself the expense and risk of a protracted war with G&H. Glorification Temple and Pilgrim Covenant Congregation could carry on the Secret Plan without him.

"Who can keep it?" asked Luca. "I thought it was yours? Why are you doing this?"

"It's ... more complicated than I can explain. You don't want to know. Trust me, there's legal stuff going on here you really don't want to get sucked into."

Luca held out both palms and turned his head away. He was in total agreement with not learning about things that might get him in trouble.

"Luca, you're always complaining about the help here, how you can't get good people. I want a job. I want to just sell people honest apples and carrots, anything, and make enough to live on doing it, and not feel like I'm scheming to trick somebody all the time. I'm tired of tricking people. I'm not going to do it anymore."

"You want to work *here*?"

Nick nodded vigorously.

"We don't pay shit. At least not until you've been here a few years. That's why we can't keep anybody."

"You did it. With a kid, and Yvonne on your case. And no—well, I've got a little in the bank. I can be ok while I'm learning the ropes."

"But you've got an education. You're a big shot, all over the news. You don't belong here."

Nick waved his hands helplessly. "I've pissed it away. It's gone. I could keep fighting, maybe even winning, but ... the thing is ... I don't want to anymore. Does anybody make you do what you don't want to do—at least, now that Yvonne's gone?"

Luca was losing patience. "Yeah, Nick, they do. Why do you think I'm fixing this bin? It's 'cause the manager's too cheap to bring in a carpenter. So I gotta do it. And no, I don't want to do it, because—"

"That's not what I mean. I didn't say it right." Nick measured his words, speaking slowly. "Does working this job, even when you've got to fix a bin a carpenter ought to be fixing, make you feel like you're the scum of the universe?"

Luca just stared. Nick knew the answer would have been no, but his older brother wasn't inclined to give in.

Nick jabbed a finger toward Luca's face. "You don't want me to go to the Giant across the highway, do you? Because I'd be good. I'd whip your ass. I'd have you begging me for a job in a couple of years, because we'd run you guys into the ground."

Luca searched for guidance from the heavens, but saw only steel girders above. "You're an idiot," he said at last.

"In that case, I'll fit right in. Do I get the job?"

"Ok. Whatever. But it's got to be approved. I've got to clear it with Earl."

"*Who?!*"

"Earl Payson. The store manager. You got a problem with that?"

Nick had no problem with that. No problem at all.

THE END

Acknowledgments

My wife, Pat, has shown preternatural levels of patience throughout the writing process. Her main complaints were about the times I would freely mingle discussions of what my characters were doing with discussions of what real-life people were doing, which caused a certain confusion.

My writing teachers were extraordinarily indulgent as well: Aaron Hamburger, Tammy Greenwood, Maureen Brady, and Martha Hughes.

I was fortunate that the one person on the planet I trusted most to edit the manuscript agreed to do so, and made many important improvements: Jennifer Bardi, the longtime editor of the *Humanist* magazine, and now the Deputy Director of the American Humanist Association.

Lots of other people made contributions as well, often without realizing it, by answering bizarre questions I would toss at them. I won't remember all of them, but a few who come to mind are: Rob Boston, Matt Bulger, Paul Granados, Marci Hamilton, Jerry Kaplan, Bill Merten, Merrill Miller, Monica Miller, Helen Morrison, David Niose, Philmore Panitch, David Schoeder, Michael Skinner, Roy Speckhardt, Elaine Stewart and Lisa Zangerl. Not all these people agree with my point of view, I hasten to add.

Finally, a thank you to the patrons and staff of the Tune Inn, Washington DC, where much of this was written. As you can probably tell.